Praise for
GET OUT OF YOUR OWN WAY

"A truly inspiring book on winning in a changing world. Filled with fresh insights, bold strategies, and practical tools, this is vital reading for leaders and teams."

—STEPHEN R. COVEY, author of *The 7 Habits of Highly Effective People* and *The 8th Habit: From Effectiveness to Greatness*

"This book deserves more than five stars. Robert Cooper has surpassed all my expectations, again! In our work with hundreds of senior managers and scores of the country's best and brightest thought leaders, Dr. Cooper's work has received the highest ratings, including inherent value, usefulness, and overall results. Get your brain to act as a coach instead of a critic; an ally instead of an antagonist; an energizer instead of a demoralizer? In *Get Out of Your Own Way*, Dr. Cooper will teach you how... and more."

—JOHN C. HORTON, founder and president, The Leadership Forum, Atlanta, Georgia

"This book is truly an inspiration! Our brains can be our worst enemies when it comes to living the lives we really want to live. Combining the latest scientific research with inspiring real-life examples, Robert Cooper shows how we can use five simple tools to recalibrate our brains and become our best selves."

—KEN BLANCHARD, co-author, *The One Minute Manager®*

"*Get Out of Your Own Way* is filled with wisdom, practical tools, and fresh ideas. This is Dr. Robert Cooper's most amazing book and will clearly exceed your expectations."

—DR. JIM LOEHR, CEO, LGE Performance Sciences, and the *New York Times* bestselling co-author of *The Power of Full Engagement*

"Once again Dr. Cooper has created an exceptional resource for unlocking your hidden potential to achieve what everyone else thinks you can't. In *Get Out of Your Own Way* he provides an enlightened look at the way your brain functions affect your day-to-day actions and gives you the uncommon tools that separate the best from all the rest. This book is a *must* for everyone looking to break their personal execution barrier and achieve big goals."

—JAMES D. MURPHY, Afterburner fighter pilot, author of *Business Is Combat* and *Flawless Execution*, founder and CEO: Afterburner, Inc.

"Dr. Robert Cooper has given us far more than a book about exceeding our expectations. He provides stories and insights about growing courage, raising our practical intelligence, and learning skills that broaden our horizons while helping us get through the day successfully. Most of all, *Get Out of Your Own Way* is a book based on the author's strong trust in the further reaches of our human potential. It is a powerful program for anyone aspiring to peak performance in leadership and life."

—CHARLES GARFIELD, PH.D., clinical professor of psychology, University of California Medical School at San Francisco, and bestselling author of *Peak Performers* and *Second to None*

"Robert Cooper delivers a powerful road map toward clear thinking that all innovators, leaders, and teams should embrace as they create the future—in business, technology, education, or their own personal lives. I will employ many of his methodologies from *Get Out of Your Own Way* in our high-level think-tank sessions to discover the next breakthroughs in leadership and organizations."

—SUSAN J. DUGGAN, PH.D., CEO, Silicon Valley World Internet Center

"Robert Cooper redefines what's possible in individual and team achievement. This is more than just a book; it's a highly credible action guide you'll want to call upon again and again."

—LAWRENCE TAYLOR, retired president, Pinkerton Security

"I wholeheartedly endorse this remarkable new book. Filled with surprising scientific insights, enlightening stories, real-life examples, and practical tools to improve our lives and work, it's a must-read follow-up to *The Other 90%*."

—DAWN SORENSON, vice president of Organizational Effectiveness, Methodist Health System, Methodist Hospitals of Dallas

"We spend our lives trying to find new ways to handle what is in front of us, never realizing that the tools for greater success are right here inside us. *Get Out of Your Own Way* puts the keys to the best future in your hands."

—MIKE DE IRALA, executive director, Powertrain Manufacturing Operations, Ford Motor Company

"An extraordinary, much-needed book! Dr. Cooper provides a pathway for better understanding ourselves and how we can achieve the seemingly impossible. He pinpoints five invaluable keys that are elegantly simple and easy to apply. This is a must-read!

—PAULA VAN NESS, former CEO, Make-A-Wish Foundation, CEO, Starlight Starbright Children's Foundation

"Dr. Robert Cooper can motivate even the most highly motivated of us. He addresses human behavior and peak performances in bold new ways that every leader and athlete can understand."

—GARY HALL JR., five-time Olympic gold medalist and the fastest swimmer in the world

"Robert Cooper has done it again. . . . *Get Out of Your Own Way* is highly energizing and encouraging advice for all leaders and entrepreneurs. Read it and re-read it . . . this book offers great hope in this crazy, frantic-paced world."

—DOUG SHARP, chairman, BSB Design

Also by Robert K. Cooper

The Other 90%

Get Out of Your Own Way

The 5 Keys to Surpassing Everyone's Expectations

CROWN
BUSINESS
NEW YORK

ROBERT K. COOPER, Ph.D.

Library of Congress Cataloging-in-Publication Data

Cooper, Robert K.
    Get out of your own way : the 5 keys to surpassing everyone's expectations /
Robert K. Cooper.—1st ed.
Includes bibliographical references and index.
1. Success—Psychological aspects. 2. Self-actualization (Psychology) I. Title.
BF637.S8C658 2006
158—dc22   2005030082

ISBN-10:1-4000-4966-0

ISBN-13: 978-1-4000-4966-0

Printed in the United States of America

Design by Lauren Dong

10 9 8 7 6 5 4 3 2 1

First Edition

To all who realize that
the next frontier is not only ahead of us,
it's also inside of us.

•   •   •

It is useless to close the gates against new ideas;
they overleap them.

—CLEMENS WENZEL VON METTERNICH

Contents

Key 4   ENERGY, Not Effort   *217*
It's not how hard you try or how long you work, it's how effortlessly you get more of the right things done.

Key 5   IMPACT, Not Intentions   *267*
It's not how lofty your intentions are or how much you want things to improve, it's how measurable a difference you are making in living your deepest values and achieving your biggest goals.

Get Out of Your Own Way

1

What Does Your Brain Want, Anyway?

*Deep within us dwell slumbering powers; powers that would
astonish us, that we never dreamed of possessing; forces that would
revolutionize our lives if aroused and put into action.*

—ORISON MARDEN

What does your brain want, anyway?

If that question amounted to the same thing as asking what *you*
want, life would be pretty simple: You'd decide what you want, and
then you'd use your brainpower to make that happen. We'd all be
all the things we want to be—accomplished, influential, healthy,
wealthy, wise, admired, happy—in the kind of world we want to live
in: peaceful, free, and just.

Singly and collectively, we have all the brainpower we need to
make those things happen. But while you are a person of the twenty-
first century, and what you want reflects your experiences in today's
world, your brain is pretty much the same model your ancestors were
using a thousand years ago, and it still wants a lot of what it wanted
back then, which isn't necessarily good for you or congruent with
what you want for yourself.[1]

You may want to change the world and, while you're at it, drop a
few pounds and maybe learn Italian; your brain would be just as content to have you pass the time watching some mindless television
show while you munch on a cheeseburger and some fries. You may

want to love your neighbor as yourself, but your brain wants to know which one of those neighbors stole your hedge trimmer.

No matter that your hedge trimmer is in fact right there in that back corner where you put it the last time you organized your garage; your brain can't be bothered with remembering that. It would rather remember the name of that pigtailed girl who made fun of you in third grade, or maybe some obscure sports statistic, or something your boss said to you three months ago that might have been a compliment but, then again, might also have been some kind of subtle criticism.

And so it goes. You want this, but your brain wants that, and your brain often wins. As the comedian Emo Philips said, "I used to think my brain was the most wonderful organ in my body, until I realized who was telling me that."

Incidentally, if your brain is right now trying to distract you from reading this by causing you to ask something like "Is the brain really an 'organ'?" there are two answers to that. The first is, technically no, but that was just a joke, so lighten up, brain. The second is, as your brain well knows, you do have true brains within your organs, particularly in your heart and your gut. Scientists have proven that. These are not "brains," in quotes, but real actual brains.

The gut brain, for example, includes more than a hundred million specialized nerve cells, a complex circuitry that enables it to act independently, learn, remember, and influence our perceptions and behaviors.[2] And the heart brain consists of more than forty thousand neurons along with a complex network of neurotransmitters, proteins, and support cells. It's as large as many key areas of the brain in your head.[3]

As we'll see, there's a certain amount of competition among your brains for your attention, and that also creates some problems for reaching your goals. You could ask Michael Eisner, CEO of the Walt Disney Company, and his former friend Michael Ovitz, who was often described as "the most powerful person in Hollywood,"[4] about that. Their failure to listen to what their heart-and-gut-brains were telling them—practically shouting at them—cost them their friendship, cost Disney amazing millions of dollars, cost Ovitz his career, and played a part in Eisner's early departure from Disney. We'll get to that.

For now, I'll refer to all your brains, cumulatively, as your brain, singular. Because, frankly, it confuses your brain while you're reading to see the word in plural form when all your life you've seen it as singular. Your brain doesn't like change, even if, as in this case, the change is closer to the truth than whatever your brain is clinging to.

Even with all its frustrating qualities, it's not that your brain doesn't want to be on your side. Of course it does—where else is it going to go? It just needs guidance. A little attention from you, at the right moments, can change a lot of its unproductive habits into positive attributes that will move you forward toward what you want, beyond what anyone thought you could accomplish, in remarkable ways and with remarkable ease.

Sometimes you have to tame parts of your brain that are holding you back today, even though they once preserved your ancient ancestors' very lives by keeping them from trying anything new or stepping forward into challenging situations.

At other times, other parts of your brain will rush you toward doing something that's good for you or important to you, whether you're ready or not. "You can't climb that big tree!" someone says. "Can, too!" you answer. "Yeah, well, let's see you do it then." And, scared half to death, you do, and your world changes. "You can't sit here in the front of this bus," someone says to Rosa Parks. "Can, too," she thinks. And she does. And the world begins to change.

A specific part of your brain, the nucleus accumbens located within the dorsal striatum, responds to challenge by flaring into action, charging your system with determination and ingenuity to help you do things others think you can't.[5, 6]

Of course, sometimes you get partway up the tree, fall, and break your arm. Sometimes, like Nelson Mandela, you get thrown in jail for twenty-seven years for believing your people should be free, or, like Albert Einstein and Abraham Lincoln, you fail at practically everything you try. Heeding the nucleus accumbens doesn't mean your life will be perfect or even easy; it just means that you'll have more gumption to stay on the path toward being the best you.

This is a good place to raise three important points that apply to this book as a whole. First, when I name the nucleus accumbens as a specific part of your brain that goads you toward doing things that others think you can't, I'm giving you my best read of the latest brain science. But brain science is growing explosively these days for many reasons, in part because its power to help improve lives is being demonstrated time and again, and in part because brain-imaging technologies are now permitting scientists to observe brain activity more and more minutely. So next week someone may discover that there's another area, even one within the nucleus accumbens, that actually provokes that reaction, or that the reaction results from several areas in combination, or from something else altogether. That won't change the fact that your brain has this resource within it; it will just change the name of the location where that resource is found.

So, then, why name brain areas at all in this book, and why make claims for what they do and how they affect us? One reason is that some functions of some areas are pretty well settled, so I assert them with considerable confidence. A second reason is that for all the areas named in the book, what I'm saying is accurate, insofar as it's the best knowledge we have now. There are plenty of endnotes for you to follow if you want to dig more deeply. Thirdly, I have observed it to be true for my clients and for me personally that sometimes having a name to relate a specific attribute to makes following the material easier, even if you don't actually remember that name for very long.

Perhaps most important, there's the larger question that leads to my third point: If it's all so up in the air and so potentially complicated, why learn about the brain, anyway? My goal in encouraging you to learn some of the basics of your brain and nervous system is based on the behavior-change fact that if you can't see it, or sense it, and basically understand it, you can't guide it, and then, indeed, you will get in your own way. Instead of you shaping your life forward, noticing and transcending certain deeply wired tendencies you have that are counterproductive, your brain would simply run you, and then you end up feeling like a victim or passenger in life, instead of the driver of your own distinctive existence and untapped potential.

TO GET OUT OF THE BOX, YOU HAVE TO SEE THE BOX

In adverse circumstances, your brain usually inherently wants you to retreat, lower your expectations, accept less from yourself and your life. In effect, to flee instead of fighting. [7] Your brain even tells you that this leveling out of feelings and compromising of your dreams is a good thing, a show of "maturity." Einstein himself, speaking from experience, expressed the alternative: "How many people are trapped in their everyday habits: part numb, part frightened, part indifferent? To have a better life we must keep choosing how we are living."[8]

There are many aspects to that choosing, but one of the principal ones is to choose when to let your brain have its way so you can ride on its coattails to higher and higher levels of accomplishment and satisfaction, and when to override the brain activities that can mire you in habit, ordinariness, and disappointment.

Neuroscientists are realizing that there are brain centers for just about everything. There's one for the happiness you experience when you solve a puzzle or a problem;[9] there's one for the desire to punish people who cheat to get ahead;[10] there's one that relates to spiritual experience;[11] there's one that can turn you from a procrastinator into a workaholic.[12]

There is even a part of the brain, called the "interpreter," that makes up stories to explain things you have done. If, for example, a hypnotized person is programmed to crow like a rooster upon a given signal, she will do so; if then asked why she was crowing, she will "explain" it with something like "It's such a beautiful day, I just felt like crowing!" The explanation always makes sense, and it's never inconsistent with the facts of the person's life—she won't say, for instance, "I play the part of a rooster in an upcoming community play, and I need to rehearse," if there's no such forthcoming play; it just isn't true.[13]

It's an amazing instrument, your brain, but it's up to you to see that it plays the tune you want. The first step toward doing that is to realize that the most dominant parts of your brain are essentially reactive and protective. As I said, your brain wants to keep the rest of you around, and so it's constantly sensing for threat and danger and steering you away from them. Like a very overprotective parent, it turns any molehill of potential trouble into a mountain of looming misery.

WHAT'S THE WORST THING THAT COULD HAPPEN?

"Try climbing that tree and you'll be lucky if the only thing you break is your arm," your brain tells you. "Speak up in that meeting and you're sure to get punished for it." "Hug your child too often and people will start thinking bad things about you." "Try that new marketing strategy and you'll become a laughingstock among your peers."

Your brain collects information about awful outcomes like the most fanatical conspiracy theorist, and delights in dredging up more and more of it. That's one reason why your brain likes television so much—one good evening sitting there and you've got plenty more information about catastrophic outcomes. "Remember that guy on the news, somewhere in the Midwest, who got stabbed when he asked his neighbor to return his hedge trimmer?" "Remember that *Seinfeld* episode when Costanza talked back to George Steinbrenner and got fired?"

Of course, you know at some conscious level that an episode of *Seinfeld* is just a made-up story, but at its core your brain doesn't really separate "fact" from "fiction." As part of a database of things to worry about, your brain treats television shows, magazine stories, movies, and gossip as seriously as it treats your actual life experiences.

Organizations, as collections of individual brains, have extraordinarily deep reservoirs of awful stories about what can go wrong when we take any risk at all or do anything differently. It's almost comical how organizational theorists keep coming up with "breakthrough" ideas about "overcoming resistance to change," and those ideas don't actually make much difference. Duh—a few million collective scenarios of what can go wrong versus one "burning platform" or some "continuous, deep, committed communication."[14] You figure the odds.

Kind of makes you want to flee instead of standing up and fighting for what you want, doesn't it? Especially in today's world, when all anyone seems to want from you is more. More profits, more work, more time, more ideas, more innovation, more efficiency, more output, more commitment, more risk-taking, more sacrifice, more, more, more.

THE SMALLEST CHANGES CAN MAKE THE BIGGEST DIFFERENCE

But here's the good news. Once you recognize that some parts of your brain are getting in your way—that the part of "you" that's made up of some parts of your brain is getting in the way of the whole "you" that's more than just those parts of your brain—you can start switching off the counterproductive parts and start making use of the other parts of your brain that are just waiting to align your best energy and brainpower with your goals, hopes, wishes, dreams, and aspirations. In fact, simply recognizing how some parts of your brain may be holding you back is a big first step toward putting them in their place.

In the midst of the din and the yammering and the demands, there are moments when a little energy applied in the right way will start positive change happening, and lead the way to more and more moments—which you will come to recognize more and more clearly—that sustain the momentum toward what you want to achieve. Your brain has been taught (of course) that there's a price to be paid for opening yourself to those moments, but people wholly immersed in the real world, from Thomas Edison to Oprah Winfrey to Estée Lauder to Michael Dell to Michael Jordan, would tell you that the right moments can come to you anytime. You just have to see them and seize them before they evaporate or get shouted down.

It's not just famous people or world-changers who are models for seizing the right moments. In this book I'll tell about some people you might not have heard much about, whose stories illustrate what your brain will do to help you reach your goals, if you permit it to. People like school principal Muriel Summers, inventor Henry Martyn Leland, attorney Inge Fryklund, social-service agency head Howard Hendrick, high-school student Frank Daily, Japanese fashion designer Rei Kawakubo, statesman James F. Byrnes, drag racer Cristen Powell, and swimmer Gary Hall Jr.

You don't need to master the latest neuroscience to appreciate the enormous leverage the right moments provide. In essence, those moments permit you to tap into sources of inner power that usually become submerged beneath the everyday bustle. It's like the difference in marketing between accumulating small "impressions"—the number of times an ad gets seen—as opposed to changing consumer attitudes in one dramatic moment.

Most impressions are fleeting and pretty inconsequential, even though they can add up to what is called "share of mind." If, for example, your carbonated beverage is on billboards, in commercials, and in print ads, all those little impressions might cause some people to remember your product when it's time to buy or order a beverage. But if you can get Julia Roberts or Tiger Woods to consume your beverage on camera at some big award ceremony with so much delight that it seems the beverage is more gratifying than the award itself, then you get a thousand times the leverage.

When you seize the right moments in the right ways, you get that same kind of leverage, which can have immeasurably more impact than what you do with the other thousands of moments in your day. I've already mentioned how the nucleus accumbens becomes active when something genuinely important to a truly satisfying life is happening, when there's a provocation to stand up for your finest ideals or to prove to others that you can achieve what they think you can't.

Then there's the orbital cortex, which "sees" without seeing, senses when things aren't the way they should be, and sparks motivation and decision-making to set things right.[15]

Along with our heart brain and gut brain, those brain areas—and several others—are the sources of inspiration, vision, commitment, and momentum toward reaching your goals. They not only keep you on track toward accomplishing what matters to you, they also provide the insight, awareness, resilience, emotional stability, and clarity that help you get there. Heeding those areas and enlivening them makes life easier. In effect, it streamlines everything you do so that you require far less energy to advance.

Why don't we all just tune in to those wonderful instruments and tune out the static? There are many reasons, which I'll discuss more fully later, but one fundamental reason takes us back to what I've already suggested: Under any kind of stress, the loudest signals your brain sends are about what's happening right at this moment and how to survive it. Anything that's not immediately critical—such as moving toward your longer-term goals—gets drowned out.

This phenomenon is familiar to anyone who works in or leads an organization: Strategic plans or mission statements or corporate visions are laboriously produced (often wholly or in part at an off-site meeting, to get away from the daily stresses), but they often have little impact on what people actually do, because everyone is much more concerned with today's "hot news" (the boss's mood, the rumors of budget cuts or outsourcing, the "squeaky wheel" customer, the Super Bowl office pool, what's appropriate to wear to the company picnic) than they are with advancing some way-down-the-road vision of the future.

ABOVE THE FRAY

In today's more-more-more world, practically all of us are fueled by stress, which has become so normal that we hardly notice it. This stress-centered drive is called "tense energy"; it's sparked by hormones like adrenaline and cortisol, which detonate small, lethal explosions in your organs and arteries as they're released, punctuated by stimulants like caffeine, sugar, rushing, tension, and deadlines. "The stress is killing me," we tell each other, and then we proudly enumerate all the things that are "driving us crazy."

That's your brain, giving you a message, because, of course, the stress truly is killing you—leading you, among other things, to heart disease and cancer.[16] And it's also killing off the "you" that is truly you, that is not just the rantings of your ancient brain. It's up to you, the real you of your unique dreams and aspirations, to decide whether that is indeed "crazy," and what you want to do about it.

So, to answer the question with which I began this chapter, what your brain wants is everything: security and opportunity, rip-roaring adventure and couch-potato indolence, solitude and community, change and stability, life and—if the psychiatrists are right—death, too. And it wants it all now, except the death part. Which ones it works toward, now and into the future, is completely up to you, moment by moment.

Over the course of three decades of research, teaching, and hands-on work with leaders and organizations around the world, I have sought the best tools and strategies to help you make the best choices in the midst of life's roar. All around us, a few exceptional individuals and teams are accomplishing the seemingly impossible—not just once but again and again, in changing circumstances and under rising pressures. They're hitting higher-than-expected targets and making it look easy, doing it with more ingenuity and fewer resources, more speed and less stress, more trust and less time—while still managing to have rich and full lives.

These top performers have learned that just going along is stifling, settling for less than your biggest dreams is draining, and furiously treading water to stay in the same place is soul-destroying.

Their secret is that they've learned to get out of their own way—to wisely work with the brain, and around it, instead of against it.

They step aside from their ancient brains' chatter and set about accomplishing what's rare and often amazing, surpassing everyone's expectations—including, often, their own.

Yet that's not really a secret at all. Star performers in all walks of life, whether they do it intuitively or with sophisticated coaching, are applying lessons that scientific research and careful observation have been imparting to us for years. Those lessons are counterintuitive, and often contradictory to the received wisdom about success that most of us have been fed throughout our lives, but they work where the traditional advice leaves most of us in a knot of tension and frustration. They're only secrets to those unable to see them.

FIVE KEYS

In *Eye and Brain*, British neuropsychologist Richard Gregory asserts that perception is "a dynamic searching for the best interpretation of the available data."[17] That, in practical terms, is my aim in this book. Along with my colleagues, I have interviewed scientists, reviewed, tested, revised, and retested the simple, practical methods that will turn your brain's amazing powers to your advantage. If you apply them, often for just a few minutes each day, you'll find yourself making the five kinds of larger choices that enable you to achieve what others think you can't—and even what you think you can't.

Those five choices are as follows:
- *Direction,* not motion
- *Focus,* not time
- *Capacity,* not conformity
- *Energy,* not effort
- *Impact,* not intentions

Trying harder is a prescription for disappointment and dissatisfaction; it's trying differently that changes everything.

Key 1 DIRECTION, Not Motion

It's not how busy you are or how fast you're moving, it's how effectively you are advancing in the right direction.

The only way of discovering the limits of the possible is to venture a little way past them into the impossible.

—ARTHUR C. CLARKE

During several summers when I was a boy, my family traveled for a few weeks to visit national landmarks. We camped in parks, in a tent. At a gift shop in one of those parks, my mother bought a small piece of wood with an acorn glued to it and a saying painted in a circle around the acorn. It read, "The hurrier I go, the nuttier I get."

Ain't it the truth. Looking back, I also think she bought it as a not-so-subtle hint to my father about the pace of those trips: Reach Site A, set up tent, unload essential items, visit every possible corner of Site A in a maximum of two days, repack, get in car, head for Site B, repeat.

There was plenty of motion in those trips, but only my father experienced them as having any real direction, because for the rest of us Site G felt pretty much exactly like Site A, except that by the time we got to Site G we were more exhausted, more irritable, and far less enthusiastic than we had been at the beginning. Instead of learning or growing or thrilling at what we saw, we paced off the battlefield or trudged along the trail or sat before the educational filmstrip with only one thought: When will this end?

Direction, as I'm talking about it here, is more than your next destination. It's some overarching purpose that inspires you and gives meaning to your activities. Without it, we live as sadly as the "hired man" in Robert Frost's poem, having "nothing to look backward to with pride, and nothing to look forward to with hope."

BEYOND YOUR SHOETOPS

Your brain is not made for today's manic pace, and it's all it can do to keep up. The more you can run on preprogrammed routines and habits, without glancing far above your shoetops, the happier your brain is—and the more it's actually in your way. It's not for nothing that the eminent scholar of consciousness Robert Ornstein can say, "The mind is a squadron of simpletons,"[1] and "The human mental system is failing to comprehend the modern world."[2]

When researcher Paul Light studied organizational adaptation to change, he found something similar. While people can handle one major change or perhaps two, after that the majority of employees, like my siblings and I on those summer camping trips, lose almost all their zest for heading toward yet another new destination.[3]

The best hope you have for creating genuine direction toward a future worth going to and toward goals that bring out your best is to make good choices about what parts of your brain to engage. For example, parts of the forebrain, which lies just beneath your temples, are stimulated whenever you look into the future—say, five years ahead—or across a distant physical or mental horizon.[4] It mobilizes your inner resources to get there, to make what you envision happen, to realign and energize your current actions along a through-line to that future.

It's remarkably easy to implement the simple actions that begin permitting your forebrain to have some say about your future amid all those simpleton brain areas clamoring for more of the same, believing that being busy is the same as actually getting somewhere. I'll show you how to do that in the next chapters.

The central message of this section is this: You must choose the right moments, not motion, and these moments must be carefully aligned on a through-line to your best possible future. It only takes a moment, a clear far-forward glimpse, a special "stretch" toward the future here and there every day, to keep the forebrain performing its magic, keeping you ahead in a changing world and positioning you to achieve an ever-better future. It only takes a moment, and few people ever know to do it.

And there's a caution here, too. If you don't engage your forebrain and its scanning of the most compelling possible future, it backs off, and even stops altogether and actually atrophies, as brain areas can do when they are not being fully engaged.[5] Then your other reactionary, survival-today-oriented brain circuitry fills the void, leaving you even less able to imagine and pursue your best future. There's a general rule here that I call the Brain Displacement Principle, which is generally summed up in Bob Dylan's famous axiom "He not busy being born is busy dying": If you are not deliberately using your most useful brain areas to move you forward, then your least useful ones will probably take over.

So fragile is this balance when it comes to your forebrain that you can permanently *lose* the capacity to truly envision a future for yourself in any but the most wishful and fantastical ways: One day that capacity just vanishes, along with your ability to realistically plot a way from where you are now to someplace you want to be in the future. Put bluntly, you become more like a machine and less like a person. You can still follow all the rules that are programmed into you—you just can't dream of something new and make it happen.

On the contrary, when you tap into the forebrain's readiness to activate and shape the way your life and your work connect to your unique abilities and passions, the forebrain is strengthened in much the same way that a muscle is strengthened by exercise, and you move forward more and more powerfully, more and more easily, less and less at the mercy of your reactionary brain centers.

Achieving what others think you can't is largely a matter of getting out of your own way, of choosing to shut off the motion for a while and permitting your brain to offer direction instead, and then building in that direction. The chapters in this section will help you with that, too, and with a range of other techniques and methods for lining up precisely the right moments on that through-line to your dreams.

ROARING OFF THE FACE OF THE EARTH

Robert H. Goddard, the driving force behind America's early space programs, is today called "the father of space flight." But when Goddard first imagined that a rocket could be propelled through outer space, the *New York Times* ridiculed his dream, saying he lacked even "the knowledge ladled out daily in high schools." With no atmosphere in outer space and therefore nothing for an engine to thrust against, the *Times* patiently explained, a rocket couldn't move an inch.[6] That was in 1920.

Goddard stuck to his dream, insisting, "It is difficult to say what is impossible, for the dream of yesterday is the hope of today and the reality of tomorrow."

In 1969, when the Apollo 11 mission reached the moon, the *Times* reconsidered its earlier scoffing and mocked itself instead, in an editorial that included these words: "Further investigation and experimentation have confirmed the findings of Isaac Newton in the 17th century, and it is now definitely established that a rocket can function in a vacuum as well as in an atmosphere. The *Times* regrets the error."[7]

Maybe it was Goddard who inspired the great psychologist

Abraham Maslow to say that when we free ourselves from the con-straints of ordinary goals and uninformed scoffers we will find our-selves "roaring off the face of the earth." That's what happens when we focus on going in the direction we want to go and not on the buzz and bustle and naysaying of everyday life. Manage direction, not motion, and the world may one day owe you an apology for scoffing at your grandest dreams.

Good and Great Are the Enemies of Possible

We must not be afraid of dreaming the seemingly impossible if we want the seemingly impossible to become reality.

—Václav Havel

My grandparents, whom you will hear about from time to time in this book, had a big influence on my life. My mother's father, Wendell Downing, was an accomplished physician and surgeon. He always took time to share his knowledge, experiences, and wisdom with me. I was his first grandchild, and he had suffered some tragic losses in his life;[1] maybe that's why he always made time for me.

During the early years when I would visit him at his medical office, I always noticed a blue index card tucked in the corner of his ink blotter. On it were these words: "Good and great are the enemies of what's possible." During one of our many conversations about this topic, he gave me that small card as a reminder to carry with me. On the back of it he had written:

There will always be a conflict between good, great, and possible.

—Henry Martyn Leland

My grandfather loved writing down wisdom he received from many sources. In this case, the author of the quote, Henry Martyn Leland, exemplified what my grandfather valued: the capacity to constantly question "good enough" and continually press beyond what the world considered "great" to imagine instead what might become possible, and then to bring a wholly new standard into reality. Among other things, Leland invented a better automobile in 1902 when most people considered it a great accomplishment just to attach four wheels to an internal combustion engine. That automobile was the first Cadillac, with many features that made it safer, more reliable, and more enjoyable to drive. Then, at the age of seventy-six, when he felt Cadillac was resting on its laurels, he invented another automobile whose brand name became synonymous with quality—the Lincoln. His design for the Lincoln engine was entirely new, based not on previous automobile design but on innovations Leland had developed while manufacturing airplane engines during World War I.[2]

Aiming just for "good enough" traps us in mediocrity. Striving toward great is better, but even achieving greatness often holds the seeds of its own downfall. Only reaching always for what's possible keeps us fully alive and fully in touch with our true potential. The author and poet John O'Donohue has said, "Always we tend to equate 'the limit' with the limits of what's possible, but it never is. If you could look at limits in a creative way, the limit would always be the invitation to the beyond that you don't know yet."[3]

Impossible is not a fact, it's just an opinion. Or a question mark. It's temporary. As the indomitable conductor of the Boston Philharmonic, Benjamin Zander, puts it, "You can choose one of three responses to any experience that you have: resignation, anger, or possibility."[4] Selecting the third response—"standing in possibility," in Zander's words—means rejecting impossibility and imagining and creating what can be, instead of stewing over what was or settling for what is.

NEUROPLASTICITY AND YOU

Your brain is your ally in this. Whenever brain cells are activated—by new sights, sounds, conversations, creative pursuits, or problem-solving—they begin to change. They produce more electrochemical energy, form new connections, remodel nerve endings, improve receptor networks, and revitalize your overall brain function.[5] You become more capable, smarter, and more vibrantly involved with life. Each time you reach further, your brain becomes better at helping you go beyond that.[6]

With practice you can strengthen and embolden the more forward-looking and inventive parts of your brain, the places that see your life and the world as it could be and ask, why not? If, at the same time, you take action to quiet down the usual outcry of your brain's other hyper-reactionary areas—the ones that tend to hijack your attention and overwhelm your biochemistry and work against you—you can really make progress toward your top priorities.[7] In a positive upward spiral, these actions turn your life and work toward what's better and deeper, not just what's easiest or most popular.

It takes rehearsal to build new skills, particularly if you're aiming to overturn deeply ingrained patterns or habits.[8] Fortunately, some of that practice requires only moments of sharpened focus, rather than hours.[9] Even just envisioning a new way to respond to a challenge activates the same brain cells that are required to perfectly perform that response.[10]

The whole structure of the brain, in fact, can be changed just by thinking, a phenomenon called "neuroplasticity."[11] For instance, recent brain scans of Tibetan Buddhist monks showed that the brains of monks who had spent many hours in meditation had acquired a far different structure than the brains of monks who were novice meditators. As the *Wall Street Journal* reported, "[A]ctivity in the left prefrontal cortex (the seat of positive emotions such as happiness) swamped activity in the right prefrontal (site of negative emotions and anxiety), something never before seen from purely mental activity. A sprawling circuit that switches on at the sight of suffering also showed greater activity in the monks. So did regions responsible for planned movement, as if the monks' brains were itching to go to the aid of those in distress."[12]

Similarly, as described recently in *The New York Times Magazine*, "Brain scans of London cabbies showed that the detailed mental maps they had built up in the course of navigating their city's compli-cated streets were apparent in their brains. Not only was the posterior hippocampus—one area of the brain where spatial representations are stored—larger in the drivers; the increase in size was proportional to the number of years they had been on the job."[13]

And here's one more startling example of the power of thought alone: A muscle can be physically strengthened merely by visualizing it getting stronger.[14] Thirty adults were tested using a purely mental "exercise routine" for fifteen minutes a day over twelve weeks. In each "workout" they imagined they were doing fifty repetitions of exercise for their little finger and elbow joint. At the end of the test, the sub-jects had increased strength in the finger by an average of 35 percent and in the elbow by 13.4 percent—literally without lifting a finger.[15] Similar experiments aimed at developing the biceps have yielded similar results.[16]

There's also the anterior cingulate cortex (ACC), which serves as one of the brain's "gear-shifters," freeing changes in behavior and helping you be open and flexible.[17] When the ACC isn't working well enough, we tend to get locked onto negative thoughts or behaviors and have trouble noticing pivotal moments or seeing options in stressful situations.[18] What your brain becomes, and how it develops to aid in serving your deepest needs for accomplishing what matters most to you, is within your control.

HOW GOOD AND GREAT HOLD US BACK

Reaching for what's possible changes you. You start becoming what you were born to be—an original in your own right who doesn't turn away but steps forward, someone who keeps wondering what might be and sets out to create it. You devise better ways to exceed the best you've ever given to the world instead of marching in place or just polishing the edges of what you're already good or great at.

Resting on what's considered great has always been a recipe for decline. I remember touring Rome once with a guide who pointed out one marvelous achievement after another of the first Roman emperor, Augustus. Augustus was said to have inherited a city of brick and left a city of marble, with twelve entrances on twelve hills. He built nearly a thousand glorious new structures—bridges, buildings, monuments, and aqueducts. As we marveled at the remnants of Augustus's grand designs, our guide exclaimed with pride that this era marked the pinnacle of Rome's greatness.

"What came next?" I asked.

After an awkward silence, the guide said, "Slow ruin."

It's much the same for individuals, groups, and organizations today.[19] For example, *Forbes* magazine annually names a Company of the Year, based on past performance and projected staying power. The winners would seem to have the right to proclaim themselves "great," yet since 1995 more than half of them have suffered precipitous declines almost immediately after being named.[20] Being king of the business hill one day doesn't tell much about a company's future—of the 1955 Fortune 500, 70 percent are now out of business.[21] Of the companies on the 1979 Fortune 500 list, 40 percent no longer exist.[22] Of those on the 2000 list, 30 percent are already gone.[23] The data show that excellent companies one year rarely sustain that excellence for long; visionary companies built to last often don't; and organizations that move from good to great get passed by almost as soon as they're crowned.[24]

Here's one of the hidden reasons why: Our brains are wired in many ways to make "great" a difficult status to maintain. Staying on top requires constant change and adaptation, and that creates pressure. Our inherent reaction to such pressure is deeply embedded in our neural pathways—as a survival mechanism, human beings are designed to do whatever is necessary to avoid stress, minimize pain, eliminate surprises, fend off uncertainty, and resist change. Your brain's deep and ancient amygdala, for instance, craves routine and promotes the repetition of habits. It wants to make sure you avoid venturing into the unknown. From its place inside your brain's limbic system (which we'll discuss later), it scans everything that happens to you or could happen to you, moment to moment, ever alert for even a hint of a change in your normal patterns, and when it detects such a change it floods you with warnings about the dangers of what you're doing.[25]

Where there are no changes, there are no worries, the amygdala seems to say. But when you take the small, specific actions in this book to reduce the panic-button tendencies of the amygdala, you make changes with less stress. You experience a second benefit, too, because the amygdala is not purely a blindly instinctive emotional reaction center; it also helps uphold your guiding values—both in living them and defending them.[26] It's not just your ancient and often misplaced fear reactions that are wired very deep inside you; your most enduring values are there, too.

Not only are your values there, they are hooked up to deep emotional resources that can propel you forward. There are far more neural connections running from your amygdala to your higher, more thoughtful brain centers (such as the cerebral cortex) than there are running in the other direction. This reflects the fact that our emotions influence our thinking significantly more than our thinking influences our feelings. Sometimes that power of emotions can be counterproductive, if unfiltered emotional reactions are permitted to run your behavior. But when your emotions are aligned toward something that matters to you, such as the enduring values your amygdala embraces, the other meaning-driven brain centers work in that direction, too.

Whatever you do, you will do it more purposefully when your emotions are appropriately engaged. A core concept here is "emotional experiential memory," or EEM. Essentially, one function of your brain's limbic system[27] is to test all your experiences and decide which ones it would like you to repeat and which ones it would like you to avoid, and it stores that information in your emotional experiential memory.

At the most basic level, your EEM contains information like "Ice cream. Good. Repeat." And "Touching hot stove. Bad. Avoid." At higher levels, your EEM contains messages about the satisfactions and dissatisfactions of achieving your goals, living your values, honoring your relationships with others, and all the other things that ultimately define what your life will add up to. The more you engage with things that inspire you emotionally, the more powerful is your motivation to achieve them. Your EEM provides a "higher gear" that stimulates forceful self-regulated action for making new choices that move you toward what really matters most to you.[28]

With the EEM and the limbic system, as we saw with the amygdala, there's a double-edged quality. There's a drive to succeed, because success feels good. And then there's a deep and enduring drive to be cautious, to not go beyond what has already succeeded, for two related reasons. First, moving toward something new and better involves change, and change involves doing things differently, and things you do differently can go wrong. So instinct tells you to stick with what you know and what you've done before. Second, we all have many bad memories associated with "failing" at things that are new to us, and the limbic system has them all cataloged. Maybe they happened in school, in sports, in relationships, at a new job or task, or in any one of many other areas, but they're all still there in your brain. So your EEM has access to a very broad category of things under the heading "Change. Painful. Avoid"[29] as well as the other end of the spectrum with powerful positive emotion-centered memories and aspirations.

I'll talk more later about getting the positive parts of your brain on your side and aligned toward achieving your deepest and farthest goals. EEM plays a crucial role in that. But for now you can see how much pressure your brain can exert on you to protect and defend success instead of seeking new challenges. That also makes "great" a dangerous place to be. Whenever we become great at something, we instinctively stop doing the kinds of new and ingenious things that *grew* that greatness and unconsciously but powerfully switch our attention and energies to *holding on* to our lead or fame, repeating what we believe got us there.

Just before he was decisively defeated by Wellington's innovative tactics at Waterloo, Napoléon said, "My way is proven superior." Success often reassures us that we've hit on the one best way to succeed—*our* way.[30] There are certain warning signs in the business world of greatness rigidifying into failure, and it's easy to see how the same kinds of disaster-inviting perceptions can take over the lives of individuals in any situation. Here are some of those warning signs:

- You start believing that you have all the best answers.
- You resent and resist anyone who is not 100 percent behind your view.
- You "go Hollywood," obsessed with your image rather than being genuine or true.
- You underestimate emerging obstacles.
- You see yourself dominating the field or environment.
- You rely on what worked for you in the past.[31]

THE NEUROSCIENCE OF WHAT'S POSSIBLE

To be sure that our greatest achievements are a series of momentary points on the rising path to what's possible, and not the beginnings of our decline, we must counteract the deep influence of the amygdala and other ancient parts of the limbic system. Fortunately, there are other brain resources that with some practice can help us do that—in particular, the frontal lobes region and, inside it, your prefrontal cortex (PFC).

The frontal lobes provide the core circuits of working memory, temporarily storing key insights that can be compared, contrasted, and integrated by the executive functions of the brain and which support goal-directed behavior.[32] But you have to consciously apply your frontal lobes to help you, or any progress will be hit and miss. It's very easy when you're living in a rushing, reactive mode to have the frontal lobes all but drowned out by the doom-and-gloom brain regions that clamor for attention and can flood your body with stress chemicals at the slightest bit of pressure or foreshadowing of change.

In order to sense a new idea or shape a better future, we must first create it in the brain as a possibility.[33] Otherwise it remains invisible to us. The prefrontal cortex is where new ideas have a chance to take hold and grow. It gives you the ability to make plans, compare concepts, and assemble your intuitive perceptions into a unified whole. It frees you from the grip of habit, custom, and fear.[34]

The PFC integrates incoming stimuli from your senses and other brain areas and then oversees the working memory circuits that move your intentions into action.[35] Every time you envision a goal or target that is emotionally compelling to you personally, you activate the PFC, and you also energize the positive aspects of your emotional experiential memory toward building new successes instead of simply defending old ones.

But it takes practice to get the PFC fully on your side. With practice you can train it to activate faster and stay more firmly in a guidance-toward-your-goals mode, which also helps keep the faster-reacting watch-out-this-could-be-bad brain areas like the amygdala from hijacking your attention. The greater the PFC preactivation, as it's called—using simple tools like those described in this chapter—the more successful you will be at performing goal-related actions.[36] If you are more oriented toward external drivers—such as the rewards of being labeled "great" and the satisfactions of repeating what's already good—than you are to internal rewards and deeper purpose, then the PFC does not come to your aid.[37]

When that happens, your brain lapses into a zero-sum game. This feels natural because it's so common—many of us have been taught that you can only find your best, and then better it, through head-to-head competition. Once in a while that kind of competition does produce dramatic breakthroughs, but more often it limits your accomplishments and hinders your attainment of what's possible. In today's world, those who surpass the best find that it's excelling, not competing, that makes the biggest difference.[38] They realize that their triumphs do not require someone else to lose.[39]

Whenever you launch into a competitive mind-set, assuming you have to defeat others in order to reach your goals, you are likely to become a victim of that very mind-set.[40] Such competitiveness has been shown to stall forward progress altogether and waste up to 40 percent of people's time at work.[41]

Competition inhibits learning and creativity because people in conditions of competition focus solely on the task at hand, paying too much attention to what competitors are doing, comparing themselves to others but not to greater possibilities, and trying to win the favor of those who are judging the contest.[42]

Even thinking competitive thoughts can interfere with best performance and increase the release of negative stress hormones.[43] In studies on athletes, for example, competitive words such as "harder," "better," "faster," and "win" stimulated more than double the normal levels of stress hormones. Researchers recommend that people "abandon competitive thinking during exercise," because "performance improves when you take pressure off yourself."[44] In fact, according to one leading student of performance, "superior performance not only does not *require* competition; it usually seems to require its absence."[45]

Star-performing individuals and teams replace the goal of getting across the finish line ahead of the other person with the aim of going beyond the best they have ever given because doing so matters to them personally, for its own sake.

TAPPING INTO WHAT'S POSSIBLE

Even before science had fully understood the functions of the amygdala, the limbic system, and the prefrontal cortex, my grandfather sensed how to tap into the neuroscience of what's possible. He would tell me, "Always be appreciative when someone calls your efforts 'great,' but only let it into your heart and mind for about ten seconds. Then ask, What's deeper? What's better? What's next?"

To do that, you have to put courage and curiosity ahead of your fears and reservations. When a 3M chemist accidentally spilled a vial of liquid fluorocarbon on his new athletic shoes, he tried desperately to hose it off with water and save his shoes. The water just rolled off. In many settings, such an accident would be an embarrassment, but not for this engineer at 3M, whose curiosity about possibilities was stronger than his desire to make excuses for a mistake. Scotchgard was born.

Chocolate-chip cookies are another example of a mistake turned into a bonanza by someone willing to take the next step beyond wounded pride. In 1930, Ruth Wakefield wanted to make chocolate cookies for the customers at her well-known restaurant. She cut a bar of chocolate into small bits and mixed it with her cookie dough, expecting it to melt. What she expected didn't happen, but she served the results anyway, and a worldwide favorite came into being. So it is, also, for the microwave oven, windshield wipers, Coca-Cola, Silly Putty, cellophane, dynamite, the yo-yo, and dozens of other products, all of which were mistakes that turned out to be gold mines.[46]

DON'T COUNT ON THE EXPERTS

The experts might scoff as you aim past the next imaginary "limit." But the experts' predictive powers leave a lot to be desired. On a lonesome high-school athletic field, Dick Fosbury realized that he could jump higher over a crossbar by turning onto his back when he was in the air than by doing what everyone had always done, which was to scissor across the bar one leg at a time. Traditionalists were aghast— until Fosbury soared his way to a gold medal and an Olympic high jump record in 1968, forever changing his sport.

Even then, the "experts" continued to defend what they "knew" to be great. "Kids imitate champions," U.S. Olympic coach Payton Jordan, of Yale, said at the time. "If they try to imitate Fosbury, he will wipe out an entire generation of high jumpers because they will all have broken necks."[47]

Before you succumb to the constricted thinking of the so-called experts, remember how inclined they often are to consider today's best as all there is. Louis Lumière, for example, had the foresight to open the world's first movie theater, in Paris, in 1895. His company's films were shown all around the world. And then, declaring that "the cinema is an invention without any commercial future," he quit the business for good in 1900.[48] And just a year before Lumière's premature exit from the movie business, the commissioner of the U.S.

Patent Office, Charles H. Duell, resigned his position, announcing, "Everything that can be invented has been invented."[49]

Other formidable experts have gone out on the forecasting limb to assert the following:

No one will ever set foot on the moon.
There's a world market for about five computers.
Plastic cards will never replace cash.
Lord of the Rings *can never be made into a successful movie.*
Rock and roll won't last a year.
Overnight delivery can't succeed as a business.
Instant messaging will never catch on.

Those experts couldn't really imagine the future, but others did, and proved them wrong. It's always wise to remember what the science writer Arthur C. Clarke defined as his "first law": "When a distinguished but elderly scientist states that something is possible, he is almost certainly right. When he states that something is impossible, he is very probably wrong."[50]

HEADING TOWARD WHAT'S IMPOSSIBLE

You can't make what's possible happen until you imagine it. Awakening and engaging your prefrontal cortex to imagine what you can achieve that is better than your best is the first step toward achieving the impossible.

Ask one question whenever you're about to settle for doing something in a certain way: *Will this choice propel me toward the outer edges of what's possible, or keep me repeating what's good or defending what's great?*

To gain insight into that question, do the opposite of what most people do: Go out of your way to talk with spirited and demanding people who are not satisfied with good or great, those who disrupt the status quo instead of settling for it. Difficult colleagues. Discontented customers. Clients who push your limits. Demanding investors. Tough coaches and persistent mentors. These men and women can provide the stimulus for you to reach for what's possible instead of settling for good or great.

The tension in our brains between changing nothing and building for a different, better future is always with us. How you manage it determines how close you come to achieving the best of what's possible for you. The future is being rewritten every day in every endeavor. Yesterday's progressive thinking becomes today's passé news. You can keep repeating what got you here, or you can keep unlocking hidden capacity to reach for more of what's possible. It's always a choice.

THE HEART AND THE HORIZON

Becoming better than the best starts deep inside you—and far outside you. To an amazing degree that we are just beginning to understand, we genuinely think with our hearts. Star performers start with a well-defined and concrete "impossible" goal they care deeply about and then they build a through-line that clearly connects here with there. In the presence of emotionally arousing stimuli that matter to your life and goals, your brain switches into what is called a motive state[51]—one that seeks coordinated information processing inside and across brain regions and that produces engaged behavior toward positive goals and away from negative outcomes.[52]

Goals that fully engage your heart—and connect it through emotional experimental memory (EEM) with a better future you can feel as well as see—change everything, shifting thinking from herky-jerky problem-solving and firefighting to a smooth, fully aligned progression toward higher-than-expected targets. We'll discuss this more in a moment.

It also helps to think about the horizon. In everyday life, the horizon is the farthest point you can see, but you also know there is vastly more beyond it than there is on your side of it. In our crowded, busy world, to gaze out at miles of open space as the sun rises or sets or the stars come out, even for a few moments, allows us to catch our breath and regain our bearings. From a window, rooftop, cliff, or highway overlook, the horizon is not an arbitrary line but the gateway into the far distance, a place from which we can fix and then extend our gaze in wonder and awe.

The horizon we perceive is more than an image, it's a catalyst that moves us forward. If you check in with yourself, especially as a first thing you do after awakening and a last thing you ponder before retiring at night, how far out do your thoughts and dreams extend?

As the German statesman Konrad Adenauer, who was arrested for plotting to kill Hitler during World War II and later became the first chancellor of West Germany, leading that country to prosperous recovery and reintegration into the world community, said, "We all live under the same sky, but we don't all have the same horizon."

Studies of the most successful men and women across industries and fields indicate that they almost invariably have the longest time horizons.[53] When you keep glancing into the future and connecting that view with your current actions, you increase activity patterns throughout your brain that drive your awareness and actions today toward your highest goals five years or more ahead.[54, 55, 56]

Here's a dramatic example of what can happen when your horizon shrinks. Far from his upbringing in a tiny impoverished village in Mexico, twenty-six-year-old German Silva was leading the 1994 New York City Marathon's silver anniversary run. He was the best runner that day, but no one back home could see him, because no one there had a television or electricity.

Silva entered the last mile of the marathon with a substantial lead, triumphantly running past the blur of banners and faces, the roar of the crowd ringing in his ears. His training partner and friend, Benjamin Parades, was not far behind, but Silva knew he could win a sprint to the finish line.

Very tired and a bit disconcerted by all that was happening, Silva decided just to focus on the car directly in front of him that held the camera that was broadcasting the end of the race. With only a few hundred yards to go, the car left Central Park South and made a right turn onto Seventh Avenue. Silva followed close behind. His lead had grown, and he no longer sensed his teammate behind him. The crowd was yelling, but the nature of its shouts seemed to have changed.

Silva sensed something was wrong. He suddenly realized that his deep inner drive had become too connected to the car in front of him. He had lost his own directional bearings. The car—which had needed to veer aside to clear the finish line—had taken him the wrong way. By the time he got turned around, there were two-tenths of a mile to the finish line, and his friend had a fifty-yard advantage.

Silva saw the true finish line and sprinted with everything he had. He passed Parades to win by the smallest margin in the marathon's history—two seconds.

German Silva managed to prevent one of the greatest disappointments in sports history. He had been better trained than his rivals, stronger and better focused. His energy was higher. But for a few crucial seconds he devoted all of his talent, confidence, and training on the wrong direction, and he almost lost the race he was meant to win.

OPEN SPACE OR CLOSED SPACE, THAT'S THE REAL QUESTION

German Silva almost lost when his vision shifted from what I call *open space* to what I call *closed space*. It's in open space where the impossible becomes possible; closed space traps us in routines and paying too much attention to what's right in front of us.

I call the place where you want to be open space in honor of a handwritten note that had been passed down to my grandfather Downing, written by his grandfather William Andrew Downing shortly before he left Dublin for America in 1800. "My life has become a closed world," the note read, "with little room left to hope or breathe. I can only struggle against endless limits, in long lines, longing for work, a morsel of food, some small advantage. It is madness.

On the horizon is where hope lives. It is open spaces I dream of, across an unknown sea. I am going there."

Even though today's world may seem quite different to us, full of distracting possibilities, I believe we all still crave this kind of open space, the chance to breathe deeply, to hope bigger and touch the horizon of possibilities.

Because our brains are hardwired to protect old habits, favor close-in perception, and play it safe with tiny incremental changes, we tend to live mostly in closed space. That's where almost all daily work and life takes place; it's where virtually everyone is, and it's more crowded in there every day. Tensions rise over the smallest and simplest of things: when we're traffic-bound at 10 miles an hour in a car that could do 120, when we find ourselves fixating on finding a close-in parking space or fuming when we make the wrong guess as to which lane will move fastest at the grocery store. When we struggle to improve our job performance by a few percentage points or to gain a few more pennies of profit.

In closed space, we inexorably become passive about the future—we put it off: "There'll be plenty of time for that later; I have all I can do to deal with things right here, right now." We find ourselves reacting to life as it drags us along instead of actively creating it as we go forward. We polish our existing habits instead of creating break-throughs.

When closed-space thinking is all you do from day to day and week to week, it creates perceptual blindness and a boxed-in way of living and leading that can—and must—be overcome to create the most successful future.

Open space is where you can move beyond good and great into something deeper, next, and more. It's where the "impossible" happens—where you can choose to step outside the usual confines of your job or role or habitual way of thinking. It's where you excel—where you devote yourself to surpassing your own previous best efforts, not by an inch but by a mile—instead of competing where someone else has to lose for you to win.

In all walks of life and roles of work, the most exceptional people commit themselves to discovering and pilot-testing open-space opportunities no one else sees.[57] In open space, you have dramatically higher chances of creating the next big thing in your life—or the next really amazing small thing with big ramifications—while everyone else is waiting around for someone else to do it.

An example from the business world illustrates the difference it makes to think in open-space terms. A recent decade-long study looked at new businesses launched by 108 well-known companies. Most of those new businesses weren't really very new: 86 percent of them were just incremental, closed-space changes in existing products or services. The remaining 14 percent were true open-space breakthroughs. The impact on profits was disproportionate, to say the least: the closed-space launches accounted for just 39 percent of total profits for their companies, while the open-space ideas contributed 61 percent of total profits to the companies that were willing and able to think and act in bold new ways.[58]

WHAT YOU SEE IS WHAT YOU WILL GET

If you can't see open-space opportunities, then you can't seize them. Unable to see open space or think in open space, we relegate our attention to closed space, reasoning, "That's just the way life is," or "I'm only dreaming if I think it could really be much different," and then we automatically, even numbly, buy an extra lottery ticket along with our convenience store purchases, vaguely hoping for a miracle but not expecting one.

It's as if you've been working endlessly and diligently to polish the walls, floors, and furniture of a small room, always believing that this is the room of life. But once you've seen today's good and great for the constraints they are, then a secret window gets opened, and all at once you realize that you've been missing the big picture—that this is only one small closed room in a vast city, country, planet, and universe. Everything begins to change.

This kind of directional self-awareness may be the single most powerful source of inner motivation to achieve what everyone else thinks you can't.[59] Brain scans show that simply imagining a complex and compelling goal will actually fire the same neurons that will be required to actually achieve that goal.[60] Even a few minutes of open-space focus can point your life and work in the right direction for you to achieve what others may think you can't. In the pages ahead, I'll show you the rare art and science of turning your impossible goals into reality, one moment at a time.

3

What You Guide, Grows

Behind every impossible achievement is a dreamer of impossible dreams.

—ROBERT K. GREENLEAF

There's a part of you, deep inside your brain and spirit, that's a bit like a heat-seeking missile, searching by instinct and feel for something of true significance, craving big goals. That part of you wants to stop meandering in closed space and grasp the full mosaic of understanding about what matters to you and your life, before it's too late. The most amazing leaders in the business world are long-term thinkers, not near-term zealots.[1] Those men and women in every walk of life who make the biggest lasting difference almost always keep looking farther ahead than they have to and continually link that longtime horizon to their actions today.[2]

We now know many of the neural mechanisms by which the most powerful open space aims emerge in the brain to mobilize and align our attention and actions. The good news is that it appears that everything you need is already in there. For one example, inside the brain's orbital cortex—where, as I mentioned earlier, you see forward without actually, literally, seeing with your eyes—you can enlist some powerful inner motivation.[3] Every time you envision the future and contrast that with your current choices for action, you activate not only the forebrain and prefrontal cortex but also the orbital cortex, and together these areas influence what you attend to and what you ignore.[4] But they only succeed at that if you actively endow your perceptions with personally relevant meaning and purpose that extends far forward into the future.[5]

The writer Walker Percy once said that a tragedy of our modern life is that everything is interesting but nothing becomes deeply important. One of the findings of the new field of neuroeconomics is that our brains easily get overwhelmed by too many "interesting" choices, and we usually end up sticking with whatever we did before, uninspiring as that may be.[6] So it's not easy to pick your large, passionate, overarching goal and aim your energy and ingenuity toward it, but that action is what changes your life from interesting to important.

This chapter is aimed at making your open-space goals so clear and electrifying that, day after day and moment by moment, your brain will naturally begin to put them front and center.

Whenever you determine that something is vital to your future or to your deeper possibilities—whenever it is *salient,* as neuroscientists say—it ignites a further stream of brain and neural actions to bring about what you deeply want.[7] For example, the sensory cortex in each of the brain's hemispheres receives the goal input and labels it as important to your future. The motor cortex primes your overall physiology for action in pursuit of that goal. The hippocampus integrates multisensory inputs from all directions and keeps pointing you—in time and space—toward the goal.[8]

Wired on a neural pathway to other goal-oriented parts of your brain, the hippocampus actively guides the way your life is moving forward, even when you're not aware that it's doing so.[9] As other brain areas feed in sensory inputs, the hippocampus helps transform them into actionable knowledge for whatever comes next.[10]

All those brain parts, and others, are lined up with each other, harnessed together, and ready to propel you toward an open space target, creating the through-line from what you will do the next minute all the way out to fully realizing your aim. As you act, receive input from your senses about the consequences of your actions, and construct what it all means to you, you can begin to automatically make new changes and see better choices.

That's not to say you become an open-space-goal-achieving machine overnight. Lots of other brain functions and habits want to derail you—and they will. But after a while you will be able to stay a step ahead, learning to shift to your deeper self each time a key moment appears, rather than being run by that squadron of simpletons clamoring for yesterday's comforts instead of tomorrow's dreams.

Open space outcomes are within reach of us all. There are no prerequisites, educational requirements, or cultural, age, religious, gender, or geographic barriers. If you can begin to look forward in an open-space way, then you free up reservoirs of ingenuity and determination you never knew you had. An open-space goal becomes real in a much larger and more powerful way than most goals. And at once you begin to grow your way into it, against all odds.

What you guide, grows. Unless you consciously intervene in your brain's processes, the voice of your biggest dreams gets drowned out by the rush and roar of the mundane.[11] The stress expert Loretta LaRoche says that most of us spent way too much time building up tension about what we're supposed to be doing—"musturbating" and "shoulding on ourselves," as she puts it—instead of delighting in doing what we really want to do.[12] People who grasp their own original goals in distinctive and specific ways are 50 percent more likely to take confident actions to achieve those goals, and a third more likely to feel a sense of control under stressful conditions.[13]

BE UNREALISTIC

The stronger your open-space vision, the more you activate the exact nerve circuits that make it all possible. Studies of highly successful men and women across all fields of endeavor show that they almost invariably have the largest far-reaching aspirations, even if others ridicule them as "dreamers."[14]

Just a few of the right minutes applied in the right way every day to creating the future will allow you to capture more and more opportunities that otherwise you would have missed. Let areas of the forebrain atrophy because you fail to stimulate them to envision the future, and you automatically, invisibly, deep in your brain's structure, become more rigid and rule-anchored, unable to change. You get mired in old habits and limitations, less able to survive change, let alone dream big and make those dreams into realities. You know people like this, and now you know why, no matter what you do, you can't get them genuinely excited about a better, different future, or truly engaged in building such a future.

Shoetop gazing—attending only to what's right in front of you—severely limits, or even shuts down, your orbital cortex, for example, whereas aiming your vision toward the future is a driver of motivation, ingenuity, and initiative.[15] The Russian neurosurgeon A. R. Luria pioneered research on the forebrain and how our perception of time affects health and performance. Among other things, Luria found that when we look farther ahead each day, beyond our immediate to-do list—reaching ahead at least five years, envisioning the life and work we wish to achieve—the forebrain's key areas are activated.[16]

What are some of the results of regularly gazing farther ahead than you have to? Consider the life of a man who actually had a daily time horizon of one hundred to two hundred years.[17] Surely what he envisioned was fantasy, but the simple act of imagining so far ahead—if *this,* then *that,* then the world would need *this*—not only deepened the perspective and jolted the spirit of ingenuity in those around him, but also freed him for humanitarian causes that have touched the world.

By many standards, that man didn't look like an imposing leader. Early pictures of Konosuke Matsushita reveal a serious young man whose ears, as one observer said, stuck out like airplane wings.[18] He never weighed more than 135 pounds or grew taller than five feet five inches. Unlike his rival Akio Morita at Sony, he was neither charismatically handsome nor internationally recognized. He didn't excel at public speaking, and his voice was frail. He rarely displayed dazzling intellect or captured an audience's attention with spellbinding humor or storytelling. Yet he lived every day with a one-hundred-to two-hundred-year time horizon, and he motivated large groups of individuals to do the impossible and, against all odds, improve the human condition.

Matsushita started his adult life with no money, no connections, less than four years of formal education, and a family history filled with trauma. He struggled with the early deaths of family members, an apprenticeship that demanded sixteen-hour days at age nine, all the problems associated with starting a business with neither money nor connections, the death of his only son, the Great Depression, and the horror of World War II in Japan.

After working as a wiring specialist for a public utility, Matsushita went into business for himself in 1917, manufacturing sockets, and tasted his first success with a cheap, reliable bicycle lamp. The still-young entrepreneur soon diversified into batteries, radios, and allied products, becoming a commercial force in his homeland's wholesale and retail markets. His company's growth in revenues exceeded that of the companies of such famous entrepreneurs as Soichiro Honda (Honda), Sam Walton (Wal-Mart), Akio Morita (Sony), James Cash Penney (J. C. Penney), and Henry Ford. Matsushita built Matsushita Electric Industrial Corporation into the world's largest consumer electronics company, turning out such familiar brands as Panasonic, Technics, and Quasar, and generating $65 billion a year.

His open-space successes provided billions of dollars in wealth that he used not for villas in Europe, but also for the creation of a Nobel Prize–like organization, the founding of a school of government to reform Japan's political system, and a number of other civic projects aimed at ending hunger and despair. During his later years, he wrote dozens of books, studied human nature with a small group of research associates, and prodded his government to do more for the citizenry. The Matsushita story demonstrates the power of a truly long-term outlook, idealistic goals backed by the daily drive to see them through, and humility in the face of great success.

Individuals with a short time horizon—wholly right now, today, or this week, for example—tend to be unable to change.[19] On the other hand, those individuals in every walk of life, like Matsushita, who commit to a longtime horizon—those who devote at least a brief time each day to step beyond their right-now accomplishments and see far forward beyond today—are more adaptable, able to change and grow, and across time significantly more successful: They are most likely to demonstrate leadership, thrive under pressure, earn higher incomes, and have happier and longer lasting relationships.[20]

TO SEE FARTHER FORWARD, FIRST LOOK BACKWARD

The brain easily forgets how yesterday's "miracles" became today's commonplace reality. One way to break the grip of closed-space thinking is to look backward first and then forward. Think of ten things that today you take for granted but that weren't even imagined five to twenty-five years ago. How about:

- Telephones that take and send photos
- ATMs
- Wireless Internet
- Overnight delivery
- Satellite television
- Your own Web site or blog
- Instant messaging
- Keyless car-door openers
- OnStar
- Personal computers
- iPod, iTunes
- Air travel for the cost of car travel

These and many other open-space breakthroughs have rocked our world. Some individual or team conceived each and every one of them and brought them into being by looking at the world everyone else saw and then looking past it into the future. They asked, What's deeper? What's next? In your own unique way you can do the same, if you choose to.

THE FICTION OF PREDICTION

Cynics contend the future is all fog, and that fixed planning fails. To a degree, it's true. If you set a rigid distant goal, chances are by the time you reach it you won't want it anymore, or the world won't need it in that form anymore.[21] It's just as foolhardy to ignore the fuzziness of the future altogether and rely on right-now hustle and good luck, hoping for the best someday.[22]

The power of pursuing open-space goals is not just what you get, but what you become along the way. Take an open-space goal of ending homelessness. Let's say you're an architect and planner and this gets you thinking up new designs that build safe, inspiring housing for a tenth of the lowest current cost. As the design evolves, things change and improve. Your first source of funding to pilot-build a neighborhood of the new homes in one of the poorest townships of South Africa changes in midstream. All kinds of other doors open along the way, creating allies who bring their own contributions to the project. It's not castles-in-the-air wishful thinking, you're *growing* your way toward this compelling possibility—alert to the next opportunities, adapting and expanding your aims and actions as you go. Fiction? No, it's one of the Change the World paths of leadership at the award-winning firm, BSB Design.

That's where open-space goals work best, bringing your emotional experiential memory into play to mobilize a host of internal self-regulation and motivation sources that guide you to persevere and to innovate your way through distractions and uncertainty in the *direction* of your meaningful larger target, which will almost surely keep morphing into something different, deeper, or more even as you approach it.[23]

SETTING AND HITTING YOUR OPEN-SPACE TARGETS

Start thinking about your own open-space targets, a year from now, five years from now. Remember, they should stretch you. They should feel uncomfortable. That's a sign that you're onto something. Make sure you're thinking in open space, at least five years ahead. Start by asking yourself what future successes are most important to you—in your work and in your life. Dig deep. Pick something that seems very unlikely or even unattainable. This stretch factor is one way that open space targets "grow" us. They have the power to light our inner fire and stretch our perspectives at the same time they get us stoked, jazzed, or revved up in the moment. And as they compel us to move toward them, doing so changes how we listen, invent, imagine, test new approaches, learn, and expand our capacities from this level to the next.

Your open-space targets could include anything—education, hope, love, achievement, invention, caring for others, security . . . you name it. What goals get you the most excited when you think about accomplishing them? You might aspire to put food on your table—or to feed the whole world. Either of those goals can be an open-space goal, depending on your situation. If you ache to feed your family, then that's the "impossible" that will move you toward your aim. When you have enough food but realize how many others don't, then you could move your open-space goal in that direction.

If your biggest five-year dream is to own your own home, then an open-space goal could be to put a permanent roof over your head. And if you think hard about it, even while putting a roof over your own family's heads, maybe you could also be helping others have a roof, too, the way Habitat for Humanity and other projects encourage volunteers to step in to help for a few hours or days at a time. That's how open space starts to unlock parallel possibilities: One open-space target may be strengthened when it's aligned with a similar but even bigger open-space target.

Or maybe you teach Third World agricultural development, like Professor Dan Clay at Michigan State University, and your open-space goal is to bring your field out of the classroom and, in a very tangible way, into the world's great places of need.[24] What happens next is you find yourself thinking about Rwanda, a place where Clay worked prior to fleeing violence in 1994—the genocide in which Hutu tribesmen killed nearly a million of their Tutsi rivals. Coffee, one of the country's biggest exports, was another casualty of the chaos and dislocation of those days. But Clay knew that Rwanda has an ideal climate for coffee, and its taste, of blackberry and dark pecans, can't be found anywhere else in the world. Perhaps, he reasoned, there could be a way to bring Rwanda's coffee industry upmarket and avoid the commodity trap that dooms many farmers to subsistence in a coffee-flushed world.

So Clay got inventive. With support from the U.S. Agency for International Development, he teamed with Emile Rwamasirabo, then rector of the National University of Rwanda, and with Tim Schilling, a Texas A&M professor. Together, they formed the Partnership for Enhancing Agriculture in Rwanda through Linkages (PEARL), which Schilling now runs. One open-space idea that emerged from the open-space goal: Create cooperatives whose farmers, one in five of whom are genocide widows or orphans, learn a multistep process for producing gourmet coffee of the highest quality.

Since 2001, PEARL has assisted a dozen cooperatives with fifteen thousand members, many of whom now earn some $400 a year, over twice as much as the typical Rwandan earns. "It's small, but it's growing like wildfire," says Clay.[25] Green Mountain Coffee and Whole Foods are eagerly buying Rwandan coffee, and this year's entire crop sold out. "Rwanda has gone from being completely unknown to being the hottest coffee origin," says Schilling.[26]

What else has the original open-space goal led to so far? New credit financing, because the farmers can't wait up to nine months between harvest and payment. Because the financial needs were too large for microloans but too small for traditional banks, PEARL partnered with EcoLogic Finance, a Cambridge, Massachusetts, nonprofit that makes loans to businesses in Latin America and Africa. Co-ops are also bringing together Hutu and Tutsi farmers, who are now working together for a better future based on their strengths, not what divides them.

An open-space shift can make a lasting difference.

In the early 1990s, I was asked to consult with a company many might consider pretty dull: Cemex, Mexico's leading supplier of cement. As we started working, the usual strategic-planning techniques were employed to try to figure out how to turn this dull and not-very-profitable business into something more profitable. Various growth rates were forecast according to traditional formulas and assumptions such as taking market share from the competition; lots of closed-space thinking went into how to eke out a few more pesos here and there from a population that generally had very few pesos to spare.

At the end of the day, I was frustrated. Standing in the hallway, I urged several of the leaders to look farther ahead. What did they see? More pressure, more competition, and even less breathing room. Not very inspiring. Then one enterprising fellow took the leap that, in the years that followed, transformed the company: What if all Mexicans could be encouraged to look far, far ahead to one of their own seemingly impossible dreams—having enough money saved to build an addition onto their homes, or maybe even a whole new house?

From that thinking—and a flood of creative ideas that followed over the next years—was born the Cemex program called Patrimonio Hoy ("Patrimony Today"), in which families pay small regular amounts—often as gifts at birthdays and holidays, and usually over many years—toward accumulating enough cement to build that addition or that new home. Today more than 5 million people participate in the program, which has changed millions of lives and, along with this, helped reenergize Cemex and its leaders. By pushing vision outward from closed-space changes at the margins to open-space possibilities, Cemex made itself into the world's third-largest cement producer, and the most profitable.

There are many open-space target success stories across the entrepreneurial, humanitarian, and corporate worlds. Here are a few of the many recent examples:

The Australian wine brand with the funny-looking name [yellow tail] that built its brand around consistently great-tasting wines at a true value price and set out to eclipse the sales of all wines from France, Italy, and California combined—and has accomplished that in five years;

Muhammad Yunus, an economics professor from Bangladesh who founded the global microfinance movement after he lent $27 out of his own pocket to a group of poor craftsmen in India, and through their shared experiences, he foresaw a pathway out of despair for 1.2 billion of the world's poorest people who, he came to believe, can be both reliable borrowers and avid entrepreneurs—resulting in more than $5.1 billion in loans to 5.3 million poor people from the institution he now heads, Grameen Bank;

Toyota, where line workers have the true power to innovate and whose quality and efficiency have won it the greatest market share of any auto company;

Ultimate Ears, the small Nevada company that makes custom-fit personal earphones and has captured almost the entire high-end music-listening market;

Curves, which reached a billion dollars in revenue faster than any company in U.S. history by offering no-frills, no-men-allowed, fitness-in-less-time centers for women;

Umpqua Bank, the small yet fastest-growing "world's greatest bank," a service slogan they bring to life every day for their customers;

John and Cynthia Hardy who, with a spirited group of local artisans in Bali, turned a few hundred dollars into a $100 million jewelry line;

Buddy Gopher, the two-person company that turned a marketing budget of seven dollars into a $250,000-a-year business cataloging instant messaging "away messages";

Keen Footwear, three partners who started in an apartment with an edgy but ultra-comfortable sandal design and sold 700,000 pairs in the first year;

Richer Sounds, where weekly ideas from employees have created a business so successful that for 12 straight years the *Guinness Book of World Records* has named it the top retailer in the world;

Cabela's, which began as a small sporting goods store in Sidney, Nebraska, and became a $1.5 billion-a-year retailing phenomenon by rethinking everything about why we love outdoor living;

Lund Dental Clinic in Australia, where the employees, fed up with working 60-hour weeks to earn average pay, stopped doing everything except what they shined at doing and now earn four times the income working about 23 hours a week;

Confederate Motor Co., a small firm devastated by Hurricane Katrina but undeterred in turning passionate design, handcrafting, and "impossible" engineering into the smoothest, most powerful, best-controlled motorcycle ride on earth.

Every day, there are new examples from all corners of the world, from individuals to small companies to the rare long-standing companies that muster what it takes to revolutionize their industries. And every day, there are onetime winners who decide to play it safe, moving back into closed space and fading or falling.

Exceptional individuals and teams have the chance to create open space all the time. One woman entrepreneur I know repeatedly set a five-year open-space aim of transforming the way she approached her daily life so she could be the best mom to her two children in her limited time with them. But then most days she would arrive home, tired from a long day leading her company, the babysitter would leave, her husband would arrive home, and, as she put it, "Things would start falling apart." She made some small progress over the months, but the big breakthroughs never happened. She brought me a cartoon that showed two people talking. The caption: "At last, success! I've cut back to 23/6."

The question I asked her next was "Knowing how important this commitment to your children is to you, what if you only had five months to live—how could you still accomplish it?"

She got very quiet. "If I had five months to live, I would work two hours a day. In those two hours, I would do only what I can best do as a leader. I would delegate everything else I'm doing now. Most of what I do I don't love doing, but I do it anyway. In that two hours a day, I would devise every possible way to get other leaders to take far more responsibility for leading our company. In all the other time, I would build up my energy and get more involved in the lives of my children."

Which is exactly what she did. She delegated everything at work that others could do as well or better than she could. That saved her thirty hours a week. She then streamlined the remaining priorities and pinpointed which innovations, and which customers, she could make the biggest difference with. Two hours a day became one hour a day working from home Monday through Wednesday, and a half day in the office or out with customers on Thursday. All the other hours she turned her mobile phone and e-mail off. Her immediate colleagues knew how to reach her, but her encouragement to them was to take responsibility for exceeding everyone's expectations and, if they called her during her off hours, "the reason you're calling me had better *really* be good." By example, she not only won their respect for *not* being a workaholic, but also inspired them to hit higher targets while working fewer hours and heading home early, too.

Her company became even more successful, she made even more money, but far more important, she at once began to know and care for her children in a deeper way that was far more satisfying to her—and to them. While it's true that in part she could do this because she was the owner, many jobs can be reexamined based on total value (time savings, productivity increases, customers won, innovations created, revenue earned) per week instead of assuming that all that really counts is showing up for *x* hours.

The open space to achieve what others think is impossible—and what *you* probably think is impossible—is *always* there.

I still smile remembering a conversation I had not long ago with a leader in Africa who has gone on to achieve extraordinary things (I'll tell you more about him later), who literally pleaded with me as we worked on five-year open-space targets, "Don't make me do this! It's not possible."

That resistance is his ancient brain talking, of course, reacting along the same old hardwired neural paths we all have. The truth is, if you're not willing to push back, hard, against your brain's desire to keep you in closed space until you die, this is a very good time for you to stop reading. If you're still with me, let's get started now with defining your first open-space target.

Consider the following contrasts:

STOP GOAL	USUAL GOAL	BIG HAIRY GOAL	OPEN-SPACE GOAL
Stop spending beyond my limits	Make $5,000	Get rich	Financially independent forever
Stop gaining weight	Lose ten pounds	Get thin	Energized, strong, fit always
Stop falling short of targets	Perform better	Win the race	Revolutionize more with less
Stop looking bad	Improve what is	Reach the top	Transform field or industry
Stop feeling materialistic	Renew the spirit	Be number one donor to good cause	Stay close to the soul always

Many of our goals, as the first column indicates, are goals to stop doing something. I won't spend much time discussing those here, except to say that goals like that are not just uninspiring, they're virtually bound to fail because of a quirk in our brains' wiring. When you tell your brain a negative, it hears only the positive part. So if you keep saying, "I'm going to stop spending beyond my limits," your brain hears that as a command to spend beyond your limits, and happily complies. I'll explain more about this frustrating phenomenon later. Most of us feel the need to make more money from time to time, or even all the time. Let's say it would be great to earn an extra

$5,000. There are a number of potential ways to do that. But if some sum of money is all you aim for, it's rarely more than an end point. You may cut corners to get there. You may work overtime or take on an extra job. And, yes, you may achieve it, but it's highly doubtful that earning the cash will fundamentally change who you are or deepen your capacity to live and work in ways that continue to produce greater value. That's one of the main shortfalls of *usual goals.*

Even if, for example, you hoped to use all the money for tuition to learn a pursuit that excites you, it would be the educational goal—not the money goal—that makes this greater possibility work. Besides, with $5,000 in hand, it's hard for most people to resist the urge to spend it on other things, so you'll need plenty of willpower. Plus, things inevitably cost more than we first estimate, so you'll need more money.

But what if you skip going for money here and money there and aim for a *big hairy goal:* to get rich. In a single move, you'll have a mountain of cash. Getting rich can be very alluring, like winning the lottery. But once it happens, if it could happen, then what? Easy street? Not according to researchers.

Like the millions of people who get thin(ner) and gain back all the weight and more, or those who become the number one performer and then, trophy in hand, begin to decline, an alarming percentage of lottery winners not only lose all the money they've won but also have lives that unravel and relationships that fall apart.[27] While indeed it's important to have enough money for your needs, less than half the people surveyed by the wealth-management firm PNC Advisors said that they became happier as their fortunes grew, and 29 percent of them said that having a lot of money creates more problems than it solves.[28]

That's one of the dangers with a *big hairy goal.* It's an end point that almost inevitably dies on the vine or unravels. As you aim for it, you are failing to awaken your inner powers to achieve more—and do it more easily. That's where open-space targets come in: in this example, to be financially independent forever. What if you could have all the necessary resources to live the life you choose, with enough flexibility and reserve to meet any unexpected needs? This might mean finding new ways to apply your talents, make extra income with less struggle, save wisely—and never fall into a financial hole again. This is achievable even for people on a fixed income or limited salary.[29] Or, looking in a different direction, you might choose to reprioritize your life and financial responsibilities in a way that you can live more simply, and earn enough to meet all of your smaller on-going needs and then some extra to build up your savings. All the while, you're not waiting to get fully back in touch with life, your family, and nature—you're doing it now: That's another way to become financially free forever.[30]

Worst case, let's say you don't make it all the way in five years or less. Instead of being financially independent forever, you become mostly or partly financially independent—which still puts you way ahead of where you were before, with another chance in the next five years to exceed all expectations. If you stay close to the soul, actively in-fusing the days of your life with more spirit and meaning, then along the way—as you're stretching toward this open-space goal—you'll un-cover new passions or ways of making a difference. By devoting parts of your energies and resources in these areas, you will discover new talents and abilities that can become new tools of financial independence.

The main problem is, we're conditioned to never seriously envi-sion or pursue such "impossible" goals. While we may *wish* to become financially independent, that is not anything the brain can relate to in this moment or create much alarm about, so it stays, quite literally, in your way and doesn't spur any action to make it a reality.

"Why reach for the stars, you'll only be disappointed," people warn us. "Play it safe." That's common advice, and wrong. Pick an area of your life or work where you would most like to see significant growth or new success, and complete the following statements:[31]

- *Wouldn't it be amazing if I could . . .*
- *When I imagine making the greatest contribution to life or loved ones, it would be . . .*

Pick one area where you would most like to make progress in your work or life. Here is a sampling of primarily personal, rather than corporate, five-year open-space targets.

Be financially independent forever. What if you didn't have to think about, or be concerned about, money? Or you could live a rich, simpler life? How would you use your time, energy, and resources? What would it look like, feel like, and so on?

Be energized, strong, and fit always. What if you could master the art of staying robust, resilient, and filled with energy? What would you do with this continual vitality? What would be different throughout a typical day and evening? A typical year? Five years? The rest of your life?

Revolutionize how you accomplish more with less. First, replace the word "more" in that statement with a specific life or work priority area that really matters to you—or just leave the word "more" if it's about streamlining and improving how you master priorities of all kinds and make it seem easy. What would it look like and feel like? How would the lives of those around you be changed?

Create a breakthrough that changes everything. Where do you most want to make the biggest breakthrough happen in your life or work? In what pursuit or passion would you most like to rewrite how it's done? This breakthrough could be an original and significant improvement in an approach, a specific new product or process, how you live or work, or any other outcome that truly matters to you—and that *lasts.* What would it look like and feel like?

Stay close to the soul always. What if you could make most, or even all, of your daily choices based on your deepest values instead of struggling to fit in with what others want from you? What if you could sense more of the true needs of the world around you and step forward to fulfill them? Using all of your senses, imagine what this outcome would look like and feel like.

ENVISION THE THROUGH-LINE FROM HERE TO THERE

With either one-year or five-year goals, once you aim the forebrain and its related neural pathways at your open-space target, take a few moments to explore the near-term actions that will move you from here to there. Doing this creates a through-line—a powerful, energized path—from the spot where you stand now to where you most want to be. It sparks an internal challenge to your brain's obstructive habits and routines, prompting different kinds of conscious thoughts and unconscious challenges to the status quo. For example: If you keep doing things this way, you'll never get *there*, so what has to change? In essence, having a through-line bugs you into wondering how to get rid of needless motion and get your forward direction moving far more effectively.

Another way to build the through-line and provoke more open-space thinking in your everyday activities is to approach each important decision you make by asking, "With this choice, what will be the likely outcome a year from now? Five years from now?"

Later I'll talk much more about the specific ways to build an explicit string of steps to reach your goal; for now, be aware of the power that an extra dose of awareness has to alter the way you approach everything important, every day.

COMPRESS THE TIMELINE

Having identified an open-space goal, now *compress the timeline* from one year to one month, or five years to five months, and then ask, How can I do it?

Whenever you face something deeply compelling to your future, a compressed timeline like this jolts your brain into full function along a clear path and wires it directly to the hippocampus and the prefrontal cortex and emotional experiential memory that were discussed earlier. Together, these are three of your most powerful allies in rising above the daily fray and taking specific actions that make your goals a reality, and doing it sooner than even you would have imagined possible.[32] Otherwise, the brain is more inclined to dawdle on goals and instead get all wrapped up attending to the current minor "emergencies" that pop up all the time around you. Why? Because it can enjoy envisioning the distant future, but it knows it doesn't really have to do anything about it now, or soon, so it doesn't. But you can cause it to make up its mind—more wisely and innovatively and in advance.

When used selectively—that is, only for open-space goals that are personally meaningful and emotionally compelling—compressed timelines create clarity. They mobilize hidden reserves and they help you more clearly see exactly what's in your way. They prompt you to get really curious about devising a path around it. Compressing your timeline toward open space goals is a powerful stimulus for ingenuity, not just airy wishing.

The hippocampus—that part of your brain that transforms inputs into goal-directed action—becomes intensely engaged when this kind of time-squeezing challenge is presented to your brain. However, it's essential to acknowledge that other parts of your brain may naturally dismiss anything other than playing it safe, and so may the well-meaning people around you. "Let's be realistic here," you will hear. But "realism" is the very mind-set you have to change in order to excel. "Realism" too often means settling for mediocrity, settling for what others think you're capable of, aiming only a notch above where you already are, or aiming just to do better than some other individual, team, or organization.

OPEN SPACE REQUIRES . . . OPEN SPACE

In order to make breakthrough achievements a driving force in your life and work, you first have to get out of your own way; otherwise, all of this is just dreaming. Telling yourself to be realistic when what you mean by "realism" is really defeatism is one example.

I don't know anyone these days who has lots of free time to do extra things. We all feel swamped. Even if we believe in open-space breakthroughs and are willing to test them or exert willpower to add them as "something more" on top of everything else, doing it that way usually fails. So, take two steps.

First, *toss at least half of your old closed-space goals.* To free up time for open-space goals, begin to ditch running-in-place activities that—when you look out a year or five years—truly don't matter much at all. Take a close look at your typical actions throughout a day. Much of what we do is geared to right now, or next-hour priorities that are mostly polishing old habits. Usually take an hour for lunch? How about every other day packing lunch from home instead, and getting fifteen to twenty minutes of sunshine or fresh air with a leisurely walk as you munch and relax and glance ahead to make the hours coming up move you forward more effectively toward your really big goals. That kind of third-person observation of yourself increases your chances of bigger success,[33] and right away it sparks creative thinking and boosts your energy.

Spend ten minutes an hour on e-mail? Check it three times a day (mute the incoming mail tones). Instead of diverting your attention from priority projects just to answer an e-mail, now you gain far greater productive momentum during the day and will have better command of your e-mail sorting and responses in three shorter blocks of time. This can free up another hour a day. Think the people around will resist? Not if you explain why you're testing this; they may follow your lead to save an hour of their own time, too.

When you start making changes like this, it's important to provide a safety net for the brain's worrywart tendencies by being clear with yourself that you're not eliminating all rhyme and reason from your to-do lists, just tossing what matters least. Go ahead and wash the car, water the flowers, do the dishes, buy groceries, pick up the dry cleaning, flash through that last-minute report, write up your priorities for that upcoming meeting. Incremental improvements in how you cope with daily tasks are necessary, of course. But wherever and whenever those tasks don't engage the best and deepest parts of your heart or spirit, find ways to dramatically cut time, reduce effort, toss them altogether, and stop worrying about it. That way you create open space and don't end up missing the core choices that matter most of all.

Next, apply the *"If this, then . . ."* rule to abbreviate what you haven't tossed away. In my work with a number of leaders at 3M, for example, we explored ways to free up as much as half of the workday—accomplishing everything required by a job or role in half the time it used to take—to redirect this time and energy so that far bigger goals and innovations became possible. To start, weekly meeting time (which averaged about thirty hours a week per leader) was cut by 50 percent with equal or better results. The leaders reexamined everything about how meetings were held, and why—what, specifically, were the outcome results desired from each and every meeting? With better preclarity about each meeting's most compelling purpose (in a few cases that question, alone, caused meetings to be canceled—because no one could remember why they were being held), higher targets, more creative friction, delegating all closed-space operational tasks *out* of meeting time, and requiring follow-up measures to track just about every meeting outcome, results soared. No matter what your job or working situation, there are ways to free up the time and energy to put open-space progress at the heart of your day, every day.

3M's ability to do this has been well documented in recent years.[34] Organizations around the world marvel at how 3M somehow miraculously makes this happen. It's no miracle—3M has managed to implement a rare blend of direction, focus, and measurement that liberates people to make new successes keep happening.

Similarly, if throughout this book I can show you ways to cut down your work time while achieving equal or better results, then you can accelerate your progress in the open-space ways that pay off with big improvements and breakthroughs instead of small rearrangements to what already exists.

Next we will turn to the insights and tools that can help make your open-space aims come true . . . automatically. Go directly to the next chapter if you wish. Or pause a moment to consider one more open-space example.

COOL RUNNINGS: THE REST OF THE STORY

Many of us are familiar with the story of the start-up of the Jamaican Bobsled Team, highlighted in the movie *Cool Runnings*. With no budget, no ice to practice on, and no bobsledding experience, a group of young athletes decided to form an Olympic team and commit to mastering the sport. Apparently all they had to do was fill out an application form to become listed as the national team. Their open-space goal? To set a world record in five years.

To all outsiders, and in a positive sense even to the Jamaican team members themselves, it truly appeared an "impossible" goal. They chose it anyway. More accurately, they chose it *because* it seemed impossible to everyone else.

In many European countries, especially the Nordic ones, bobsledding is a long-standing tradition and point of great pride. Walls of past gold medals shine in fancy training centers, with plenty of room on those walls for the new medals that will be won with the help of blade-sharpening specialists, ice-physics analysts, cold-weather sport physiologists, and any other exotic expert that winning seems to require. One European champion said aloud about the Jamaicans what everyone else must have thought: "Their country has never seen snow. They have no chance to ever win in this sport."[35]

The Jamaicans' results in the 1988 Olympics seemed to prove the experts right—they finished in distant last place—but the team persevered. They began to train differently than everyone else in the world, pushing old wagons down heat-soaked Jamaican streets and up long winding hillsides, lunging with weighted packs on their backs, and more. They built speed-strength, lung power, ingenuity, and courage in ways others did not.

They did all that with very few resources. The annual budget for the team in 2004 was $40,000, scarcely enough to fly them to the Olympics and pay for uniforms, let alone hire experts. The team captain, Winston Watt, uses his daughter's e-mail address to communicate with the world; there's no official Olympic office or phone number.

Other teams have huge budgets. They have arm-length lists of closed-space goals to tinker with well-grooved "great" performance habits and to slightly improve their equipment and training. They are "polishing the past," as I see it—mostly motion, no breakthroughs.

It's much the same in any field or walk of life. Look around you. It's the rare person who sees things differently. But the Jamaicans saw things differently. They committed to delivering the open-space future.

How? Every minute of their training-on-a-shoestring had to move them forward—all direction, no wasted motion here. "We didn't know what was impossible," Winston Watt said to me with a brilliant smile when I met him. When I pressed him about his training philosophy, he said, "It's really very clear for us. We love speed and we *hate* cold and ice. Our motto is 'Get off the ice as fast as you can!' "

I love the stark clarity in that motivation. All of the current icons in the sport are fully accustomed to cold and ice, not irritated by being *on* ice.

Yes, the team improvised much of its training in Jamaica. When it finally had the chance to do some on-ice training, it made the most of every moment of that time, learning from each crash, simply glad at first to make it from the top to the bottom of the run. But there was a deeper ingenuity at work. A stretch beyond what anyone else believed could be achieved. "How can we break the world records?" was asked in some way every day, even when they crashed.

Perhaps you're thinking of the Jamaicans in the way they have often been presented in much of the media coverage, as well as in the *Cool Runnings* movie—as lovable losers. Well, after their disappointing 1988 finish, the team competed in the 1994 Olympics and defeated both U.S. teams. In 2000, 2001, and 2002, the Jamaican team broke and rebroke the all-time start-speed world record in the bobsled. They won several World Cup events and narrowly missed winning an Olympic medal.

The same past European champion who had said they had no chance then had to confess, "I have no idea how they broke the world record." I do. They set an open-space target that everyone else thought was impossible, and aimed their ingenuity toward it, and then moved to accomplish it, making every action and thought count.

4

What's Automatic, Accelerates

Small seldom-seen habits have the power to bear us irresistibly toward our destiny.

—WILLIAM JAMES[1]

It's fine to have positive thoughts about the future, but it's concrete actions that make the difference.[2] The people who are most successful at achieving open-space aims devote *about fifteen total minutes* every day to thinking about their big targets, considering their current actions and how well they relate to achieving their aims, and deciding what they can do to improve.[3] The rare people who revise and tailor their actions every day to better align them with their open-space targets are the ones who actually improve themselves, instead of determinedly repeating old habits while hoping for a different result.[4]

Among the most powerful but least-known engines for achieving open-space outcomes are *automatic drivers*. Your automatic drivers will likely not be the same as mine, and later in this chapter, I'll help you devise the ones that work best for you, but it may help your understanding of what I'm talking about if I share a few that have worked for me over many years.

Every day I'm the first to get up in my house. As quietly as I can I slip from bed, trying not to disturb my wife sleeping beside me.

I pull on a faded sleeveless T-shirt and some old blue jeans. I pick up two pieces of paper I placed on the nightstand the night before, slip out the door, and go down two flights of stairs to a small basement room, where I'm surrounded by old exercise equipment.

It's still pitch-black outside, but there's a hint of orange and blue in the east as the first slice of dawn comes. It's quiet: no ringing phones, no voices shouting for attention. The mind is rested and most open, and the world is poised for a new day.

There's a voice at the back of my brain yelling at me, "Are you completely crazy? Not again! Don't do it!" Within moments, other brain-area "logical" voices chime in, urging me to come to my senses and go back to bed. I know these voices and they know me. They know I don't listen to them, not that it ever quiets their clamoring.

I slip on a pair of stiff old fingerless leather weight-lifting gloves. For me, this is automatic driver number one: *New Beginning.* It's not the exercise that is to follow—it's pulling on those gloves, stained and torn from years of clutching barbells, grasping stacks of weights, squeezing handrails on the dip and pull-up bars, and the daily flow of my own sweat.

I hear the old clock ticking on the wall: Today it's 5:05 AM. The little brain voices begin shouting again: "You don't have to do this. No one else does this. Only a fool like you." Then the rationalizing voices chime in, "Remember that study on how you need extra sleep? Sleep in instead. It's far wiser. Besides, no one will ever know."

But I will know. Once my gloves are on, I know I won't turn back.

There's a general principle here that brain scientists have given a catchy shorthand expression to: Neurons that fire together, wire together. There are about 10 billion interconnected neurons in your brain, almost all of which were formed before you were born at the rate of about 250,000 a minute. Each thing you learn activates neurons and links them to other neurons. The more strongly neurons are linked, the stronger is the brain's commitment to the linkage.

Every time you employ an automatic driver that generates momentum toward a personal open-space goal, you enlist some extra motivational power from the key forward-motion parts of your brain. They encourage you to *live* your values and *achieve* your goals, instead of just hoping for them.[5] The key is to structure your day in such a way that every time your autoreactive brain wants to sidetrack you over things that don't matter in the big picture of your life, you can take a small action that redirects your energy and attitude from right now to where you're most wanting to make progress.

Over the years, my brain has learned that when I pull on my lifting gloves a sequence of thousands of neural actions begins, automatically signaling other brain centers to come alive. Memories are triggered, too—emotional experiential memories—and so are the parts of my brain that know that I'm doing this not just for today or in honor of yesterday but to be at my best for all I want to achieve tomorrow and five years from now. All these things have become wired together because those neurons have fired together time after time after time.

While many people believe that their attitudes are determined by their thoughts, there is extensive research that the opposite is true: Attitudes follow behavior. The old saying "The thought is father to the deed" can just as accurately be reversed—your deeds give rise to your thoughts.[6] When you use automatic drivers related to specific behaviors, you are also altering your attitudes toward your present and future.

For me, it begins with push-ups, moving slowly and surely up and down, warming into it as I go, for sets of 80, 60, 40, and 20—200 push-ups in all. It's a simple thing I can do just about anywhere, a challenge picked up long ago as a Marine during the Vietnam War, and my arms still shake as I press through the final push-ups. Why is this valuable to me? For one thing, it helps silence the doubting voices in my brain as it also joins me with the possibilities of the day to come. It's a simple way to get my blood flowing, creative juices stimulated, senses awake, and metabolism turned way up. For me, that's a small way that inside my heart and mind I earn the right to have today—instead of letting life pull me along, away from my open-space goals instead of toward them.

(In case getting up and jumping into exercise sounds appealing as one of your own automatic drivers, here's a brief caution. For a variety of reasons, you are more susceptible to certain kinds of injuries first thing in the morning, so you should wait at least half an hour before you get really physical.[7, 8] Push-ups are one possible exception because the spine is held in a stable position. But use care and find out what works best for you. First thing in the morning is a fine time to engage in other things to ramp up your metabolism and vigor, such as walking, soaking up some extra light, taking deep breaths, and eating a light breakfast.)[9]

In ten minutes, rarely more than twenty, I am finished with my morning exercise. After a few brief preparations, I am ready for the next step, and the next automatic driver. With a cup of hot tea in one hand, I walk to the door and open it. I do the same thing every day I'm at home, even in the deepest Michigan winters. On a table next to the door I keep a pad of paper, a pencil, my schedule for the day (which I prepare the night before), and a list of my open-space goals. I pick up those things and step outside.

The specific automatic driver number two for me—what I call *The Horizon*—is opening the door and stepping outside. That's it. That's all it takes to get the neurons to start firing together.

Outside, I gaze off at the horizon, watching the clouds move and the daylight creep into the sky. I squarely face the day at hand and how it connects to the future—my future. Days can slip past all by themselves, becoming weeks and months of undirected or misdirected action, and I don't ever want that to happen to me.

As intently and vividly as I can, I think about five years from today and picture the best possible future I can imagine for my work and my life. As you prepare to take action to move toward your goal, you activate the prefrontal cortex in a special way, priming this area that moves good intentions into action. The greater the prior activation by the brain, the more effective you are at accomplishing your goal; the aroused prefrontal cortex centers the brain's energy and focus on the desired outcome, and making it a reality. Without this preactivation, we tend to revert right back into old undesirable habits and behaviors.[10]

I catch glimpses of things being far different, deeper, better. New ways, for example, that I would be able to help more people make a difference around the world and still have a life. New ways to do that in far less time than I now devote at my current best to doing it. A deeper and richer family life, being there at more of the moments that matter in the lives of my wife and children. And better ways to do more of the community work I love. What I glimpse about the best possible future varies from morning to morning, but what I do with this view doesn't.

Next I ask myself, If I keep doing what I've been doing the past few days, will this best possible future automatically happen? If so, then fine; I'll just keep repeating what I've been doing. But for me that rarely happens. Instead, my stomach knots up a bit and my instincts say, "No way you'll ever make that happen if you keep going the way you're going. You have to test better ways to get there, to position your life and work so this naturally happens."

And it's that inner voice, or catalyst, that I see as a gift and carry into my day. It moves me to next reexamine my upcoming schedule. Sometimes I cancel things set up some time ago because now they don't seem to matter. For example, if some time back I agreed to join a conference call about something that was a priority then but no longer is. Or a "Yes" to helping someone else do *their* work that should have been an encouraging "I know you can handle this amazingly well yourself. Go for it! I'm available if you need me, but I'm guessing you won't." Or working an hour too long catching up on the minor to-do list and missing out on the change to grow one of my open-space goals, or one of my wife's or children's. You get the idea.

If you want to change your brain to more readily get out of your way, you have to think differently.[11] So even while I'm writing this passage, late in the evening, I can feel that automatic driver at work, taking on a life of its own inside my senses. In my memory, I can instantly recall the exact feeling of the pad and loose pages in my hand. My brain has learned to stop stalling and shift into a higher gear, anticipating what's ahead, conditioned, even poised, to help me follow through instead of resisting. I can feel my brain working on my side, not against me: When my mornings begin this way, I don't give my amygdala any excuse to get above "low alert" while I get extra activation from the brain areas that shape and drive my future.

After a few minutes of my every-morning routine, I walk back inside, already thinking about what's next, anxious to get going, to stop "wasting time." The ancient brain loves to play this emotional trick on us, making everything thoughtful feel like it's a waste of time. That's because the past three hundred years have conditioned the brain to be on clock time and endlessly worry about time. So when there's nothing else to be "alarmed" about, the amygdala and its cohorts conjure up imaginary evils about time getting away from us, which surely means something bad. So I stop myself from heading upstairs into the bustle of an awakening household and instead turn to one of the mirrors in my rough basement gym to activate my automatic driver number three, *Have a Word with Myself:* looking into my unshaven face, deep into my own eyes.

Time for a few moments of soul-searching. I used to hate this because it made me feel guilty when I didn't follow through. Perfect, because that's one thing automatic drivers do. So I ask myself, in a quiet voice but out loud, "Do I deeply, truly commit this day to uncovering every possible new way to be better than the best I was yesterday, or the best I have ever been? Do I commit to my open-space goals, now, not later, and get extra ingenious about faster, truer ways to reach them?" Why out loud? Because it is far more powerful than just silent thoughts. When you make a verbal commitment to another person—or to yourself in the mirror, eye to eye, in this case—you are as much as 70 percent more likely to take the actions that honor that commitment.[12]

Next, it's time for my morning chores and precious minutes of being with my family before the children are off to school and I head to the office.

There are a number of other automatic drivers that I have put in place throughout my day—for my work as a leader, in my travels, in my writing, and in working with others. For one example, I preset several text messages to myself to ring through the screening functions on my BlackBerry and mobile phone. Short encouraging reminders like "Take five seconds. Soak in the bigger picture of life and your open-space goals." Or "Shift gears for five minutes. Move. Breathe. Bring your energy and focus up." Or "Step away to a window. Remember what you're working toward, and why." I create an assortment, some in very cryptic shorthand, just enough for a positive spark, and I mix them up and add more wherever they make sense.

At the end of each day, there is always one vital automatic driver. One of my constant five-year open-space goals is to discover and apply every way for me to be the best possible father to each of my unique children. They're different from each other in a thousand ways, and I know it. I have to keep learning more about who they are and what they need and what they dream. I have to keep learning how to get out of their way while still loving them with all my heart and supporting them in living the fullest life they were born to live. It's one of the most "impossible" goals I know and, for me, the one most worth trying to accomplish.

To keep making progress toward this open-space goal, I have chosen an automatic driver that in my family we call *Two Questions:* at their bedside, or on the phone if I am away on business, each of my children can ask me two questions about anything in life they want to know more about.

In hundreds of ways, my children have each asked me, Why am I here in the world? What was I born to do? How will I know when I find it? Why do people behave in certain ways? What is electricity? How many stars are in the sky? After you die, will I still be able to talk with you? I'll never forget the night our youngest daughter, Shanna, asked, "Dad, how do they make plastic lunch boxes? And how did God hang the moon in the sky?"

I would never trade these day's-end interactions with my children. And I realize how easy it would be to rush right past them, exhausted from the day's tasks and ready for lights out. This automatic driver makes me pause and tune in.

ACTIVATING YOUR OWN ADS

One of the key reasons that people fail to come anywhere near achieving big goals is that they start off with good intentions but fail to execute daily actions that create forward momentum.[13] That's where automatic drivers come in. They tie some kind of cue to some activity you can be doing to move closer to your biggest dreams. You already have plenty of fired-together/wired-together cues and actions every day, but most of them are counterproductive or at best just dedicated to getting by. The morning alarm rings—hit the snooze button. It's lunchtime—pack in some calories that will probably make you drowsy later in the day. A meeting's coming up—rehearse all the reasons you haven't achieved all you wanted to.

In a few pages, I'll describe the kinds of cues you can use—time cues, energy cues, deadline cues, sound cues, and a lot more. The key is the action you hook them to. Your automatic drivers can have some or all of the following content (I recommend starting with just a couple and then adding more).

• A reminder to think forward more than you might otherwise have done, whether it's five years ahead or at your upcoming schedule.

• An unavoidable nudge to do something simple that boosts your attentiveness or energy in the moment or revs up your stamina and resilience for later.

• An irritating and guaranteed way to distract yourself into thinking about, and acting upon, a specific open-space aim that would otherwise be easy to miss in the crush of daily pressures.

• A high-priority "appointment with yourself" (treat it as importantly as you would a doctor's appointment) to make progress today on a skill related to achieving your open-space outcomes.

One of the simplest automatic drivers to start with is to post your open-space target in plain sight where you practically trip over it. The brain pays the most attention to what demands the most attention.

Until you can clearly keep seeing and making progress on one of your open-space aims, the mental and emotional anarchy of too many other small closed-space goals competing for too little attention will thwart you.

In a similar vein, make sure your open-space targets bug you, constantly. Word them in various irritating wake-up ways. One of my friends who has become financially free forever has little Post-it reminders that say things like "Stay off the beaten path"; "Go in the opposite direction from the crowd"; and "There's no excuse for missing simple pleasures today." I'm sure his brain still resists all of it, even though he's way into open space now.

Once you have found lots of pithy, can't-miss-it ways to state your open-space aims, post them on the refrigerator, above your desk, atop the television, taped to the front of your iPod, dangling on a small colorful note from your glasses, inside the opening to your purse, wallet, or briefcase, on the dashboard of your car. You might also record the coolest ones as an opening message on your iPod, PDA, mobile phone, or computer—and, as I mentioned, to also come your way at key points during the day as text or e-mail reminders.

Then keep asking, Am I living and working today in ways that make this come true? If not, what small specific thing could I do to conform the moments in my life more to my goals—to make my life more my own?

As you look at your open-space targets, consider what new habits or new skills would get you closer to that outcome the fastest. Then devise automatic drivers to make those different habits and skills unavoidable in your daily life and work.

One way to speed this up is to ask the question I asked the woman leader I wrote about in the preceding chapter: What if you wanted to achieve your goal in five months, not five years? What would you do differently? What powerful shortcuts would you find? Who else would you involve? What habits, skills, or attitudes would become more urgent for you than just things you'll get to some day? Your answers to each of those questions can become tied to automatic drivers, even if you don't explicitly change your goal's time frame.

ACCEPT NO EXCUSES

By and large, the old reactionary pathways in the human brain prime it to be an excuse-making machine. When it comes to setting specific drivers, the deeper the channel of the new habit you can form in your mind's eye and daily behaviors, the easier it is to overcome inherent excuses and the greater the forward momentum this automatic driver will generate.[14]

A friend of mine, aware that excess weight was slowing him down physically and psychologically, found that he could still ignore even the most irritating reminders he could think up. So he purchased a small battery-powered device with a light that's timed to flash briefly every thirty seconds after it's been turned on. He sets it in front of himself while he's eating, to remind himself to be conscious of what he's putting into his mouth, and how much of it. He's lost eighteen pounds just from paying attention differently, and he now uses the device less often, since new neuronal pathways related to eating with awareness have been taught to fire together in his brain's wiring.

Psychologists would call my friend's new relationship to food "present moment awareness," and it's also memorialized in a catchy way: You must be present to win. The more you attend to the moments in your life with consciousness, the more aware you will be of the opportunities to move toward what you want, and the more able you will be to direct your actions toward surpassing the best and reaching what's possible.

There's software that will pop up regular reminders of your automatic drivers on your computer monitor or on a handheld screen. You can set your watch alarm to go off at a specific time as a cue. You can e-mail yourself reminders. There are plenty of ways to be sure you're present.

Even without these kinds of mechanisms there are many other daily cues to which you can tie automatic drivers. Here are some of them.

Time Cues. We all do certain things at certain times, and we all, to varying degrees, watch the clock: lunchtime, quitting time, bedtime,

time for the kids to come home from school, time for a favorite television show. Why not tie an automatic driver to certain specific times? For that matter, paste your goal at the center of your clock's face. Create drivers related to time: Each day at noon, without fail, I will . . . When you back them with auditory stimuli (the ringing of a mobile phone or a quick positive music riff in an e-mail or text message), touch (like a vibrating mobile phone), or visual prompts (one of my friends has small green lights that only flash on his laptop screen when one of the AD e-mails arrives), your brain tends to stop being so caught up in the worrisome minutiae and gets into the swing of this automatic forward movement toward your open-space results.

Action Cues. For me, it's pulling on those old workout gloves, or opening the door to step outside in the morning, or having one of my mentor's faces flash on my computer screen with a message to "Think deeper," or having a friend ring my doorbell Saturday morning to go for a fifteen-minute jog while we brainstorm about the bigger picture of the world and life, or tucking each of my children into bed at night before they ask me their two questions. These are all action automatic drivers. Once I engage in the action, the fired-together neurons pick up the process from there.

Energy-Level Cues. When your energy dips during the day and you start longing for a jolt of caffeine or a splash of cold water (or a nap), that can be an automatic driver. Instead of drooping, what can you do that turns your energy back on, whether that's a physical action or shifting your thinking briefly to something that truly energizes you? The more attuned you become to what your best energy level feels like, the more your brain centers will jolt your awareness when you drift below that level—so you can raise it back up on the spot. I'll talk more about the tools and skills to do that in key 4.

Deadline Cues. There's nothing like a looming deadline to get the blood rushing. As I mentioned earlier, compressed timelines can be very positive at sparking unexpected ingenuity and helping you accelerate progress toward open-space goals. But too many deadlines drive anyone crazy—so filter what deadlines you allow into your life and work, and get rid of those that are counterproductive or trivial and distracting. And pause just for a moment as you face a deadline to ask, What's next? How can my work on this necessary task position me, or my family or my organization, for a step toward the goals that matter most to me? Then, how can you make an automatic driver out of every deadline you face, so each time your adrenaline rises you take a moment or a minute or five minutes to prepare in some way for a better future?

Sound Cues. When the phone rings, it catches your attention—it's an automatic driver. So is the attention-getting signal when e-mail comes in. But why not prescreen certain priority levels of e-mails with a special music chime? I do that for messages from my children and wife, and my own AD reminders. Then there is the sound of a doorbell, a knock on the door, a car horn, an alarm. Instead of getting irritated, why not use at least some of these sounds as a prompt to get up and change your posture—something research shows we should be doing every twenty minutes or so all day to prevent low back pain, flatten our abdomens, and raise our energy?[15] When you hear a sound automatic driver, you respond automatically. Maybe you can make some of those specific recurring sounds a reminder to breathe more deeply, for example, to keep the best supply of life-giving, energizing, stress-reducing oxygen flowing into your body. Or to wonder, Five years from now, who would I *want* to be getting e-mails or phone calls or doorbell rings from, and how can I start that future happening at this very moment?

Awareness Cues. A lot of our habitual ways of thinking and acting are very strongly wired, and a challenge to change. But it's not impossible. You just need to alter the stimulus-response pattern, and that begins with awareness. So if you begin to notice, for example, that certain events make you anxious, you might use that very first twinge of anxiety as an automatic driver to get up and move (to burn off stress chemicals, boost circulation, and gain more energy), or at least calmly but firmly redirect your mind and feelings toward something very positive that if you attend to it diligently will one day move you beyond the tendency to be anxious.

Buddy Cues. When a friend invites or asks you to do something, or steps through your doorway, it will usually spur you into action. Friends, spouses, children, clients, and customers can help us as automatic drivers themselves, encouraging us at key moments to maintain future-building momentum when they check in, remind us, nudge us forward, or help us make up our minds when we're wavering or beginning to lapse into old habits.

When I'm traveling on work assignments I always call home, or Leslie calls me, first thing in the morning, as well as last thing in the evening. The sound of her voice always anchors me to my family goals. In its own unique way for me, this deepens the genuine drive I have in my work with leaders—and revives my awareness that my goals are not all about work—and it prompts me to redouble my ingenuity at finding new ways to treasure more of the moments that matter with my wife and children.

I'll provide more examples of automatic drivers and future-creating actions in chapters to come. But for right now, decide what automatic drivers seem to make the most sense for you and your open-space targets.

What are the difficult times of day when you tend to fall off track from your biggest goals? When can you capture fresh momentum at the right moment? Test a few automatic drivers in these spots, and see what happens.

Once all of this is up and moving ahead just fine, the unexpected inevitably rears its head. That's what we turn to face next.

The Shortest Distance Between Two Points Is a Curve

How one meets change reveals all.

—Heraclitus

There are no straight lines between where you are now and your goals. Things change. Life happens. *You* change. That's why the shortest line between you and your goal will always be curved. It's just a matter of how curved, and that depends on luck and fate and how well you adapt. It's best to face that fact early and prepare yourself to adapt with the best. In a later chapter, we'll take a close look at some of the myths about change and how to overcome them, but for now I want you to sharpen your awareness and skill at making the most of the unexpected twists and turns that inevitably arise in life's path.

Your brain will want to turn your goals and automatic drivers and all the other strategies and tactics we'll cover in later chapters into rote routines and fixed end points and march you toward them, squeezing out any complications and uncertainties. Life won't cooperate. You'll have to teach your brain to get way better at accepting change and handling it not with what is called *crystallized intelligence*—intelligence that has hardened into rules and set procedures—but rather with *fluid intelligence,* which, like water, adapts and adjusts to the circumstances it finds itself in, using change as a catalyst to reach even higher successes.[1]

There aren't any straight lines in nature, either. We surround ourselves with artificial straight lines, partly because they're simpler or more efficient, and partly to create order or at least the illusion of order. In our buildings, our highways, our organization charts— plenty of straight lines. But we don't really like them very much; they rarely engage our energies or our imaginations.

Car commercials, designed to engage us emotionally, show their products dealing with curving mountain roads, or bringing new vistas to drivers as each corner is turned. Gridlike city streets may make it easier for us to find our way and get there fast, but when it's walking for pleasure we want, we head for pathways that wend. When Frederick Law Olmsted designed New York City's jewel, Central Park, he waited before putting in the walkways until many people had used the park, and then he built the sidewalks where people had walked the most: There's barely a straight line in the place.

You see this, too, in the designs for the new buildings that will go up at Ground Zero. Where the World Trade Center towers were starkly functional, serving their commercial purposes efficiently, the new ones will sweep and arc, displaying emotional content beyond mere functionality.

Organizations? Well, everyone knows that their silos and hierarchies don't reflect reality: People make their own paths to accomplish what they want, or they steam at how the structure keeps them from getting things done.[2]

Like so many things in life, most organizations are designed for the presumed needs of a squadron of simpletons, to keep you and your unpredictable brain from wandering off the path that someone else has set for you. And even in the most unexpected places, people are discovering how unproductive such regimentation can be. Consider the U.S. military, which for a long time has been the virtual model of tight hierarchy and linear thinking. Today's military leaders probably receive more advice and training on adaptability than the leaders of any other organization, public or private, in the world.[3]

My grandfather Downing, the physician and surgeon, evoked the inevitability of change and stress in what he called "Morton's law," which he described in a doctor's terms: You have a wound that's finally starting to heal and, sure enough, despite the odds against it, someone walks by with a saltshaker in their hand, turns, and inadvertently spills salt right onto your wound. It may hurt; it may make you angry; but it's reality, and you have to adjust. Eventually, you heal.

Open-space goals may be the most susceptible to being disrupted by change because you're already reaching for something big, and any disappointment will, of course, reinforce your brain's "I told you so" mechanisms. It's in times like that that your ability to calmly adapt will help quiet those reactionary brain areas and make all the difference in how successful you are at reaching your dreams, however much the line toward them might bend.

IT'S WHAT YOU *DO* WITH THE UNEXPECTED THAT COUNTS

When the brain's nucleus accumbens wakes up at the appearance of a big yet meaningful challenge or a gnarly but surmountable obstacle, it wires directly to emotional experiential memory, and together they provide a vital neurological impetus to move you "off neutral" and head you forward despite the hundred reasons why you're too busy or tired or preoccupied right now to do so. They prompt you to improvise, adapt, and overcome. They embolden you to face unexpected changes by picking yourself up after getting knocked down, and to pour yourself into whatever it takes to achieve and then surpass "impossible" goals.

Your prefrontal cortex (PFC) watches, guides, supervises, and focuses much of your attention and behavior. You want to enlist it to actively aid you because it helps you change course and improvise in the face of obstacles and setbacks, and to do that with self-guided motivation in the absence of external direction or control (by external circumstances or other people).[4] But you need some simple tools that help keep the other reactionary brain areas like the amygdala from hijacking the PFC's attention away from your goals.

Here's where the anterior cingulate cortex (ACC) comes in as the brain's "gear shifter."[5] It helps you make intelligent, intuitive, goal-oriented decisions that can occur without conscious thought.[6, 7]

With clear, goal-oriented focus, the ACC and basal ganglia enable you to effectively change your attention from thought to thought and between behaviors.[8] You can do a better job of shifting your attention from that distracting but unimportant thing you were concentrating on a moment ago to the new thing that all of a sudden matters more.

The basal ganglia are a group of nuclei that sit atop your spinal cord. They help control your body's idling speed—ideally, as I will discuss in key 4, to keep you calm and alert rather than tense and hyper—and provide a boost to motivation toward higher goals as they help integrate your feelings, thoughts, and movement.[9] The basal ganglia help you absorb new learning, initiate action, and better prepare for the next time in life you face a challenge, uncertainty, or decision point that's similar to the one in front of you now.[10]

In light of this, it isn't really surprising that we don't always handle difficult situations as well as we could. Consider that the most exceptional people in many fields—athletes, teachers, and artists, for example—spend more time rehearsing than they do performing, whereas for most people it's just the opposite: almost no time practicing and most of their time performing.[11] In the rush to achieve today's objectives, there is little attention to actually learning, in advance, better ways to live and lead. It takes serious rehearsal to build new skills, especially when the task involves overturning deeply ingrained brain patterns and habits.[12]

Some of this practice requires only moments of focus at a time, rather than hours, and you can do some of it without actually "doing" anything—it's one of the wonders of your brain that even just envisioning a new way to respond to a challenge activates the same brain cells that are required to perfectly perform that response.[13] Mentally rehearsing a new way that you might behave in the face of adversity activates the prefrontal cortex,[14] and your imagined activities begin firing neurons and wiring them into brain patterns that can be activated whenever they're needed. Without attentive rehearsal, your brain will not mobilize in advance, and despite your best intentions you will act out old, counterproductive routines instead—or new counterproductive ones, fired not by calm effectiveness but by frustration, anger, and other emotions that can distract you from giving your best. When you prepare the prefrontal cortex to activate ahead of time, you will be better at calmly, effectively performing the right action.

To increase your ability to get more of your brain on your side and fluidly adapt to changing conditions along the way to your open-space targets, try some of these simple, practical strategies.

- *Identify the path you prefer, and then take a different one.* In science, we favor "test loops," the process of making changes so that you can ascertain immediately whether the new way worked better than the old way. Insert some test loops into your own life by first becoming aware of what you take for granted. For example, do you always prefer a certain route to work, school, gym, or grocery store? If so, change your route and see what happens. That's improvising. Do you enjoy one kind of exercise or activity more than others? Abandon it once in a while and test an entirely new one. The idea is to find small ways to strengthen your skill at bypassing the brain's inherent change-avoidance tendencies.

- *Adapt by anticipating change.* Success usually comes to those who appreciate that adjustments in course or tools will be called for along the way, and who remain more curious, flexible, nimble, and attentive than those around them. One way to develop your anticipatory skill is to notice "All because of . . ." experiences.

One of the classic accounts of "All because of . . ." is how the invention of the first leather stirrup by the Scythians in about 1000 BC led to the later invention of iron stirrups, which changed, in a global domino effect, the course of warfare and power across Asia, Central Asia, and Persia, and ultimately changed European history. By AD 600 the stirrup-less Avars had been pushed west into Europe by the stirruped Turks, and by AD 700, European nobility combated these and Nordic intrusions with a new social structure, feudalism.[15]

According to historian Lynn White, before the stirrup, warriors on horseback could not brace themselves to use lances; they could only ride up to the enemy and throw things, or swing at them with swords. When warriors started using lances, it was a very lethal military technology, resulting in great, easy victories. So now everyone needed lots of horses, and the horses needed a reliable source of food, and feeding that many horses required a lot of land. The land required reliable people to work it. The political structure that provides lots of people to work lots of land to feed lots of horses is feudalism. The rulers that implemented feudalism grew more powerful, and feudalism expanded.

Ergo, over the course of fifteen hundred years or so, the stirrup led to feudalism. The story doesn't end there, of course, because feudalism begat many more things, but it makes the point.

As Harvard Business School professor Richard Tedlow has said, "Nobody said, 'Now, what I need is feudalism; what I think I'll invent is a stirrup.' And nothing came down from the sky when the stirrup was invented and said, 'Hey, this is a whole new paradigm.' "[16] Tedlow was speaking at a conference on the future of the Internet; the point he made to the conferees was the same as the one I'm making here: that often we don't recognize the seemingly small changes and trends that are likely to add up to big impacts on our lives and our worlds, but if we use our fullest powers of awareness to be on the lookout for them, we can get a great jump toward achieving our goals.

- *Break the rules—and practice adapting to the changes that follow.* Lots of us are experts at becoming defensive whenever something goes wrong—"It wasn't my fault, and here are all the reasons that my approach should still be working, even though it isn't . . ." In a split second, that ingrained defensiveness starts a chain reaction of wasted time and energy, distracting you from the innovative thinking you need in order to get back on track or make new progress.

One way to step outside that ingrained reaction is to deliberately break some rules so you accustom your brain to going outside its normal patterns and help it see that the way you've always done things, or the way things are "supposed to be done," are not the only ways. Here's one of the everyday life examples I enjoy with my own family: Pick a game you usually play by the rules, and then, in midgame, when you least expect it, complicate things so you are forced to adapt as you go. If you're playing basketball, tennis, soccer, volleyball, or Ping-Pong, you might have someone toss a second ball into play, or keep going after dark or create darkness by suddenly turning out the lights, or create tag teams that randomly substitute for each other while the game keeps going.

At work, you might hold a "We never take yes for an answer" meeting once a week. In this meeting, you take some long-held assumption or way of doing things and deliberately turn it inside out and upside down. Practice staying calm and enthused and creative. What might be better, and how could we do it? What might take half the time and be even better than *that?* You get the idea. This brief but regular "growth laboratory" strengthens the ingenuity and resiliency pathways in the brain and body—remember, you have to use them to develop them—making you better able to handle pressure adaptively and calmly.[17]

In a similar vein in your personal life, you might experiment with taking one old habit every week and tossing it out the window. For example, if you sleep in on Sunday mornings and are pretty attached to that, consider rising early enough to watch the sunrise or head to your favorite coffee shop to savor a copy of *The New Yorker* or *New York Times,* or take the dog for a walk through your favorite stretch of a nearby park. Your brain's don't-change-anything areas will probably do lots of squawking at first, but let them and do it anyway. Watch what happens. This suddenly found "free hour" may turn out to be a godsend, helping you get your bearings back and your spirit up. Besides, sleeping in on weekends gives your body and brain the equivalent of one time zone of jet lag for every hour you sleep in beyond your normal awakening time. That's because the body clocks cue on awakening time, not when you fall asleep.[18] Net result: As vital as sleep is, it's usually better to get up at about the same time as usual after that weekend night of staying up late. Your health and energy will also be better off for the week ahead. So you can win in many ways from this small habit-breaking test.

And there is medical evidence that such novel experiences not only make us more adaptable, they also can actually help slow or reverse many aspects of biological aging in the brain and body: scientists call it "enriching heredity."[19] When you test new things, the sensory cortex for example increases its activation level and sparks the development of new neural pathways throughout the brain, in essence making you more alive—tuned in more fully by the senses to life—and allowing you to transcend the aging-related slowdown of other brain areas.

• *Give up something.* Once, on his way to Washington for a medical conference, my grandfather included a stop to meet with some surgeons at the University of Michigan Medical School. He made that arrangement partly so he could visit my mother and father and his grandchildren where we lived nearby in Ann Arbor.

When he showed up at our doorstep, he was still wearing a suit and tie. Dinner was ready, so the six of us sat down, said grace, and began eating. The three of us kids were hungry, as usual. Because it was a special occasion, my mom had okayed our having chocolate milk. We stirred in lots of Hershey's powder and got out some straws.

My younger brother, David, my younger sister, Mary, and I were laughing about something. David was truly funny. He got on a roll. Grandfather was laughing, too. Something happened with one of the straws and my sister shot some chocolate milk my way.

Being the oldest, I felt compelled to demonstrate some sense of responsibility, so I called for a halt to the craziness. As usual, my brother and sister ignored me. I decided to take matters into my own hands. I jumped to my feet, ready to take their straws away, but my hip bumped the edge of the table as I rose. A full glass flipped over and splashed the front of my grandfather's blue suit—and his white shirt and red tie—with chocolate milk.

Silence ensued. All eyes were on my grandfather's face. David brushed his napkin off the table and ducked down to get it, avoiding eye contact—a practiced strategy of his.

"It was my fault," I admitted, blushing.

"That's right!" chimed in Mary.

I noted that my grandfather was still smiling. With a shake of his head, he dismissed the accident: "Nothing the dry cleaner can't take care of . . ." We breathed a collective sigh of relief. "Except," he added, "it's my only suit, shirt, and tie, and my flight leaves tomorrow morning at seven."

He was traveling light—something he loved to do. The dry cleaner was closed for the night. Was there any way out of this dilemma?

My mother took command. "Why don't you change out of those clothes?" she urged. "Let me see if I can dab off most of the chocolate stain. Then I can wash and press your shirt."

I'm not sure how many fellow doctors at his medical meeting the next day noticed the big brown chocolate blotch across the front of my grandfather's suit and tie. But at least his white shirt was clean.

Later, he told me that none of it mattered. During his speech, he said something about how doctors needed to keep being reminded about fun and life. He told me he felt a bit smug, knowing he was wearing the evidence.

One of his tools for learning to travel light was the following sentence: To _____ more, _____ less.

How would you complete it?

Among the answers I remember most of all:

To climb more, carry less.
To hear more, talk less.
To succeed more, assume less.
To invent more, resist less.
To excel more, compete less.

In almost every case of adapting to life's unexpected changes, you can advance more freely if you first let go of something.

GROWTH BECOMES YOU

At every moment, each of the trillions of cells in your body is either growing or dying. There is no staying the same, no matter how hard you try. As biologist George Land says, "The nature of a cell, just like what we call 'human nature,' is not something that is, but something forever in the process of becoming. . . . If conditions and feedback permit new growth patterns, the result will be growth. If not, regression."[20]

As history teaches us, it's not the strongest that survive, nor the most intelligent, but those that are most adaptive to change.[21] The origin of the word change is the Old English *cambium*, which means "becoming." No matter who you are, no matter how hard your life has been, no matter what challenges you are facing right now, one of the greatest powers you have—at every turn and in every moment of your life and work—is to shape what you become.

Remember that fellow I mentioned a couple of chapters ago who pleaded with me not to make him think hard about what his future could become, because he was already very accustomed to the busy routine and stress levels the way things were? I'll call him Walter. It all started with a session I was leading for a group of international bank executives in Africa. When I asked everyone to imagine an open-space goal five years from now, the best Walter could—or would—come up with was to increase customer satisfaction survey scores by a few percentage points.

Since most of the other participants had come up with pretty bold goals, I asked Walter to think again. This time he did what some of us naturally do—he came up with a goal so far-fetched that he imagined I would just leave him alone. He said, "Within five years, I want to win as customers every new and growing business and every single hardworking honest person in my entire region of Africa."

He was very obviously surprised when others in the room started to pitch in to help him think about ways to go about doing exactly that. Energy crackled as people came up with new ideas and challenged him to try them out. After a while even Walter started playing, and within the next couple of days he got pretty excited about his big dream.

Then he went back to work, and that's when the kinds of obstacles he'd never imagined started to arise. Naturally, the bigger your dream, the wider you're going to cast your nets, and the more snags you can expect to experience. Among other things, his geographic area was quite large, and the infrastructure was quite run down. Everyone seemed to have some logical reason to think smaller, not bigger, and to just make do with the way things were.

But then, a week later, his managing director happened to notice in the newspaper that the king and the president of a neighboring country shared a dream to build a new bridge over the Zambezi River, but had no way to do it. Overnight, the managing director phoned Walter, and within days they created a meeting with trusted partners from around the world—in finance, construction, engineering, and road planning and development.

In one open-space choice, they eclipsed the long line of other bankers waiting to have traditional we-want-your-business meetings with the powers that be, and won the trust of the king and the president. The open-space attitude and adaptability to notice unexpected opportunities has since led to a wave of other opportunities that, a month before, would have seemed all but impossible.

That's the power of open space. It changes how we see the world, how we define success and work to create it, and how we adapt to the constant changes along the way. Walter and his team now devote time every day to pioneering their next improbable open-space solutions to other big challenges.

As one of my automatic drivers to be more open to life's currents, I keep the following poem posted above my desk:

> *I sense it coming but cannot avoid it.*
> *My boat strikes something.*
> *At first sounds of silence, waves.*
> *Nothing has happened;*
> *Or perhaps everything has happened*
> *And I am sitting in my new life.*
> —RUMI

Key 2 FOCUS, Not Time

It's not how well you plan your time, it's how effectively you put your attention on what matters most . . . in advance *and* as it unexpectedly appears.

Oh! do not attack me with your watch. A watch is always too fast or too slow. I cannot be dictated to by a watch.
— JANE AUSTEN, *Mansfield Park*

My grandfathers always made me aware of how fleeting my opportunity to achieve what really matters would be and I have always been determined to try to make the most of every minute.

Even when I was just a boy, I read time-management books as though they held the secrets for not wasting a single second, and I put their ideas into practice. By the time I was into my twenties, I had developed my own comprehensive system for—I thought—squeezing every useful second out of every day.

Once on a consulting assignment, I found out that the revered statistical-quality-control expert W. Edwards Deming was working with the same company and leading a workshop for managers on how to operate more efficiently. Deming's methods for getting more quality while using fewer resources made him one of the most sought-after and influential business thinkers ever.

I wangled the opportunity to pick him up at the airport. When I dropped him at his hotel, I asked if he would take a moment to look at my personal efficiency system. Famously gruff, he nonetheless agreed to sit in the lobby with me.

Out of my briefcase I retrieved my thick, worn leather day planner, with notes bristling from every corner. I opened it to a page full of tick marks, priority rankings, alternative activities to fill any unexpected downtime, inspirational quotes, observations about inadvertent time wasters I needed to eliminate—everything I had built into my one-step-after-another-no-faltering system.

Dr. Deming took the book from my hands. I thought he was about to ask if he could take it with him to his room and study it. Instead, he walked to a trash can and dropped it in with a resounding thud.

Sitting back down next to me, he said, "If you focus on that, there's no chance to pay attention to these." And he retrieved from his breast pocket a list he had created on the airplane, of unexpected opportunities to advance his work that he had noticed during the day.

I believe I still remember the exact words he said next: "You can get so busy being planned by your planner—writing everything down, afraid and guilty whenever you don't, worried about the clock and not about whether you are truly making any difference in the world. You master the minutiae and miss life along the way. I can see that's not what you want, but it's what you're doing."

The brain wants to take you in a hundred directions and make you worry about unimportant details. This section shows the importance of focusing on what is important.

WHAT REALLY MATTERS IGNORES THE CLOCK

If the vital moments for moving your goals and dreams forward could be counted on to appear at scheduled times, then you would be carrying a daily planner everywhere you go and cramming it with every detail you could imagine. But what I learned from Dr. Deming is what those who consistently excel know intuitively: They loathe traditional time management, knowing that it wastes time and creates unproductive guilt.[1]

They come to understand that many important moments come during day-to-day humdrum; during an evening walk; or as an unexpected opportunity to learn something new and important from serendipity.

Moving steadily toward what's possible means putting the right parts of your brain in control at the right moments and not getting stuck in counterproductive routines and habits, ruled by the clock and the brain's inner timekeeper.

Eons of neural wiring prime your brain to move in lockstep with daily survival demands, especially those of the clock. Whenever you become truly focused with real momentum on something that really matters, your brain wants to snap your attention back to what time it is and what you're *supposed to* be doing right now. Your momentum becomes lost, and then you waste time trying to regain it, only to get interrupted by your brain's neurotic time-watching all over again. And so it goes. The more this happens, the more your sensory cortex—the brain part that helps you feel engaged and tuned in to life—seems to disengage, as if shrugging its cerebral shoulders, and it relinquishes what little control it once had to those ancient hypervigilant panic-button areas like the amygdala, so you can become trapped in an endlessly reinforcing spiral of time anxiety that hijacks your attention and yet leaves you endlessly worried about what time it is. When this happens you may find yourself burrowing into a time planner and trying to run your life from there.

HOW MUCH ARE YOU MISSING?

The busier you get, the harder it is to see anything except what's in front of you. You may not realize how much you're missing, but it's a lot. In a recent experiment conducted by professors from Harvard and the University of Illinois,[2] people were asked to watch a videotape of two three-person teams of students passing a basketball back and forth, and count how many times the ball was passed among the members of one team.[3] On that tape, while the students are passing the ball, a person in a gorilla costume walks slowly among them, stops, turns to the camera, thumps his chest, and then walks on.

So busy were the subjects with counting passes that fewer than half of them even noticed the "gorilla" at all. When they were shown the same videotape again but without the instruction to count the passes, they all saw the gorilla—and most of them refused to believe it was the same tape they had just watched.[4] When a professor repeated the same experiment, live, before a group of four hundred people, fewer than 10 percent even noticed a dark shape, let alone the gorilla.

Scientists call this phenomenon "inattentional blindness." You can be paying so much attention to one thing that you're blind to a whole lot of other things. That's one way in which your brain can misdirect you when it thinks it's doing things right.

There's another, related, service your brain performs that can turn out to be very limiting. In order to know what to pay particular attention to, your brain is continually scanning, trying to create patterns and meaning from the barrage of sights and sounds around you. Maybe that need to see and interpret patterns is an adaptation to the necessity of knowing for sure whether that hazy shadow at the back of your cave was made by a boulder or a saber-toothed tiger, or whether Og, that mean guy in the next cave over, was threatening you or inviting you in to share some mammoth-meat leftovers when he made that gesture toward you with his club yesterday.

Most of us go through the same kind of thinking all the time in everyday life. Is my boss out to get me or just bad at showing his admiration for my work? Will this product really do what it says, or are they just trying to take my money? Is that journalist telling the truth or just grinding some ax? Does this doctor really care about my pains, or is she already thinking about the next patient? Are my kids just going through a phase, or are they going to turn out to be juvenile delinquents?

Your brain wants answers to all these questions, and so very many more. Not only that, it will often make up that answer based on a worst-case scenario.

Again, this negativity is a very sensible adaptation. If you don't learn effective new ways to redirect your attention, these brain areas will run your life in neural autopilot based on the better-safe-than-sorry principle. If I don't know whether the shadow is a rock or a predator, much better to assume that it's a predator. Better to keep my distance from Og until I have a better read on what intentions his club-waggling was meant to communicate.

But reflexive, unexamined negativity and fear detract from your focus on accomplishing what's possible. They get you stuck, defensive, self-protective, and untrusting. New research has identified a brain region, yet unnamed, that plays a special role in controlling thoughts and behaviors. Acting as an early warning system, it monitors environmental cues, weighs possible outcomes, and is wired like a hair trigger to sound the alarm bell to help us avoid dangerous situations.[5]

But here's the problem: While we need this function, it appears to base many of its evaluations of situations primarily on past experiences and deep-set routines, not future possibilities. It is linked to lightning-fast brain areas that lean toward instant fear and avoidance reactions. So when this part of the brain senses that we are about to make a "mistake" (by diverging from past behaviors, for example), it warns us to stop, hold back.

Your brain's amygdala scans everything that happens to you, alert for any change in normal patterns or routines.[6] In this compulsion to keep you unchanged, the amygdala has good company in the reticular activating system, or RAS, which sits as a gatekeeper at the base of your brain atop the spinal cord. The RAS filters all input coming up the brain stem and tends to dramatically amplify negative sensations, comments, and signals while minimizing and all but ignoring any positive encouragement you receive. Sound familiar? On a day when a hundred things go right and one goes wrong, what do you think about? That's the RAS at work.

Along with the amygdala and other limbic areas, the RAS regulates arousal, stress and relaxation, wakefulness and sleep.[7] But if you can stop the here-there-everywhere clock-watching long enough to use more calm, clear focus, you can tap into another little-known part of the RAS: Its ability to awaken the brain to consciousness and new growth, especially during times of pressure and change.[8]

Here's the crux of the challenge: Seeing details—including life's most precious moments—takes sharp powers of attention, which are hard to muster consistently. The RAS and the amygdala are continually screening sensory input for possible negative emotional content, and at the instant they sense danger or threat or potential alteration of your patterns and habits, they can hijack your attention away from your desired focus into something else, usually something trivial that doesn't move your life forward in any way. Every time that happens—which can be as often as every few seconds or every few minutes—your focus is no longer guided by your prefrontal cortex or the other areas where life is aimed at your best future, but by the brain functions that promote panicky survival but miss the deeper, important details.[9]

You have to know how, and when, to override this inherent tendency that keeps warning you not to try anything different or new. To do that, it's essential to see context and work for clarity. Without context, we have to understand and evaluate every event or circumstance in and of itself. Without clarity, we imagine the worst. In both cases, the brain's negativity steps in to depict things in terms of closed-space threat and danger, not open-space opportunity and possibility. Such thinking halts you in your tracks toward achieving what's possible and limits you to the perspectives I described earlier: settling for or defending what is, instead of looking for what's next.

Emphasize the Right Moments,
Not the Clock

Tell me, what else should I have done?
Doesn't everything die at last, and too soon?
Tell me, what is it you plan to do
with your one wild and precious life?
                    —MARY OLIVER, "A SUMMER DAY"[1]

On a summer afternoon when I was nine years old, I was sitting alone on a wooden bench under a window at the end of a long hallway at Sacred Heart Hospital in Le Mars, Iowa, where my grandfather was chief surgeon. Earlier that day I had gone swimming with some friends at the local sandpit, which had been converted to a community pool. My grandmother picked me up there and drove me to the hospital. After my grandfather finished his afternoon surgeries, he planned to take me to a nearby park.

A long time passed. Usually my grandfather met me promptly with a hug and a hearty "Let's go!" That day, he was very late. Five o'clock came . . . five thirty . . . six o'clock . . . and still no sign of him. Finally, I saw him walking toward me. I jumped to my feet, then stopped, stunned to see that he was still in his surgical gown. His scrubs were soaked with sweat and covered with blood. Something was wrong.

He sat down on the bench, obviously exhausted. I'll never forget the look on his face.

"Are you all right?" was all I could say.

"Yes," he said. "Sometimes I learn a lot about life from people who are dying."

"Did someone die today?"

"Yes."

"Who?"

"A man and woman."

"What happened?"

"They were in a car accident," he said. "Luckily, their children weren't in the car with them."

As usual, he talked to me more as if I were a grown-up than a child.

"They made it to the hospital in the ambulance," he went on, "but I couldn't stop the bleeding inside them. It was remarkable, though. They talked the whole time we were prepping them for surgery." He shook his head at the recent memory. "Side by side on the emergency carts, they talked to each other and to us."

"Weren't they afraid of dying?"

"Yes," my grandfather nodded. "They could feel the blood flowing from their wounds. But they were fully awake. Hemorrhaging is like that sometimes. But what they talked most about was not being afraid of dying but being afraid they had missed everything that mattered most about living."

I must have given him a puzzled look.

"They talked about being so busy all the time, distracted by all the things that weren't the most important, falling into ruts and routines instead of seizing every chance they had to give their best to each other, to their work, to their family . . ."

He went on. "Robert, it's a strange thing. Sometimes people have to be dying before they realize they haven't been living. I was doing everything in my power to save their lives, but at the same time, listening to them, I thought to myself, everything they really needed all along was right there, within their reach, but they had failed to see it. If you could have felt the pain of their regrets . . ." His voice trailed off. "It got to all of us who were there."

TIME'S TYRANNY

One of the things my grandfather taught me was that seizing one right moment can matter more than a hundred days of just putting in your time. But he died when I was fifteen, and it was only years later that I finally understood what that meant, in real terms. At first, I mistakenly thought the answer was to organize my time to the last detail, so it might free me to notice the right moments. But the harder I tried to control time, the more I found it controlled me. My grandfather had an expression for that: "Standing knee-deep in the river and dying of thirst." I finally caught on only after Dr. Deming did me the favor of tossing my overstuffed time planner into that trash can.

The full focus of our attention is the most precious resource any of us possess, yet in our distraction-packed world, the scarcest thing of all isn't ideas or talent or money or willpower, it's attention itself. "Focus is the base of a mental pyramid," says neuroscientist Sean Drummond. "If you boost that, you can't help boosting everything above it."[2]

Neurologically, we are synchronizing beings, tuned to ancient biological rhythms of nature and cycles of life, as studied in the medical field called chronobiology.[3] Those rhythms are natural—when a mother and daughter live in the same house, for example, their menstrual cycles tend to synchronize; when we spend time walking with a loved one, holding hands, our biological rhythms tend to naturally align.[4]

But a clock-based sense of time has literally made its way into our bodies and brains. For example, if we sleep in a room where a clock ticks, our hearts adjust their beating to the ticking of the clock: sixty beats a minute instead of the more desirable thirty or forty beats that we would experience if the heart found its own rhythm—and which would be much better for deep rest and restoration.

Our innate rhythmic orientation goes haywire when the clock takes over. We worry when we're late, we space out when we're early. Life becomes about keeping time instead of living to the fullest.

It's worth remembering that the clock is a pretty recent invention. There are no clocks, no "I'll meet you at two thirty," in the Greek tragedies or the ancient wisdom literature or in Shakespeare. For thousands of years, the sundial kept a rough approximation of time. It was Galileo's observation of the constant spacing in pendulum swings that cleared the way for the first pendulum clock to be invented in the seventeenth century by Christian Huygens, and for the transformation of time from a personally meaningful perception into an objective, external measure.[5]

We take working by the clock for granted now as the model of how business should be run. But even in recent American history, that model was vehemently rejected. In the 1860s, New England textile mills began harnessing the power of steam engines to drive mass-production looms. To make the most of that technology, it was necessary to ensure reliable attendance by the mill workers, so the owners of one mill posted a new set of rules: All weavers were to enter the plant at the same time, after which the gates would be locked until the end of the workday.

Deeply offended by what they called a "system of slavery," the weavers—who until then had worked whatever hours they pleased—went on strike. The rules were withdrawn, and it was not until several years later that they could be successfully reintroduced.[6]

It hasn't really been very long that the tick-tock of the clock has provided the drumbeat for our lives. Its sound doesn't have to drown out everything that's really important in yours.

THE ATTENTIVE BRAIN

Over time, the human brain has become remarkably large and complex remarkably quickly. It's a phenomenon unparalleled in evolutionary history: As one researcher describes it, "To accomplish so much in so little historical time . . . requires a selective process that is perhaps categorically different from the other typical processes of acquiring new biological traits."[7]

That fast growth has had roughly the same effect on your brain that fast growth can sometimes have on a teenager—not everything is always as coordinated as it could be. In terms of paying attention to what actually matters, there's a distinct lack of coordination. The brain's nearly random drive to focus on whatever your instincts say is important (which one of my neuroscience professors called "the sensory-cerebral circus") makes it a real challenge to pay attention to any one priority for very long.

A story in the satirical magazine *The Onion* captured what the primitive brain's most delightful project would be—a catalog of every single thing that could possibly go wrong, ever.[8] What a treat it would be for our brains to have all this to contemplate! We might laugh at the mix of the trivial, tragic, far-fetched, and everyday scenarios included in *The Onion*'s "excerpts" from the purported page 55,623 of that purported list (see Figure 1), but to our brains, it's all real enough.

PROJECT AWRY   page 55,623

run in stocking; nuclear annihilation of planet; phone system down; balloon floats away; glass eye falls out during speech; condom breaks; hairdresser quits; wolverine attacks child; White Stripes release bad album; lose $60 at bus stop; fatal heart attack; meat goes bad; floor collapses; tsunami; train wreck kills hundreds; computer crashes during lengthy download; Statue of Liberty falls over; grain elevator explodes; comet hits earth; ammo runs out; gored by moose; fan belt breaks on interstate; sour cream runs out; gassy; mother-in-law hates you; hamburger tastes charred; ignored by waiter; check gets lost in mail; $2 winning scratch-off washed with pants; get caught in middle of knife fight; humidity makes hair frizzy; cola explodes all over you; UPS package isn't for you; gas grill explodes all over you; neck breaks while clowning around; Livestrong bracelet gets caught in revolving door; everyone finds out you're a fraud; leg cramps up in middle of big game; strike out with bases loaded; boss catches you masturbating in your office; earth gets thrown off axis; plane gets hijacked; girlfriend's new friend cuter, funnier; pen dries out in middle of class; laptop battery loses charge; favorite bill gets vetoed; asshole paints swastika on Hillel center; oversleep on first day of work; neighborhood goes to seed; double-dutch jump rope; meeting with ambassador postponed; greeting card not a Hallmark; water doesn't taste like water at all; attempts to help poor perceived as racist; suffer second-degree burns trying to set toppled candle in jack-o-lantern upright; rescue operation fails when helicopter blade tips strike water tower; die of exposure after unknowingly taking more arduous path to summit; bite violently down on inside of cheek while eating sloppy joe; get shortchanged at charity bake sale; blind date repulsed by toenail parings on futon; mother throws out beloved old stuffed hippo; leg gets amputated by dredger chain; wrong backing-vocals tape played; final exam directions misinterpreted; real mother appears out of nowhere; friends, family learn the truth; drunk tattoo artist uses Dremel tool instead of needle; president roofied; lycanthropy turns out to be real; one of your legs grows four inches; pants stay unzipped all day; nosebleed unnoticed for first 10 minutes of wedding; batteries in remote control die; favorite song used in aerosol-cheese ad; toilet paper stuck to shoe when firemen rescues you; tacky plastic animals at gift

---

Figure 1 (Reprinted with permission of THE ONION. Copyright © 2005, by ONION, INC., www.theonion.com)

It's a cardinal rule of the brain that whatever captures and holds your attention grows stronger.[9] Ten or twenty thousand years ago, worrying about everything that could go wrong was a big asset, but today all this jumpy, reactionary stuff wears us down and leaves us with very little focus power for what actually matters most.[10] Even before adding caffeine, rushing, and deadlines, perception arises mainly in what Abraham Maslow once called "random flashes, ricochets, whirlybirds, and briefly guided beams of attention."[11]

Here's a test: What is your brain focusing on right now? True, it sees these words, at least in a fleeting glance, but chances are it's mostly back on one of the items from *The Onion*'s list, or on how wrong today's weather forecast was, or on one of the other things vying for your attention from the catacombs of memory and cacophony of present stimuli. That small dent in the door of your car, now *that* really irks you, and speaking of irksome . . . And off it goes, exactly where, only it knows—certainly not, except by accident, in the direction that's most important to you.

Unless you actively guide your powers of attention, they'll run on their own, largely in circles. It's no surprise that despite all the attention to time—staying on time, making the most of time—on average, only about three minutes out of every hour are used with maximal focus.[12] Simply being aware that we are wired to chase after negative images and magnify them helps you guide your thinking in the opposite direction. To focus on what matters most, you have to be able to switch off the brain's all-that-could-go-wrong search engine and get more of a grip on what's right in front of you.

SCANNING WINS THE DAY

Thoreau loved to say, "Time is the stream I go fishing in." That is precisely the right vision for overcoming the brain's time trap.

To live an exceptionally rich life, you have to be respectful of time while also being attuned to seizing the right moments, both as you plan for them and, more often, as they appear from out of nowhere. Unless you can learn to let go of marching to the clock, you will continue getting in your own way, missing life and many of your deeper chances to make a difference along the way.

Try as we might to be productive and stay focused on what's in front of us, the brain is mainly wired to notice the details, richness, and threats of life by shifting its attention from one area to another—using the gear-shifting ACC and the basal ganglia, along with other brain centers—by scanning, not by staring. We implore ourselves to zero in, not knowing that it makes us all but blind, so that we may fail to notice life passing us by, just inches away.

History tells us of many great people seizing the right moments that changed everything: Archimedes in his bathtub pondering water displacement, Newton under the apple tree calculating gravity, Marie Curie in her laboratory harnessing radiation, Mrs. Fields in her kitchen baking up her first crowd-pleasing cookies. What was going on that enabled them to see opportunity where others had seen only what everyone else saw?

In his autobiography, Bob Dylan described exactly what the moment of deepest awareness can feel like. Tired from touring, exhausted from the expectations his adoring public held him to, and feeling artistically empty, he realized in 1987 that he had gone as far as he could along the track he was on: "Many times I'd come near the stage before a show and I'd catch myself thinking that I wasn't keeping my word with myself. What that word was, I didn't exactly remember, but I knew it was back there somewhere. . . There was a missing person inside of myself and I needed to find him."[13]

Dylan could have kept himself distracted from what that "missing person" was telling him with a million details of his life and work, from tuning his guitar strings to haggling over concert details or finances or trying to write more songs. But he didn't. He heard the call to keep his word with himself, and that revitalized his creative energies and brought him to new levels of accomplishment. After that day in 1987, he won six Grammy Awards, an Academy Award for best original song, and scores of other artistic honors. In 2003, forty-one years after he recorded his first album, he received three Grammy nominations, including Best Male Rock Vocal Performance.

SEEING WHAT'S THERE

Your brain very much likes chugging along on autopilot, doing what it thinks needs to be done and sidestepping anything that's new or challenging. Even when the brain scans, the RAS is a magnet for the negative and tends to automatically lock onto things it considers big, urgent, and awful—easily missing anything that's small, important, and positive. All the while, it's patting you (and itself) on the back: "Look how hard we're working!" "Look how focused we are!" If you buy into that, you're sunk in terms of getting the big stuff right.

As mentioned earlier, the kind of attention you need to stop rushing and tune in to a key moment arises from emotional experiential memory (EEM).[14] But the moment must mean something special— it must evoke strong emotion in you that connects to something that excites you, personally, and not just right now but forward, into a better future.[15] I'll always remember something that Dr. Karl Pribram, longtime director of the neuropsychology laboratory at Stanford, once suggested to me as a rule of thumb: We remember 10 percent of what we read, 20 percent of what we hear, 30 percent of what we see, 40 percent of what we do, and 100 percent of what we feel.[16]

Whenever EEM is activated, it enables you to judge information and opportunities more effectively, to turn down irrelevant distractions and persist through obstacles toward your more deeply desired outcomes.[17] As soon as such an internally relevant goal appears— even in a split second—EEM provides a surge of necessary motivation to seize it. It does this by instantly activating brain areas involved with arousal, positive mood, attention, and constructive action.[18]

Ultimately, EEM is the primary brain function that spells the difference between goals that work and those that don't. The usual internal motivation approach comes from the ploy known as *self-control*. We all use it, and once in a while it works. "Lose those ten pounds like your doctor told you!" "Pay attention!" "Make more sales!" "Be positive!" All of these are aimed at self-control, just like New Year's resolutions.

But it's hard to force yourself to do anything, even getting to your doctor for an annual physical or dental checkup, let alone changing your life, unless what you're doing is emotionally compelling and you then set automatic drivers to make sustainable progress toward them. Self-control fails us because it can't sustain the motivation to achieve large dreams. Resolutions vaporize amid everyday hassles and distractions.

Instead, what you need to make big progress is *self-regulation,*[19] which taps into emotional experiential memory. Rather than relying on your thinking brain to spew reminders—"Get to that meeting by three o'clock today!"—if the meeting matters to your most emotionally meaningful and compelling future, EEM will move your attention toward being at that meeting. Not because you have to be there; because being there matters to you. That's the kind of motivating power that open-space goals tap into.

Back to the self-control demand to "Lose those ten extra pounds *now* because being overweight is unhealthy, just like the doctor said!" Other than a fleeting moment when you honor your good intentions, such impositions rarely generate or sustain any action to make it happen. Instead, you may just feel worse about yourself for not doing anything about it, and your reactionary brain areas fire up, making you even more stressed and less likely to go exercise or make any other change. Self-regulation driven by emotional experiential memory, on the other hand, moves you past the reactionary brain's automatic resistance field. If, for example, "I want an attractive, sexy figure filled with energy" or "I want to be trim and strong with the stamina to conquer any obstacle" are emotionally compelling goals for you, then EEM will provide the necessary motivation to keep you going to lose those ten pounds, especially if you take a few moments at the start of each day, and then here and there throughout the day, to intensely imagine that outcome—envisioning yourself out there in the world with this goal already achieved and using all your senses to see it, feel it, touch it, hear it, and even taste it—and you use other automatic drivers to keep your EEM engaged.

To enlist more of your EEM's power, you also need to boost your skill at third-person observation of how you meet daily challenges.[20] One tool is to carry a daybook and jot notes whenever you notice events or actions that evoke positive emotional drive to take actions toward a goal. Then find a way to do more of those kinds of things.

Your EEM deflects the usual siege of distractions that have nothing to do with your deeply felt priorities and open-space goals. It keeps you motivated and more capable of both sensing and seizing the pivotal moments each day that move you toward them. That means a crucial determinant of how you notice and handle defining moments and other pivotal experiences depends on your skill at the relation, in working memory, between the current moment or experience and instantly recalling your deeper emotionally based sense of your true best self.[21] In other words, how exactly does this moment connect to your deepest values and biggest goals?

With practice, you can make EEM more effective. Every day you make a multitude of choices that impact your future. Many of these choices are minor and affect only the next minutes or hours. But a vital few each day have the power to reshape and uplift the course of your life. EEM links to your prefrontal cortex and hippocampus, continually monitoring feelings and sensory inputs about your preferences. Circuits in this part of your brain are home to positive feelings, reminding the rest of your brain about what matters most in your struggles to pursue a goal and urging you to keep going, firing circuits that remind you of the satisfaction in achieving things others may not believe are possible.[22] Maybe one out of every ten thousand moments—on average, perhaps one golden moment every half hour—reaches this level of significance for you, giving you the chance to:

- *Live your values* by speaking out or stepping up or taking a stand or going it solo when everyone else is getting set to head off in another direction that's at odds with your deeper principles.
- *Raise your vantage point* to catch that bigger future-oriented set of possibilities when everyone else seems to be dragging you back into shoetops gazing.
- *Convey caring, respect, or recognition* to individuals you interact with and do it spontaneously and genuinely and specifically, right when it matters, not later at some predetermined holiday or recognition session once a year.

- *Listen deeper, learn differently* by taking frequent pauses, even in mid-conversation, to stop talking (or stop thinking about what brilliant thing you're going to say next) and get out of your own way. Empathy is something that the best leaders bring, and it's this rare quality that makes you invisible, at least for a few moments, while it makes the other person's dreams, challenges, and travails the only things that matter.[23]

There are two questions you should ask regularly, not just because they're vital in themselves, but because the more you ask and answer them, the more you train your brain to address them without your conscious guidance. They are *What do I want above all?* and *What am I doing right now to make that happen?*

Think about a recent day. Which three or four moments stood out at the end of the day? Which of those moments did you plan for, and which appeared unexpectedly? Did you notice them and seize them? Or did you miss them?

Think about the rest of today and tomorrow. How can you be better prepared to take advantage of the key moments that will come your way?

These simple actions, combined with others we'll discuss later in this chapter, will move you toward where you want to go.

SEIZE THE RIGHT MOMENTS, PLANNED AND UNPLANNED

Most of your brain lives very intensely in the here and now. Just imagine all the inputs the RAS and the amygdala are constantly scanning—sights, sounds, feelings, ideas, physical sensations, thoughts, smells . . . Over many years of training by you and many millennia of history, your brain has learned to set aside 99.9 percent of what it perceives in favor of what it thinks are the really important things.

How much we disregard is summed up by sayings like "Stop and smell the roses" or "Wake up and smell the coffee." In general, you teach your brain to lock onto whatever will get you through the upcoming day—or the morning, or the next few minutes—and disregard everything else as an unproductive distraction.

You won't find the big things that can change everything there, so you have to teach your brain to notice the moments that can mean the most to you.

First, there are the *defining moments you can plan for.* Look at the remainder of today and tomorrow. What handful of moments are coming up that are likely to have the greatest significance? One way to get at the answers is by asking yourself, "If I had to accomplish everything important that matters to me but I had exactly half the waking hours I now have to do it all, how would I make that happen?" "By working twice as hard" is the wrong answer. "By finding ways to do the right things better" is much closer.

You're looking to use your focusing powers to create more of what matters most to you in the moments you're able to schedule. When you realize what's really important, then say no to anything that consumes time but doesn't bring you closer to what matters most to you. If you can't say no, delegate it, speed through it, or eliminate it. It's valuable to recall what my grandfather used to remind me: "Doing a thing well is often a waste of time." A hardworking, perfectionist friend of mine, who normally would try to do anything in front of him as excellently as possible—thereby giving up his focus to many things that don't really matter—now has an expression he uses to wean himself from such admirable but ultimately unproductive obsessiveness: "If it's not worth doing, it's not worth doing right." Writing ten drafts of a letter on some minor issue—where a scrawled fifteen-second note would have sufficed. Expertly surfing through five hundred Web sites or television channels trying to find the one "just right" to take your mind off work when a glance at that photo on your desk from your favorite vacation would have nicely done the trick. Those kinds of things.

Then there are the *defining moments that appear unexpectedly.* Just about the time that you think you're getting it right about concentrating on the right moments and letting the rest flow, your brain can play another trick to trip you up. The thing about the brain and its ancient tendencies is that it has a lot of energy but often doesn't have very good judgment. So when you've told it that moments are important, at once all kinds of neural forces get marshaled around moments—what they are, where they've been hiding, and how you can horde your fair share. In no time at all, this escalates into what you might call *momentitis:* an acute inflammation of the brain's new-found desire to seize every moment and not let go. That way you're certain to have corralled the winning moments in there somewhere. So the pendulum swings from not enough right past just enough to all and more.

It's something like that old *I Love Lucy* television episode in which Lucy is working on the chocolate factory assembly line and gets a compliment from her boss about how effective she is at getting all of the little chocolates in all the right compartments in each box.

Then she inadvertently hits a switch that speeds up the conveyor belt. She can't keep up, but she sees all these chocolates coming her way. She's trying faster and faster to get as many as possible in the boxes but falls behind and starts to eat all the extras so she won't look bad. She can't eat them fast enough, either, and begins jamming them into her apron, and then the boss appears. Uh-oh. Despite the brain's frenzied harder, faster attempts to gain control and grab every moment, like those chocolates whizzing by, it can't keep up.

So get really good at saying no to all nonessential moments. This is just as important as seizing the right ones. Detach and more closely observe life, and your behaviors in it, as it whizzes by. Observe yourself when things are hectic. Keep peering into the whir of moment-to-moment choices and reactions. Cherry-pick the best, let go of the rest.

The act of saying no to the trivial many in favor of the critical few isn't just a time-management strategy—it's a way of taking advantage of that neuroplasticity we talked about before to alter what your brain focuses on in the future.

If you're shaking your head right now and thinking that I don't know the real world, because you really can't say no to tasks, I'd advise you to think again, and ask yourself how committed you are to your most important goals. Because when our commitment is deep, we do say no to things that get in the way. When our romantic commitments are deep, we say no to other involvements that might compromise those commitments. When we are financially committed to some goal—buying a home, let's say—we say no to expenditures that stand in the way of attaining that goal.

We say no to many things in order to be able to say yes to our children, to our spiritual obligations, and even to recreational activities, such as our weekly bowling league or golf game. Heck, we say no to things just so we don't miss our favorite television shows, even though we probably won't remember one important thing about those shows a week after we've watched them.

Once you have placed something on your schedule because it's important, be sure you derive the most from it by using two questions that keep you linked to your emotional experiential memory. Ahead of that interaction or activity, ask yourself, *How can I seize this chance to become more of the person I most want to be?* And immediately following it, ask yourself, *Have I just acted like the person I most want to be? What did I miss? How can I do it better the next time?*

Start now to build defining moments into your schedule. Think about small specific things that give you the most hope and drive toward a better future, the simple specific actions or interactions that boost energy and spirit in yourself and in each of the four or five individuals who are vital to your success in the year ahead. Pick one or two of these by-plan defining moments every day: Put them in your brain's awareness, not just on your schedule, and then make them happen.

Also, think about the places in your life or work where you could make a very small change that might bring the biggest reward or return. Then place that in your brain's awareness, plot it on your schedule, and make it happen.

TELL WHAT MATTERS FROM WHAT DOESN'T

To live most fully, you have to learn to differentiate defining moments from the blur of other activities that make up your day. Emotional experiential memory can be a powerful ally in accomplishing that: once you attach a meaningful emotional charge to something, you're much more likely to notice it and respond to it.

The Ovarian Cancer National Alliance (OCNA) is saving lives by subtly altering the emotional experiential memory pathways in the brains of future doctors. Here's how. Unlike many other diseases, there is no simple test to detect ovarian cancer. The warning signs, which can include a bloated feeling and frequent urination, can easily be attributed to many other conditions, and doctors, busy as they are, can easily fail to connect those symptoms to the possibility of ovarian cancer. Fifteen thousand women in the United States alone die each year from ovarian cancer, and many of those lives would have been saved by an earlier diagnosis.

Now, through an OCNA-sponsored program, teams of two or three ovarian cancer survivors travel together to medical schools, where, as part of the regular curriculum, they meet with small groups of third-year medical students. The survivors describe their experiences and, often, their misdiagnoses. They tell what it's like to live with the probability that their cancer will eventually return. They explain how an extra step of focused attention in a doctor's office might have lessened not only their suffering but the risk of death they now live with every day.

The medical students, so often up to their eyeballs in dry books, detailed lectures, and demanding examinations, respond very powerfully to going beyond textbook abstractions and talking with real people about their emotionally charged experiences. These future doctors' sensitivity to the crucial moments when future patients will describe their symptoms is greatly heightened, because that sensitivity now is woven into their emotional experiential memories. Lives will be saved in the defining moments in doctors' offices when that heightened alertness causes a doctor to take one extra diagnostic step and recognize ovarian cancer in its earlier, more treatable stages.

In your own everyday life, you can easily miss the moments that matter the most. Try some of the simple yet uncommon methods below to make more of unexpected pivotal moments.

Keep an eye on yourself. Your perspective can have some very significant influences on whether you are able to change and grow in life or stay stuck in old views and habits. One practical strategy is to imagine yourself sitting on your own shoulder watching how you tune in, or not, and how you manage your attention. Switch your view from the first person, "This is me working toward my own goals," to the third person, "I am observing myself work toward my goals."

The brain is lightning quick at jumping to assumptions, and is often wrong.[24] So the ability to observe your own natural reactions and rise above them—to follow your own natural flow of focus and then guide it in new ways—is one of the key things that separates the best from all the rest in any field or endeavor.

Keep remembering that taking a third-person perspective on your own behaviors accelerates change and progress.[25] Pause more often to observe yourself. Ask, What's working? At once, move beyond whatever isn't. Keep testing small new ways to center your focus powers on the desired line of energy that intersects with your highest priorities moving you into the best future.

Get out of your head. The smarter you are, the more you may think you know where to focus your attention and what to ignore. But this creates what scientists call the "mind-set problem."[26] Whenever we have special expertise at something we have to be able to step outside it, or else our narrow brilliance cements our view of the world, and we can't make room to see things any other way. We miss changes. We refuse to look deeper. We pass by unexpected opportunities. We ignore potentially useful strategies. Whenever you're applying something you're already good or great at, watch out. Practice letting go of that all-knowing view and, instead, take the frame of a beginner for a few moments. See what you sense. I'll bet you'll be amazed at what comes to you.

Bring all your senses into play. All-sensory imagery can have "profound effects on improving physical performance and psychological functioning."[27] The brain loves its one small way, but there are always other ways, if you pause and prompt them.

You may have seen images of pre-Colombian Incan or Mayan people with large ear decorations. The ears were pierced and decorated at the end of lengthy ceremonies celebrating the culture's history and the importance of being attuned to the "voices" of the natural world. As one anthropologist writes, "The piercing of their ears and the insertion of ornaments served to ensure that the lessons they had received would 'penetrate' their hearing and be remembered. . . [T]he ear-piercing ceremony was designed to 'open up' the participants' ears."[28]

As it turns out, we are now recognizing the crucial role of the brain's hearing-related systems—particularly the auditory cortex—in providing us with true balance and orientation in the world.[29] Not just physical balance and orientation, it turns out, but also emotional: A part of the auditory cortex known as Broca's Area centers our senses and balances our focus.[30] You don't have to go as far as the Incans, but it's good to keep remembering how much difference sharpening your attentive hearing can make.

Your vision can be a great source of insight, but limiting as well. Blind people who have had their sight restored show how much brain capacity goes into highly sophisticated routines for distinguishing and relating to what we see—and how much potential observation power we lose because we already have those instant categories for everything. A scientific journal's account of a man who had his sight restored after forty-three years of near-blindness shows how powerful those categories are: "Although he has seen faces everywhere since the first day his vision was restored, they simply don't coalesce into recognizable people. Their expressions—their moods and personalities—elude him entirely. Even his wife is familiar to him only by the quality of her gait, the length of her hair, and the clothes she wears."[31]

While being thankful for what our brains can do with visual input, it's also worth imagining how much more we might perceive if everything had to be figured out anew. A restaurant in Zurich, Switzerland, called The Blind Cow, is always fully booked months in advance. Its success secret? Food is served in pitch-darkness. Every bite is a taste experience unfiltered by the expectations that sight creates: "blind tasting" at the highest sensory level![32]

All-sensory imagery programs tailored to individual needs and goals have demonstrated some dramatic success.[33] The application of your senses to recognizing important moments is subject to the rules of neuroplasticity—the more you do that, the better you become at doing it.[34] In order to mobilize all of your hidden capacities to succeed, all-sensory awareness must be fully linked to your desired outcome.[35]

What's next is the test, not what's past. Once you have committed to making the most out of whatever comes your way, you'll think of lots of ways to retain your best focus. My grandfather used to ask me a great question for paying attention: "What has become clear to you since last we were together?" Knowing that he was going to ask me that—and then probe more deeply—made me much more attentive.

Hook moments to personal meaning. Almost always, the world is way beyond our brain's limited powers to make meaning from complexity. In our mind's eye we can see the phrase "One billion hungry children," and it has little emotional connection for us until we sit at the bedside of a single dying child. Are all snowflakes really different? The brain cannot tell and does not care.

The celebrated poet William Blake wrote, "If the doors of perception were cleansed, everything would appear as it is, infinite." No, it would appear as nothing at all—our brains would be completely overwhelmed and thereby tuned out. Keep looking for the specifics—the individual sick child, the one snowflake that lands smack on your nose, the single recycled container that connects you to caring for the earth—that your brain and its emotional experiential memory can relate to.

There are many stories of breakthroughs happening when someone sees something that everyone else has missed. On a purely human level, this is also where we learn to value what's beneath the surface of life.

Years ago my wife, Leslie, kept a box in our hall closet where she saved wrapping paper and ribbons from past gifts so we could reuse them. In the box was a particularly lovely, large piece of silver embossed wrapping paper that we had agreed to save for a special occasion.

I arrived home late one night from a business trip, a few days before Christmas, and I was surprised to find my daughter Chelsea, who was four years old then, awake and kneeling in the hallway with a small box in her hands. With her preschool scissors she had cut apart the entire large piece of silver wrapping paper to make a small wrapping for the little box. I got angry, thinking how she had wasted the paper we had been saving.

By the next morning, I was over the incident, and Chelsea never said another word. On Christmas morning, she handed me the little box wrapped in the silver paper. "This is for you, Daddy," she said.

I opened the box, and it was empty. I must have looked perplexed, and I guess I was thinking about all the wasted wrapping paper for an empty little box. She sensed my disappointment, and there were tears in her eyes.

"It's not really empty, the box," she said. "I didn't have a gift, so I blew kisses into it and filled it with my love for you, Daddy."

I felt terrible. I still have that little box to remind me that some rules are to be broken for the right reasons, and it's up to us to value the right moments when that happens.

All it takes is a single pause, a moment's question, to guide your focus deeper so your brain can get to the core of things and understand more of what's real, instead of staying lost in its own worries or locked into believing its surface assumptions are indeed reality.

What You Frame, Engages

When at last you see the lens you're looking at life with, you're finally free to change the view.

—Tom Robbins,
"The Day the Earth Spit Wart Hogs,"
in *Wild Ducks Flying Backward*

The comedian Lily Tomlin once said, "All my life I wanted to be somebody. Now I see I should have been more specific."[1] She was so right: Unless you can say specifically what you want from your life, you'll become whatever life makes of you. People who carefully frame their goals into the meaning and path of their lives are at least twice as likely to achieve their goals compared with those who fail to make that connection.[2]

As Goethe wrote, "Things that matter most should never be at the mercy of things that matter least." If you have no screen for separating what matters most from what matters least, you're at the mercy of your brain's ancient deeper wiring. And as we've seen, your brain often turns what actually matters least into what seems to matter most, the better to keep you safely harbored in closed space rather than venturing into open space. If you let your brain decide what really matters, you'll likely spend your life in a narrow little corner of your true potential, sifting through gossip, assuming the worst, comparing yourself to others, spacing out on trivialities, and numbly trying to clean the flyspecks off the windows of your life.

Your brain quickly turns off to anything that seems new or complicated, switching into a defensive, learning-resistant "stonewalling" mode.[3] It shows, too, how quickly and fiercely any hint of fear mobilizes the ancient RAS and the amygdala,[4] and how fast your body's amazing "alertness switches" (which we'll discuss more in chapter 14) can become frozen in the off position when the brain decides it's not going along with some new approach.[5]

When you can more clearly see the world and your place in it, you become invested, interested, engaged, involved—more focused. If you are blind to where you fit into the landscape, there's no good reason inside the brain to care much about what's not right in front of you.

Breaking through rarely happens by accident; it happens by plan. *Your* plan. Nearly two-thirds of people who feel they've failed to achieve success in their lives attribute it to being unable to live up to standards they chased that were set by others.[6] So the power to grow and change must be guided by you, on your own terms, in your own best way.

YOUR ARC IS A LINE

In all worthwhile literature there exists what is called a "character arc"—the development of a character from one thing into something else. In the original *Star Wars* film, for example, Luke Skywalker starts out seeking only revenge for the deaths of his aunt and uncle, but by the end he has become a warrior with noble motives, fighting for good against the "dark side." The *Godfather* trilogy shows Michael Corleone in an opposite trajectory, from idealist to brute. A reviewer describing the 2005 remake of *The Longest Yard* wrote, "Adam Sandler has no real character arc: he begins the film as an amiable goofball lacking direction and ends it as an amiable goofball with slightly more direction."[7]

Your life will have some kind of arc: positive, negative, or indifferent. The more clearly you understand what you want and the more you approach circumstances with that in mind, the more that arc will be as you want it to be.

For me, a scene I observed in Tibet many years ago provides a vivid metaphor for that message. I still have a photo on my desk that I took back then. It shows a horseman hanging far off the saddle of a galloping horse, aiming an arrow from his long bow at a faraway target.

Archery has been practiced all over the world, but never with the degree of precision amid daunting conditions of Tibetan archery—on the flat-out run from immense distances over constantly changing terrain in strong, shifting winds. A physicist for the Smithsonian once remarked that such accuracy was impossible.[8] If that's true, then the Tibetan archers have found many new ways to accomplish the impossible in front of thousands of witnesses over many years.

I can still see the archer—a man named Litang—bow in hand, drawing the long crimson arrow as he swung wide off the saddle of the galloping gelding whose hooves thundered across the uneven ground. It was as if he was floating in the air as he smoothly drew back the bowstring and let the arrow fly. Across fifty yards, the arrow sliced the moving air and struck the bull's-eye within a hand's width of the first arrow he had shot, from even farther away.

I couldn't stop thinking about how complicated it all seemed, yet how simple and effortless the action appeared. Later that day, Litang and I climbed a steep hillside together, up through crumbling rocks to an old temple on the side of a mountain. As we sat in the temple's arched entrance gathering our breath, I asked, "How did you do that?"

"Climb the mountain?"

"No, shoot the arrow."

"Same way I climb the mountain."

He was smiling at me. "No," I went on, "how did you balance the movement of the racing horse, read the winds, hold yourself steady, aim perfectly, and release the arrow to the center of the target?"

"I saw the target. Then I simply sent my strongest line of energy toward it. Which is the same way I climb the mountain."

"But how . . ."

"The arrow goes where I send it, where the deepest drive inside me sends it. It is not luck or faith, but an act of precisely gathered focus. That's my strongest line of energy."

For more than thirteen hundred years, there have been archery contests on horseback in Tibet, and the winners hold to one central teaching: The arrow of life always follows the strongest line of energy. It goes where you commit every fiber, every molecule of your being. Wishes are just feathers on the wind, those archers would say—it's nice to have them, but they amount to little. What matters are commitments of being. Those commitments form the unseen channels that guide you toward the results you desire.

NEUROCHEMICALS GO EXACTLY WHERE YOU SEND THEM

Our capacity to summon up our strongest lines of energy is shaped in large part by the high-speed communication among neurochemicals that form a dynamic information network linking mind, body, and emotions.[9] When you get out of your own way and onto your strongest line of energy, where purpose gathers itself into a far more formidable force, a kind of inner switch is thrown to help you turn off past negative mental patterns, shut down old habits, and activate a laserlike focus of all of your senses for breaking through the barriers to success.[10]

In your nervous system, one of the main reasons what you focus on grows is because neurochemicals go exactly where you send them. "You" is either your conscious focus of images, thoughts, and feelings toward specific moments and actions and outcomes that matter most to you, *or* it's your brain's unconscious instincts running on thousands of years of spooky shadows and reactionary tendencies, doing whatever *they* think is best. Which are you choosing? The targets are there, even when the world seems to be moving beneath your feet. What are you aiming your attention at? That's where a cascade of neurochemicals is going.

One thing that gets in the way of staying on your strongest line of energy is keeping your dreams to yourself. You can multiply the strength of your line of energy just by stating what you want to others. That is, to speak your goals aloud, in specific actionable language, to at least one other person is a major impetus to actually achieving them.[11] The emotional charge generated by saying aloud what you really want fires up the brain centers associated with goal attainment in ways that just wishing about them cannot.[12]

HOW MANY OTHER PEOPLE'S BRAINS ARE YOU LUGGING?

I've made it clear in this book that caring about others can be central to a life properly lived, but that doesn't mean you have to take on everyone else's problems as your own.

My youngest daughter has a little game called Who's Got the Monkey?[13] Inside a small box are one hundred plastic monkeys in different colors. I was thinking about it the other day, and if I were asked to write a note to go inside that small box, it would frame the choice this way:

> Do you continually find yourself falling behind in reaching your own goals because you're repeatedly solving everyone else's problems? If so, then every time another person comes up to you with a problem, ask yourself: Is this person truly in need of my help, or do they want me to take away their problem? If they genuinely need a few moments of your attention or encouragement or wisdom, then fine, that's what you should give them, and then wish them well and get on with your own deepest commitments and priorities. But if you're not *very* focused, you may find yourself automatically taking on *their* problem and doing *their* work. It happens all the time—and now the monkey that should be theirs becomes yours. Decide when that's fine, and when it isn't.

On the one hand, your brain wants to look out for number one—itself—yet being partly a social brain, it also needs to win points with others to survive. If left to its own instinctive devices it can get lost in winning points with others by saying yes to taking on their headaches and problems when actually, if you paused to weigh the outcome of what you were doing, you would be saying no. When you say yes, you are essentially agreeing to lug around their monkeys—or as I prefer to think of it from a conversation I once had with the pioneering neuroscientist Dr. Karl Pribram,[14] their brains. It's a wired survival instinct in the brain stem based in part on the fact that forever saying no gets you thrown off the team—or worse. In the times when our ancient brains were forming, banishment meant not just loneliness and isolation, it also meant death, because no one could make it on his or her own. So yes is the default in the neurological wiring.[15] Set the framework of your awareness to catch yourself saying yes when that might not truly serve the best in the other person or the best in you.

DO MORE OF LESS AND LESS OF MORE

We try to fool ourselves into thinking we're tricking time by multitasking. It backfires. Multitasking—both in the sense of doing more than one task at a time as well as switching frequently among many tasks—has been shown in numerous studies to in fact be an enormous waste of time, cutting productivity by 29 to 53 percent,[16] destroying focus, and undermining spirit.[17]

There's only so much brain capacity available to us at any given time. Tasks can be performed simultaneously with efficiency only insofar as the required attention for those tasks does not exceed what the brain has available. As people divide their attention between two even seemingly simple tasks—reading their e-mail while talking on the phone, for instance—comprehension, concentration, and short-term memory nosedive. Switching from one job to another doesn't work any better; it eats up more time than waiting to finish one job before beginning the next—an inefficiency that increases as the tasks at hand become more complicated.[18]

Shuttling among two or three different pieces of work can be accomplished efficiently provided each one is relatively simple and that they are adequately differentiated from one another. Where trouble really rises is with problem-solving tasks, the kind that require creativity, integration of thoughts, and the generation of new ideas—the kind that are most important to reaching your open-space goals. Switching among such tasks demands a certain degree of downtime; the fuel cell of imagination can only be drained for so long before it needs to be recharged. Attempting to solve a problem or grasp an opportunity with a dead imagination is a recipe for failure.

Companies that see multitasking as part of the solution to their staffing issues are actually making their problems worse and are not, finally, doing more with less. They are doing less with less. Individuals who are multitasking too much experience various warning signs; short-term memory problems can be one. Intense multitasking can induce a stress response, an adrenaline rush that when prolonged can damage cells that form new memory.[19] If your brain's gear-shifter, the anterior cingulate cortex, gets multitasking fever you're in even bigger trouble—with your attention firing all over the place at increasingly high speeds, something like highly caffeinated Web surfing. Other red flags are changes in your ability to concentrate or gaps in your attentiveness.

Of course, railing against multitasking isn't going to make it go away, in your life or in mine. But there are ways to sidestep it, at least at those key moments when you want to be fully engaged and fully open to what's possible. Here are a few.

Create islands of focus. If you work more than twenty or thirty minutes straight on one task, your focus wanes and your problem-solving time increases by up to 500 percent.[20]

So it makes sense to set aside at least one "protected" hour—or even a half hour to begin with—during the day when distractions and interruptions are avoided, when you can work sequentially on the two or three different tasks or relationships with the highest priorities for moving your life and work forward. Dr. Deming recommended this approach, urging, "Do one thing exceptionally well. Make progress, then change your focus to something else that matters."[21]

During each of those periods, stay intently tuned in to what matters above all. Devote twenty to thirty minutes, tops. After that, your productivity starts sliding, whether you recognize it or not. Then deliberately and fully let go of that and move to a different focus.

Give your brain a break. Knowing that half an hour of intense concentration is about all your brain can handle at a stretch without starting to lose its powers of attention, it pays to get really good at stepping back and regaining your focus. Despite its reputation for logic, reason, and linear analysis, the thinking brain all too readily unravels, spinning out of control and losing much of its analytical power.[22]

Make room in your schedule for "doing nothing." Get up and leave the room on a "doing-nothing walk," or some such carefree act—because when you do that, a lot can happen, none of it the way the brain had planned. We'll explore this further in chapter 16, but for now, recognize that when you do nothing—or nothing hurried or the same—the brain slows, even for a few moments, and all of a sudden, the hyper-reactionary brain areas seem to chatter less and other deeper ways of sensing and knowing can appear.[23] Ellen Langer, a psychologist at Harvard, has found that just pausing to "tune in" increases solution-finding and creative energy.[24] She calls it "soft vigilance"—back off the effort to see more, more deeply.

It's often intelligent to be less busy and more productive in the right areas for your own goals—so take hunch breaks, vantage-point pauses, perception shifts. Thinking too hard, overconcentrating, interferes with new learning, applied expertise, and creative insight.[25] Pausing actually speeds us through difficult tasks, uncluttering the brain's neural firing chaos.

Whenever you make a mistake, pause and shift gears. Take a moment to place your attention on what's right—and how you can build on that—instead of getting stuck on what's wrong. Bypass the brain's natural tendency to overstress or overfocus on mistakes, which just reinforces neuronal networks that aren't useful.[26] Instead, take a little break and then shift your attention to something constructively different that moves your attitude and life forward.

Pauses help you see critical moments that can arise unexpectedly. I am reminded of something that Laurel Schneider, head of a theological seminary in Chicago, once wrote about the spirit: "What I have begun to notice among people who are open to such things is that divine presence seems, quite simply, to occur. And the least we can do . . . is to be there."[27]

Whatever it is that you're hoping to find, learning how to "be there" makes all the difference in whether you're continually engaged with your deepest goals or just skating across life's surface. We are engulfed with new possibilities. Receptiveness to such possibilities is all but absent from the brain, so you have to create it by reaching out and overriding the brain.[28]

Jot notes. Carry a small daybook so you get at least some of your brain's juggling cerebral images onto paper and out of your way. A new thought, however trivial, in the midst of an important thought can put your constructive attention into a tailspin. It can start you multitasking even when there's no need to. The second you turn your attention away from your main focal frame, it rushes outward in all directions. Your brain's happier that way, but your goals recede. Your brain does not have the active memory space to keep advancing several streams of thought at once.[29]

Take quick notes if important things (or seemingly important ones) distract you—and then turn back to what you were doing. Save your notes for another time, when you can give them proper attention. Move your attention onward, and come back to reflect later. What you wrote down might seem utterly inconsequential later, in which case you can toss it. If there's good stuff there, you can turn back to it and build that one good idea into three more when you're in the proper attentional frame of mind.

It's no coincidence that many of the world's most innovative and successful people carry daybooks. For example, Richard Branson, founder of the Virgin Group; Howard Schultz, creator and chairman of Starbucks; and Doug Sharp, president of BSB Design, have each filled many notebooks with ideas, questions, and reflections. They have all recognized how to free their brains' focus powers to hatch the next great idea without missing what matters along the way.

IF IT IRRITATES YOU, LOOK DEEPER

Your nervous system has a capability that can be seen as a "depth finder"—the orbital cortex that sees without seeing,[30] Broca's Area that hears beneath listening,[31] and the brains in the heart and gut (which we'll discuss more in key 3) that sense beyond thoughts and words. As you move through your busy day, keep your overall sensory awareness *calmly open* to what's happening in the larger picture of life all around you.

Your senses extend into the air beyond your physical body, like a kind of neurological radar. With practice, this awareness range can extend from a few inches beyond your own skin to across the room or street. Elite martial artists develop this natural skill, and you can, too.[32] This two-tiered awareness is not multitasking; it's a way of being *in* the world instead of just *on* the world.

What bugs you may be what builds you . . . if you let it. All it takes is a simple switch in how you respond. When another person frustrates you, or you're hit with a sudden problem or challenge, it's easy to get distracted, tensed up, and gloomy. You can lose lots of time and energy here if you're not careful. The highest-performing leaders and teams have developed the skill to turn these small crises into breakthroughs that move them forward, while everyone else is fuming and just hoping to get it over with.

Whenever your attention is about to get hijacked by some frustration or irritation, consider these choices.

"It's a momentary setback." This simple phrase can keep you moving forward instead of getting stuck. The brain loves to catastrophize, taking something small and negative and quickly esca-

lating it into a dire scenario. Tell yourself, "This is a momentary setback, and now I'm choosing what happens next." Then choose what happens next to move your life forward.

"Am I willing to give power—and a piece of my life—to this?" When you let someone else's bad mood or gnarly personality set you off, you give them power. Decide instead to keep your power—and your calm ability to make different choices to keep you moving forward.

"Come back to life." I got this from my youngest daughter, Shanna. When she was three or four and would see that I was distracted by something, she would say, "Come back to life, Daddy!" Then I began to notice how often distractions took me away from life and dumped me into a whole separate world in which petty annoyances, instead of grand opportunities, absorbed my energy and attention. I didn't want to live there, and looking into my daughter's eyes, I could see that she didn't want me to, either.

TURNAROUND

The brain's hardwired intolerance for anything different can be deep and swift. The brain often tries hardest when it should flow, and learns least when it should learn most.[33] In terms of focus, what we love is what our brains want us to love—routine and what's comfortable. Stretching your mind is stressing to the reactionary parts of your brain, and therefore, like all of us, you have a deep and often hidden aversion to new learning.[34]

So, in each defining moment, pause to suspend judgment on a new possibility or approach. Remain open and more curious. Ask yourself, How would this idea be profitable and serve a human need? Or ask yourself, If this idea were true, what would be its potential value?

No matter where you are, your openness to what's better may

even start something going that could change the world. Not long ago I sat in a Johannesburg office with Dominic Bruynseels, CEO of Barclays Bank in Africa and the Middle East. I have worked with many senior executives around the world, and Dominic is one of the leaders I respect most.

He had said he wanted to consider new, open-space possibilities for building the bank's business in his region and also for serving some of the region's deep social needs. So throughout our meeting we scanned the future, sparking ideas, taking a different view of possibilities that might advance his open-space goal of helping 300 million people in Africa achieve their ambitions.

Dominic is not just an idea person; he's an implementer, and so everything we talked about had a through-line to execution and measurement. For a few moments, halfway around the world from my family, I found myself thinking about my two young girls, wanting the world to be a better place for women and girls than it has been in the past, and I asked, "What about starting a Barclay's Bank for Women?"

At once Dominic said, "A bank with global resources run by women, for women, beginning here in Africa. Yes, it could make a huge difference." The next day, during a session with the bank's forty top leaders, he conveyed his vision and asked if they would take responsibility for making it happen. Within twenty-four hours, the bank's women leaders had set about making Barclay's Bank for Women a reality.

World-changing moments are available to each of us, when we're open to them. Dominic Bruynseels has a relatively large platform from which to make a difference, but let me tell you about two people who changed the world, whom you won't read about in the history books or in the business press—Robert Hendrick and his wife, Geneva, of Bethany, Oklahoma. When Robert died in 2005, they had been married for sixty-three years.

After finishing high school in Mississippi and marrying Geneva there, Robert moved to Oklahoma, where he gained part-time employment as a mail carrier. He then went on to work for the postal service his whole life. He and Geneva raised five children.

I am privileged to know Robert and Geneva's son Howard, who has been the director of the Oklahoma Department of Human Services since 1998. Howard, who like his brothers and sisters credits all he has accomplished to his parents' ethic of hard work, commitment to excellence, and deep personal values, has been recognized as one of America's premier public servants. In 2004, he was one of only four individuals to receive our country's most prestigious honor for public leadership, the National Public Service Award.

Howard Hendrick has worked in closed space, greatly increasing the productivity with which his department's $1.6 billion annual budget is administered. And he has worked in open space—many of his innovations have become national models for providing more services, more effectively, to people in need. The Swift Adoption program he pioneered, for instance, resulted in more adoptions being completed in a five-year period than had been accomplished in the preceding twenty-five years. It's almost impossible to find anyone among the Oklahoma Department of Human Services's eight-thousand-plus employees who has anything negative to say about their director, and it's easy to walk into a room there and find ten people who will tell you that Howard Hendrick has strengthened their commitment to innovative, efficient, compassionate service to those in need.

So, do you not think that by the way they raised their five children, Robert and Geneva Hendrick changed the world? Among them, those five children earned five postgraduate degrees. Do you not think that by the way he has done his job, the programs he's begun, the people he's inspired, the lives he's changed for the better, Robert's son Howard is changing the world? None of them may have set out to do that, and each of them might have laughed if you told them that's what they were doing—but the world is being changed by all of us, all the time, in ways visible and invisible.

I'm reminded of a note I wrote to my grandfather Downing the year before he died, when I was fourteen. In part, it read:

You may not remember the time you let me ride on your shoulders.

You may not remember the time you clapped when I finally made a basket.

You may not remember the time your smile beckoned me on as I first recited the whole alphabet without forgetting any letters.

Or the time we walked together and I was falling behind and you let me catch up.

You may not remember, but I do.

REFRAME DELAYS AND SHIFT GEARS

With a relatively small amount of practice, you can be effective at reframing a typical aggravation—like slow drivers in front of you or being in a slower line at the grocery store or bank—into an unexpectedly positive gift. In part, that's a matter of gaining perspective. Murphy's Law—which states in essence that if anything can go wrong it will, and probably to you—insists the universe is against us. And guess what, it partly is.

Scientists have long dismissed Murphy's Law as little more than our selective memory for those times when things go badly. But using a wide range of mathematics and science, from probability theory to dynamics physics, studies of Murphy's Law show that it just conforms to the normal laws that govern everyday life.[35]

For example, according to Murphy, the line that will finish first in any situation will probably be one that you're not in. But that's to be expected: Your actual chance that the line you picked will be the fastest is just $1/N$, where N is the total number of lines. If there are five lines, you have a four in five chance that yours won't be the fastest. So delays are inevitable.

The lightning-fast reaction in more and more people's brains is to get down on themselves for picking the wrong line, and then fume about it, looking disgusted, murmuring under their breath, and otherwise getting all worked up. It's amazing how things can be going along just fine and then when traffic slows down unexpectedly or the line stalls in front of us, the cascade of angry, counterproductive neuro-chemicals that follows can completely throw us out of sorts unless we deliberately guide our energy where we want it to go. This is particularly true for folks called "hot reactors," of which you might be one.[36]

In fact, the whole thing can quickly multiply as a neurological process called "state-dependent memory"[37] kicks in: When you're tense and slumped, you far more readily recall memories of being tense and overloaded. When you stay loose and calm, you recall easier times when you were loose and calm. It's that literal. This is a simple choice I have seen some of the highest-performing athletes and leaders use with consistent success.

The instant a delay happens, treat it as though someone handed you a gift of unplanned breathing space. At once, with this single choice, you head off your brain's negative reactionary tendencies and create instead a sudden and unexpected "island of calm" to recharge your energies and move forward. Instead of fuming and tension, you relax and flow; instead of being upset about the choice of line you made, you feel good that you get an extra chance to gaze forward in the midst of your busy day.

It takes some practice, but it works. If you're late, by all means call ahead and let people who are expecting you know you will be late— "It's a momentary setback, and I'll keep you posted when the traffic gets moving again"—and then let go of the delay as an issue that could otherwise gnaw at you. You consciously detach, shift gears, loosen up, think of the best possible outcomes your overall choices and actions are building toward. As these unused neurons—the ones that switch from frustration space into breathing space—fire to-gether, they wire together. This is, in fact, a perfect practice ground for training yourself to excel under pressure. Each time you do it, it gets easier to go calm and feel renewed anywhere, anytime.

BOLDLY FOCUS WHERE NO ONE ELSE IS LOOKING

It's worthwhile to consider one example of a person who knew what she wanted and then saw and seized the right moment in a bold, ingenious way that changed everything.

Josephine Esther Mentzer was born in Queens, New York, where her family lived above her father's hardware store. She started a cosmetics business in New York in the midst of the Great Depression, selling facial creams that she and her uncle cooked up in pots on their kitchen stove. Eventually, she changed her name to Estée Lauder. By the time she retired in 1994, she headed a business empire that employed more than ten thousand people in 118 countries, controlled 45 percent of the cosmetics market in American department stores, and enjoyed annual sales in excess of $3 billion.

As her company grew, she decided to tackle international markets. In 1960, her company opened its first overseas outlet, at one of London's top department stores, Harrods. Paris was her next target, and she aimed high there, too, determining to place her company's products—particularly its hottest-selling perfume, Youth Dew—in that city's fanciest store, Galeries Lafayette. To establish her business in the premier store in a country famed for glamour and world-class scents would carry her "impossible" vision even further—a very long way from her beginnings.

But the perfume buyer at Galeries Lafayette was uninterested in this upstart American woman—so uninterested that he refused even to meet with her.

Esther didn't go home to New York in dejection, she didn't rant and curse her bad luck, and she didn't fight to get another appointment, either. One morning as Galeries Lafayette opened, she walked into the store and took one small action that made a huge difference. She poured a large bottle of Youth Dew onto the carpeting in the perfume section.

Nancy Koehn, a Harvard Business School professor who has chronicled Lauder's career, tells what happened next: "Over two days, shoppers repeatedly asked Galeries Lafayette saleswomen where they could purchase the scent. Some of these conversations took place in the presence of the store's cosmetics buyer, who was impressed with women's enthusiasm for Youth Dew. Within a few weeks, Estée Lauder opened her first counter in Galeries Lafayette."[38]

Estée Lauder did three things in Paris that resulted in her achieving something most of us might have given up on as "impossible": She looked beyond the minutiae of her situation to focus on, and then seized, a rare opportunity; she acted in a way that advanced what mattered most to her; and she calmly sensed the precisely right way of acting to do so. Her passion and commitment opened a path for boldness and ingenuity. As *Time* magazine wrote about her in naming her one of the hundred most important Americans of the twentieth century, there's a word that constitutes "the very definition of Lauder: focus."[39]

8

What You Clarify, Unlocks

A great many people think they are thinking, when they are merely rearranging their prejudices.

—William James

To save time, brevity is vital, but not at the sake of clarity. What if you had to pay for e-mails or spoken communications by the word? Remember telegrams? My favorite exchange of short and to-the-point telegrams was between the playwright George Bernard Shaw and Winston Churchill. The two were friends, and titans of repartee. Once Shaw sent a telegram to Churchill announcing the opening of his new play. It read:

Have reserved two tickets for my first night. Bring a friend, if you have one.

Churchill replied:

Impossible to come first night. Will come second night, if you have one.[1]

So you might want to pretend that a few more of your e-mails or text messages are telegrams, and here and there awaken your soul of both clarity and wit. It can instantly capture attention and infuse a difficult day with a spark of humor and hopefulness. For example, think of four people who are vital to your success next year. When you last communicated with them, how could your message have been briefer but more heartfelt, and clearer in content and context? With practice, you can sharpen your focus, save time, and communicate your message with more impact.

VP FOR CLARITY

"You don't see the world as it is, you see it as you are." This line from the Talmud aptly expresses why you need help to create accurate perceptions of life as it moves forward. Clarity in understanding each circumstance that presents itself to you enables you to stay on your strongest line of energy. If you can accurately perceive what's in your way on the path to what's possible, overriding your ancient brain's tendency to shape the world into a grotesquely distorted series of fun-house mirrors, then you can get past obstacles and make the most of the opportunities they present.

For example, as obvious as it is that you should treat every person and situation as unique, most of us tend to do exactly the opposite. Instinctively, we usually assume that every point of difference is an attack on us or a resistance to the "right" view, and it's usually only after conflicts and confrontations are over that we say to ourselves: "I wish I'd done something different." "If I just hadn't raised my voice . . ." "If I just hadn't panicked . . ." These thoughts, these regrets, haunt us all.

The ability to rapidly gain clarity before proceeding can make all the difference in how you respond. A simple technique that I've developed, the Vantage Point, or VP, helps your brain establish clarity more quickly. VP is counterintuitive—like turning the wheels of your car into a skid on an icy road. Turn *into* the skid? Yet if you ever started to lose control of your car, it can save your life.

The challenge is to recognize the moment of conflict and then *respond* instead of *react,* so that you have a very real moment of choice that will affect the outcome. By increasing your level of awareness, you are actually changing the entire situation even before you do anything.[2]

This instant inner change gives you the widest range of options for influencing what happens next by using four simple steps:

1. Acknowledge reality
2. Release the past
3. Go with what's different
4. Guide your focus

1. Acknowledge Reality

Many people skillfully put off facing whatever's in their way—a bullying boss, a friend with an anger problem, an employee who's not up to his job description or role, a spouse who's insecure about their value in your life or the world, or a child with great potential but serious gaps in applying it. The way the brain's wired, many of the things we resist facing grow bigger and harder to overcome later on.

Start by facing forward. This straight-on honesty, the spirit of confronting reality, is a hallmark of exceptionally successful people the world over.[3]

2. Release the Past

Practice setting aside hardened attitudes and releasing old patterns. One simple way to break free of past habits is engaging in a sustainable calming activity, such as focusing inward on your breathing. Get away from the situation for a few minutes by going for a walk or run or pedaling a bicycle or stretching out on the sofa for a quick five-minute "think and rest" session.[4] The repetition or gear-shifting in these simple activities clears the way for a completely fresh mind-set, blending areas of stillness in your brain with areas of intense focus and decision-making power.[5]

During this simple getaway activity, notice when a past unproductive pattern arises—such as feeling stuck or automatically getting incensed or anxious. Whatever the past reaction, ask yourself something simple and clear, such as, *Could I let this go? Could I let it go right now, even for a few moments? Will I?*

The power of these simple questions lies in letting you test releasing the grip of past habits on your current mood and thoughts. Even if the challenge you're facing seems especially perplexing or daunting, could you let go of feeling perplexed or daunted, even for a few moments? Just to see what happens? It's safe to release the past briefly. You can always grab back your old habits and reactions. But will you want to?

3. Go with What's Different

One of the priorities in clarity is managing your insights rather than simply managing your hours. *"If I knew _____, then I could improve _____."* This simple sentence completion is one of my favorites because it cuts to the core of issues and challenges, clarifying what you need to know to move forward. Once you know, you can save time and energy as you redirect your focus to accelerate progress right away.

This forces you—and frees you—to get intensely curious about what else might be possible as you peer past obstacles and step from now into your future.

This also helps elicit what I call the *uniqueness principle.* When you start *every* interaction by pausing for a moment to focus on what's unique—what, exactly, is different about this person, challenge, opportunity, or instant in time—the brain can readily shift into the higher level of functioning known as fluid intelligence, when you are most open to, and skilled at, solving new problems with new solutions.[6] You bypass the brain's more embedded drive to solve new problems with old solutions—the habitual approach known as crystallized intelligence. It is a sign of strength, not of weakness, to have your brain admit to itself that it doesn't have all the answers.

4. Guide Your Focus

Like that Tibetan archer in chapter 7, choose exactly what you're aiming at right now and concentrate your energies and focus there.

Now take your focus a bit deeper. For example, as my grandfather taught me, when you sense upcoming delays in traffic, challenge yourself to decide when to choose an alternate route. If that route doesn't work and you start fuming again, choose a different focus until the traffic clears—immerse your attention in something else that really matters, and make some kind of progress there.

I've built on this lesson from my grandfather by adding some related steps. First, *focus intensely.* The act of seeing takes the image through the lenses of your eyes and reflects it on the retina, most importantly on the fovea, where what you see comes into perfect clarity. You should try to achieve this kind of crystal-clear vision about your goals. To focus intensely is to use relaxed but concentrated attention.

A second facet is to *be relentlessly constructive.* Even when something is extremely difficult, put your attention on seeing exactly where you want to go or envisioning specifically what you need. In other words, never stare where you don't want to go. The one and only time in his fifty-year career that the great high-wire athlete Karl Wallenda focused on where he didn't want to go, he fell to his death. His wife recalls, "This was the only time he began worrying about, 'What if I fall?' "[7]

Whatever you try not to focus on, your brain focuses more on. If you're hiking in Yellowstone or Glacier National Park and you try not to think about falling or grizzly bears, that's what you immediately begin thinking about.[8]

So *direct your mind's eye to the positive.* This calls on emotional experiential memory and drives you toward best possible outcomes. If you allow your mind to focus on preventing a negative outcome instead of bringing about a positive one, your brain gets entrapped by the negative, making the bad outcome even more likely to occur.[9] What you think about is what you get. The brain can't dwell on the reverse of an idea. It has to focus in one direction—a clear, clean line of energy aimed at a specific target—in order to be effective.

No matter how you say it—I want to stop doing that; I want to prevent that; I want to avoid that; I don't want that to happen—and regardless of what the "that" is—you want to stop losing sales, stop spending unwisely, avoid gaining weight, stop getting bad grades, avoid being late, keep from feeling tired, no longer running out of new ideas—your brain only hears the content, not the negative. And so it thinks—it really does—that losing sales is your goal, or spending unwisely, or gaining weight, or getting bad grades, and it's very happy to help you.[10]

Focus on exactly what you *do* want—the direction and the constructive realm of outcomes: more new sales, financial freedom forever, that svelte strong body full of energy, creating new learning at an A+ level, being early and fully attentive, attracting or creating more new ideas than ever. Draw all your energy toward your desired outcome: a specific direction or specific result.

TO GET CLARITY, GIVE IT

Ambiguous communications from others subvert your focus by causing you to spend time figuring them out, and, as I've shown, they often lead your brain into negative speculations about others' intentions, which are counterproductive for finding the best solutions together for the real problem. Everyone's time is wasted by ambiguity, yet often our communications fall into a kind of shorthand that leaves everything fuzzier than it should be.

The more complex the language, the more rambling the message, the more vague the instructions, the harder things are to implement, learn from, and improve.[11]

In my experience, when I give clarity in my communications with others, I usually get it back from them in their communications with me. Being specific in your language, images, and intentions leads to more accurate and fast results.[12]

So, every time you communicate anything that matters, pause to clarify the context. Explain why it's important to you, and exactly why you think the other person will care about it. Take the time to answer questions. Link what you're communicating to the most compelling emotional outcomes in the future.

Own the perspective, feelings, and ideas you're communicating as your own, recognizing that others may not see things as you do: "I could be wrong, but here's why I believe this matters, and here's how I feel/see things/envision the best future, and here's specifically what I think I/we need to do next . . . Now, how about you, how do you see things/feel about things/see the best future?" An approach like that leaves instant room for others to have differing views, allows them to clarify their understanding and help you clarify yours, and makes it possible for you together to make even better future choices.

STILL HAVING TROUBLE? GESTURE

I remember being in a television studio during a national news broadcast. I was there to give a brief scientific update. Next to me at the anchor desk were two men and a woman. Perfect hair, makeup, sitting like statues. I felt like I was in a morgue. As the cameras rolled, I could see the anchorpeople each stare at the camera lens and only move their lips, reading the words as they scrolled by on the teleprompter. I didn't want anything on the teleprompter, so when the camera turned to me I talked extemporaneously, in short practical statements with excitement about my subject. Problem was, I was moving my hands, not just my lips.

The producer was incensed, and I never got asked back to that network. It didn't bother me. I realized that while not ideal for a talking-heads anchor desk, making hand gestures can improve your ability to recall things in your memory and communicate them genuinely to others. Dr. Elena Nicoladis has conducted studies of hand gestures used in storytelling and concluded, "[T]he very fact of moving your hands around helps you recall parts of the story—the gestures help you access memory and language so that you can tell more of the story." She adds, "Initially, we thought gestures were related to meaning—that they meant something on their own. But now we believe they are more related to language. If you're in a situation where it's important to get the language out and you're having difficulty, it may help to start making gestures."[13]

This isn't surprising. Spoken language is a recent development in human history, emerging only about five thousand years ago, so the brain has a great enduring capacity to work with nonverbal signals. By some accounts, at least 80 percent of human communication is nonverbal, so messages and meaning come in words only about one-fifth of the time.[14]

E-TRUST

Of course, one of the biggest challenges to clear communication today is that we often can't see each other at all when communicating. There's no medium except words. Hand gestures don't do you much good in that setting, except maybe as a way of remembering what you meant to say. E-mail correspondence has taken over so much of so many of our lives, and it's a medium fraught with risk of misunderstanding.

In every text and e-mail message, go out of your way to be clear. Ask for what you want and need; be clear about what you expect or hope for. If no reply is necessary, say that! It's amazing how many hours in a week can get wasted when people wonder if you're expecting some witty reply to their message when actually you're not and there's no need.

Most important, provide context. Many of us have had an experience something like this, whether the other person in the story is a boss, an acquaintance, or a loved one. You receive an e-mail from your boss at noon on Sunday:

CANCEL OUR MEETING ON TUESDAY.
GET GOING WITH THE FOLLOWING 5 PRIORITIES
[LISTS THEM].

In the world of bosses, e-mail and text messaging are breakthroughs. Save time, jot out quick notes . . . perfect! But as you've seen, such messages are actually a huge source of danger, considering how our brains are wired. The next Internet will be heart, eye, and voice connected, very much in the way that human beings need to trust. But for now, cyberspace is mostly filled with flying words, and the brain doesn't do well with words alone when it can't look in your eyes, listen to the tenor of your voice, read your heart's intent, and ask questions to make sure there is clear understanding.

On the receiving end, such an e-mail from a boss is universally condemned and resented. "How dare you send me such a message on a Sunday when I'm off from work!" the brain immediately reasons. "It's hard enough to get a meeting with you, and on Sunday you're canceling Tuesday's meeting? What, you hope to never see me again?"

Then the brain escalates the guessing of intent—"There's no further hope of promotion for me!" Then the brain catapults into the ancient internal war cry: "I'll bring you down by Tuesday!" A purely informational message from a boss incites a passive-aggressive rebellion. What went wrong here?

Whenever you receive an e-mail or text message, your brain gives it a temperature rating: warm or cold.[15] This attribution, or rating of both the message and message sender, happens in a split second. If the message feels warm—genuine, human, caring—you keep reading, at least a bit longer, because it feels trustworthy. If the message feels cold—dictatorial, dogmatic, all capital letters, bullet points, exclamation points, misspellings, shorthand—you instantly infer manipulation. You can lose twenty years of trust in one cold e-mail, and you can have a very difficult time winning it back.

So in every message that matters—when you're not just sending some attached document or forwarding information—always begin with genuineness and context. If I were coaching the boss in this example, I'd say, Wait to send the e-mail until you provide human warmth and context. Something like this.

HOPE YOU'RE HAVING A RESTFUL WEEKEND. SORRY TO E-MAIL YOU ON SUNDAY, BUT I WANTED TO BRING YOU UP TO DATE AS SOON AS THINGS CHANGED FOR ME. HAVE A CHILD WHO'S SUDDENLY ILL. NEED TO SEE A SPECIALIST. ONLY OPENING IS ON TUESDAY, RIGHT WHEN WE WERE SUPPOSED TO HAVE OUR MEETING. NEED TO RESCHEDULE.

[Or, Got called out of town at the last minute to meet with a key customer/board member. Hate when that happens.]

Because we have to meet later in the week, here are five priorities I have been focusing on. Perhaps you can think about them, too, so we will be farther ahead when we meet later this week.

Practically everything in your reaction to this e-mail would be different. You'd have immediate empathy. You'd know why your boss needs to cancel the meeting. You wouldn't imagine the worst or get angry or resentful. You might e-mail back:

Sorry to hear about your child. Anything my family can do to help? By the way, if those are your five priorities for the meeting, here's a sixth one I've been thinking about. Look forward to the meeting later in the week.

Remember, context is two-way: If it's not there in a communiqué you receive, ask for it. "Why did you think I would want to know this?" is one example? If you don't ask for what you need to move forward, chances are the other person won't know you need it and therefore won't give it.

With e-mail or text-message correspondence, as with everything else, the future is largely determined by what you focus on, and what you don't.

Race Your Own Race, Together

We lack peace because we are not whole. And we are not whole because we have known so few of the vital relationships we might have.

—D. H. LAWRENCE

During the time Albert Einstein was at the Institute for Advanced Study in Princeton, New Jersey, his best friend was the brilliant logician Kurt Gödel. The two spent many hours together. As one historian recounts:

> They were very different in almost every personal way—Einstein gregarious, happy, full of laughter and common sense, and Gödel extremely solemn, very serious, quite solitary, and distrustful of common sense as a means of arriving at the truth. But they shared a fundamental quality: both went directly and wholeheartedly to the questions at the very center of things.[1]

While you might think that genius flourishes best in isolation, quite the opposite is usually true, as these two geniuses recognized.

That's because your brain is in part a sensory and social brain, changing throughout your life in response to your interactions with the world and people around you. Enriched environments increase the brain's thickness, the number of neurons, and the number and strength of connections between and among neurons.[2] Moreover, the very act of openly responding to a challenge or change alters your brain through feedback loops that in millionths of seconds inform your response patterns to help you be more effective the next time.

Almost all actions and responses affect the pathways of nerve response for future function.[3] The more you, like Einstein and Gödel, join together to go "directly and wholeheartedly to the questions at the very center of things," the more your overall capabilities expand.

What you make of your one go-round with life is up to you. But you're not in it alone, and it can be a lot richer and a lot more fun when you're doing it with others you care about, for a reason that matters deeply. The brain's natural drive is me first. You have to override that. If you don't, the world will increasingly leave you behind, because in this age of the Internet and globally linked businesses and other endeavors, the growing power of all of us to collaborate is shaking up not only businesses, government, and education, but also the way we achieve our goals and live our lives.[4]

THE BIGGEST WINS ARE US, NOT YOU *OR* ME

My grandfather Downing was the one who first said to me, "Learn to race your own race, together." He explained that we never achieve what we could in life if we're racing someone else's race—the boss's race, the bully's race, the superhero's race, the way a race has always been run, or the Hollywood race.

To really shine, you first have to discover your own best race, where every ounce of your strengths, talents, passions, and ingenuity can come through in pursuit of the best possible outcomes *for you*. Then you also need to clearly understand what "Run your own best race" means to others who might join with you. Only then can we work with the right people on a group or team and align our own best races in a specific direction where we all win by uniquely contributing the best we each have—and we all have—toward getting there.

Thinking back to when I served in the Marine Corps during the Vietnam War, I have many recollections of teamwork. Some center on running. Every day we ran at least three miles—sometimes alone, but often in pairs, or as a squad, a platoon, a company, or a battalion. We ran through rain, heat, dust, exhaustion, steep hills, twisting trails, and, during intensive training, gunfire. In combat gear, we ran. In T-shirts, battle trousers, and jungle boots, we ran. On days off, we ran.

One rule was drilled into us: Know your target and get there with teamwork, and leave no one behind. If you happened to be the one who could sprint most expertly and alertly through a particular kind of terrain, you took the lead. If you were struggling for any reason, you stayed in the middle of the formation and someone else took the lead. It had nothing to do with rank or title, it was about who could lead best *now*. Everyone had his moments to lead. We ran our own race—each responsible and committed to run that race at our personal best—while, just as crucially, we ran together.

One predawn morning while we were on training maneuvers in the rocky vertical draws and ravines of the Marine Base at Camp Pendleton, a Marine named Miller, all 240 chiseled pounds of him, fell and hurt his knee. At that moment, I was at the front of the platoon and I glanced back, sensing something was wrong. The Marine on Miller's left scooped him up and carried him. We ran on. While running, the Marine on his right pulled off Miller's pack and slung it on top of his own. The Marine behind him took Miller's rifle. The Marine in front dropped back a few steps to spell the first Marine in carrying Miller.

We left with a goal. We had our aim on the goal but also kept our attention on the route and changing conditions before us, as well as each other. We left together. We finished together. Together is better. Problem is, most families, groups, and organizations don't commit to together. They may preach teamwork, but in reality each person mostly works independently and often at cross-purposes to the others.[5]

Yes, there's a me-first set of ancient reactionary drives in the brain, but, luckily, deep down the brain is socially wired.[6] That quality has helped us survive for eons and, although you might not have tapped into it lately or even know your own neighbors for that matter, you can train your brain to become much better at collaborating—and each member of your group or team can achieve significantly more than solo efforts alone would normally produce.[7]

Think about where you are right now in doing the best work of your life and living the best *life* of your life. Jot down some notes.

Know your own best race. Right now, what's the race you're running? Is it your race—or someone else's? Is it toward your highest goals—or someone else's? Is it the best race you're capable of running? If not, why not?

Know the best race of your vital allies. When you think about a few of the key people vital to your best possible success in the next year, what is the best race they are each running as individuals? Is their best possible goal similar to yours? How is their own best race related to, and different from, *your* best race?

Expand your most effective social network. Success often depends on incorporating yourself into unofficial social networks that allow you to gain access to necessary information and to collaborate with the colleagues who can open doors, shine where you're weak, and actually get things done. If you deepen your observation of the social networks around you and get more curious about how you might collaborate better on the path to your goals, you can better pinpoint individual bottlenecks and breakthrough partnerships, and then tap into the right people at the right times to speed your progress and help theirs as well.[8]

Determine the best alignment of your races together. When you line up each of these best races with the best possible future outcomes— the outcomes that really motivate each of you—what does this look like? Is this how you collaborate now? If not, how can you make improvements?

THE LAST KID PICKED

Summers when I visited my grandfather, I'd join in pickup sports games with the kids who lived in his neighborhood. Even though I was a familiar face from my frequent visits, I wasn't really one of them—I was an outsider. That, plus the fact that I wasn't great at most team sports and many of the others were older than me, resulted in a familiar experience: As sides were chosen up for the game of the day, I'd stand around shuffling my feet, knowing that I was always going to be the last one picked.

I tried not to show it, but my stomach was all jumbled up inside me as I stood there alone, pretending that being passed over didn't matter.

One evening as the team captains were choosing sides for a game of softball and pointing at everyone except me, the hurt just became too much. I walked away, choking back sobs.

When I reached my grandfather's house, he was sitting in his den, and he noticed me as I came in. "I thought you were going out to play," he said, getting up and coming toward me. Then he noticed my red eyes.

I explained why I felt so bad. As he always did, he empathized with me and told me something about his own experiences with the hurt of being disregarded. I recall him saying, "It happens to almost all of us at least once, in some situation, and it's not telling you you're a failure, it's just telling you it's time to try something new. When you feel that sting, try a different way, or learn to thicken your skin, to stick up for the underdog and say no to popularity contests."

"What's a new or different thing I can try when I'm just not very good at those sports, and everyone else is bigger than me?" I asked, focusing on the little picture of my immediate sadness instead of the bigger one of my life as a whole.

My grandfather answered, "There's something I learned that's helped me a lot in situations like yours, something about fighting back." I must have looked surprised, imagining my grandfather putting up his fists, but that was not what he meant. "Want to know how you fight back?" he asked. When I nodded, he said, "Change the game. Whenever you get to pick a team, always pick the last kids first. Then watch what happens."

I didn't get a chance to do that while I was visiting him, since, of course, no one ever named me captain of anything. But when I returned home to Michigan for the school year, there were times when a gym teacher or playground supervisor would designate me as captain, in charge of picking one team. The first time I picked all the "losers" to be on my team for a game of touch football, other kids acted as though I had lost my senses, but I came to see what my grandfather meant.

It might make a good story to say we won that game and taught our detractors a huge lesson, but that's not what happened. I don't remember the exact outcome of that game or of any of the other games where I applied the same personnel-selection strategy, but I do vividly remember the experience. Instead of what usually happened—that we would be judged by the better players on our teams and found wanting—we all were in the same boat, and that gave us a different kind of energy.

Instead of giving in to the playground philosophy that every up or down moment in a game must be practically a life-or-death matter, we got ingenious and played for the fun of it. Every caught pass was an occasion for celebration. A touchdown was like winning the Super Bowl, and here and there, for at least a glorious moment or two, we managed to outplay the most talented athletes around. We walked off the field with a new appreciation of one another, and of the meaning of "play" and "game."

A bigger change happens, too, when you shift what people expect. Change the way people understand what choosing a team for a game means, for example, and pretty soon people may see the whole game in a different light. It can become more fun, more energizing, more satisfying. The focus shifts from the same old same old—who's better and who's worse, who's winning and who's losing, who's the hero and who's the "goat"—to something refreshing, invigorating, liberating. It shifts from the energy-depleting grind of worrying about failure to the energy-boosting prospect of novelty and ingenuity and fun.

Easy for me to say, you might think. Fretting about winning and losing, about looking good and not failing, are built into our lives by the cultures and attitudes of those around us, and it's not easy to change all that. Can changing how the game is played, or even changing the game itself, actually be acceptable and practical anywhere, in this day of hypercompetition and win-at-any-cost attitudes, aside from a bunch of kids on a school athletic field?

Well, just sticking with sports for a moment, it could help you re-define what you think is possible. One of the most talked-about triumphs in recent memory owed a lot to a similar approach, albeit with more skilled players. The members of the Boston Red Sox team that overcame a decades-old "curse" as "losers" by winning the 2004 World Series delighted in referring to themselves as a "bunch of idiots." One sportswriter wrote about that team, "The self-proclaimed 'bunch of idiots,' whose grooming habits fall just this side of Tarzan's, took the softball beer-league approach to their profession: Have as much fun as you can, as often as you can. . . . Playing for a franchise with extreme media scrutiny and so many years of post-season baggage, the Red Sox players decided an 'Animal House' atmosphere was the best way of coping. Thus, the beards, the long hair, the practical jokes, the guffaws in the dugout when a teammate made a mistake."[9]

"Idiots," outcasts, just plain different, at ease with their failings—and world champions. As another sportswriter observed, "[T]he 'bunch of idiots' exhibited a love of the game—and each other—which enabled them to do what 85 previous Red Sox teams could not accomplish."[10]

Find your way to love the game, find teammates you love, and whatever you're doing, great things can flow from the energy you generate. There's value in remembering what Richard Bach said: "The more I want to get something done, the less I call it work"; and in what Tim Sanders, author of *Love Is the Killer App*, says: "Your network *is* your net worth. And the power of your relationships—the friendliness, warmth and emotional content in those relationships—will define your happiness as well as how you're going to do in business."[11]

A CAUTIONARY TALE

Even in seemingly strong relationships, there can be signals that things are going wrong. It pays to heed those signals, and to use context and clarity tools to set things right. One of the most dramatic business stories of our time involved two brilliant, successful, even visionary people who somehow missed what was not just right in front of them, but right inside of them. If Walt Disney Company CEO Michael Eisner and his very good friend Michael Ovitz had only listened to what their instincts were saying—saying loudly and clearly—Disney would have been spared some huge financial losses, each man would have been spared serious embarrassment and career damage, and their friendship might still be intact.

Ovitz, the talent agency dynamo whom the *Wall Street Journal* had called the most powerful person in Hollywood, went to work for his friend Eisner in 1995 as Disney's president. The two had been close friends for many years; their families often spent holidays together; their wives were also best friends. When Eisner became convinced that he needed a powerful, trusted second-in-command, he offered the job to Ovitz. Because the balancing of so much power at such a high-profile corporation among two successful and ambitious individuals was very hard to put into words, the two men eventually agreed to proceed as much on trust as on delineated roles, responsibilities, and authorities. As they came closer to a working arrangement, Ovitz told his friend Eisner, "I'm putting myself in your hands."[12]

Moments after hearing those words from Ovitz, Eisner called a business associate and said, "I think I just made the biggest mistake of my career." The next evening, after meeting with some Disney executives at Eisner's home, Ovitz said to his wife, "I just made the biggest mistake of my career."

But still they went ahead, and the formal hiring of Ovitz was announced with fanfare at a press conference a few weeks later. Within less than eighteen months, Eisner fired Ovitz, who received $140 million in settlement. Disney shareholders sued the company's directors; some Disney board members turned against Eisner in unusually virulent and public ways; the company's stock languished; Eisner eventually was forced to announce his early retirement. As for Ovitz, *New Yorker* reporter James B. Stewart says, "the career of the man known as the most powerful individual in Hollywood was effectively destroyed."[13]

How different might things have been if either Ovitz or Eisner had simply been willing to say to the other, "Michael, something's bothering me and I think we should talk about it"?

THE POWER OF ONE PASSPORT

Over the past five years, my research group has been studying star-performing leaders and teams, the men and women who consistently accomplish the "impossible" in challenging circumstances. We've been asking what distinguishes the best teams from all the others during times of wrenching change and rampant uncertainty. We have learned that exceptional individuals put their social brains together to move beyond everyone else by applying some simple yet powerful perspectives that overcome the natural categorization tendency of the brain and instead permit them to embrace each other's uniqueness and be far better at racing their own race, together.

We found six key factors to that uniqueness, and I summarize them as the Power of One Passport—a two-way passport that details several essential insights that each person must share with and learn about others in order that their teams will zoom beyond business as usual and life as usual. The name "Power of One" comes from the realization in our research that once you have gathered these insights, all it takes is one person to apply them to change any relationship or team for the better.

Here are the six elements of the Power of One Passport:

1. This is the work I'm best at . . .
2. These are my values . . .
3. This is what energizes me . . .
4. This is what I need in order to learn and work at my best . . .
5. These are the results I can be expected to deliver . . .
6. This is what I need to feel genuinely respected and recognized . . .

How accurately can you describe each of those things about yourself? How much do you know about others? The more clear you can become about these things, the more effective your performance will be.

Use the items in the Passport to open dialogue. It's a very powerful way to launch any team undertaking. We recommend that each team member write down his or her responses to the six items and then sit down with every other individual to discuss them. You will detect places where you're getting in your own way by trying to do things in ways that aren't most effective for you, and all the team members will learn how to stay out of each other's way by not imposing what they like best on others who may work very differently.

1. *This is the work I'm best at . . .* These are my strengths—the kinds of work I believe I do best. What are your strengths? In contrast, here are several kinds of work I like least. What are some of your least-favorite pursuits?

2. *These are my values . . .* You don't put your heart into things you don't value or that aren't a fit for you personally. Organizational, or shared, values are useful, but they're not as fundamental or significant as individual values. Individuals' commitment to exceptional work rises most significantly not when they're clear about the organization's values but when they're clear about individual values.[14] We need to be able to say—and demonstrate—to others, "These are the values that matter most to me." Most leaders stumble by emphasizing organizational values and ignoring personal values.

3. *This is what energizes me . . .* This may have nothing to do with

work, and that's fine: "Here are some of my most compelling life interests and passions." "These are activities or pursuits that I have a blast doing and that make me feel the happiest."

4. *This is what I need in order to learn and work at my best . . .* When you recall the times you have learned and worked at your absolute best, what were your resources and environment? For example, were the lights bright or dim? Was it quiet, or was there music in the background? Were you near a window? What was the temperature? What time of day was it? What was your work or study area like? I'm amazed at how seldom—if ever—people in workplaces discuss this, and yet what a huge difference it can make in how focused—or more likely, distracted and ineffective—we are.

5. *These are the results I can be expected to deliver . . .* We're going to explore this in detail in Key 5, but the theme here is "When I do my best work, you can count on me to deliver the following specific results, and here's when." "What can I count on you to deliver, and by when?" There is also another aspect to results that often goes unnoticed. Just by being present, we can each make a contribution to any group or effort. Whether we have content expertise or industry savvy, we each contribute to group processes by having a unique perspective on the world, our own network and ways of accessing resources, and a one-of-a-kind way to ask questions and make things happen: "Just by being present, this is the contribution that I plan to make. How about you?"

6. *This is what I need to feel genuinely respected and recognized . . .* When you look back across your life, how would you describe the time you felt the most genuinely respected and recognized by another person? Is this how you feel at work each day? It should be—and, in more instances, could be. We need to be able to talk with those above us and around us and clearly say, "To give more of my best at work, here's what I need to feel genuinely respected and recognized. How about you?"

Competing is hard and unproductive work. Collaborating—racing your own race, together—can feel like flying. In fact, an aeronautical phrase makes sense to me in this context: You use the force of the lift, not the push. That was the breakthrough discovery that allowed humans to take flight, to roar off the face of the earth.

The next time you're feeling pressure to compete instead of collaborate, notice it and change the game.

BEHIND THE GREEN BAG

If you imagine that your organization, field, or profession can't really be reinvented in an open-space way, or if maybe you imagine that doing so wouldn't be much fun, I ask you to consider a small but rapidly growing publication that's shaking up the whole world of legal scholarship. Yes, legal scholarship. And if three farsighted law students can start a movement that changes and energizes their whole cynical, hidebound, competitive profession, and then enlist hundreds of others to join joyfully in furthering that change, what's stopping you?

Legal writing has become so long, dry, and dense in the past few years that practitioners and academics alike have got up in arms about it. Federal judge Richard Posner has written, "The result of the system of scholarly publication in law is that too many articles are too long, too dull, and too heavily annotated . . ."[15] The *Harvard Law Review* recently announced the results of a survey of nearly eight hundred law professors by saying, "[T]he survey documented one particularly unambiguous view shared by faculty and law review editors alike: the length of articles has become excessive. In fact, nearly 90% of faculty agreed that articles are too long."[16]

The publication that's changing all that is called the *Green Bag*. Three young men created it while they were still students at the University of Chicago Law School, a top-ten law school that is so demanding and rigorous that it's sometimes referred to as the "boot camp" of law schools. The three—Ross Davies, Montgomery Kosma, and David Gossett—were not just ordinary students, they were very busy ones: two of them were married with children, one of them was editor in chief of the *Law Review*.

Davies, deep in the drudgery of checking the hundreds of footnotes in an eighty-five-page book review he was editing, chanced upon a unique, charming turn-of-the-last-century publication also called the *Green Bag*. Instead of doing what most of us would have done—glancing at it and then getting quickly back to his mountain of work and other obligations—Davies decided that the world needed a new *Green Bag*. He showed the dusty old version to his friends Kosma and Gossett, and they agreed.

Long story short: Today's incarnation of the *Green Bag*, whose cover proclaims it "An Entertaining Journal of Law," publishes short, pithy articles that legal professionals love to read. While subscriptions to academic law journals are sagging (Yale's have decreased from about seven thousand to about four thousand, for example), *Green Bag*'s subscriptions are doubling every two years. The editors have fun—the Supreme Court justice bobblehead dolls they give away to subscribers being just one example (one of those dolls sold recently on eBay for over a thousand dollars).[17]

And the work is done as a community: hundreds of lawyers and academics, excited by the *Green Bag* vision, volunteer their time to get out each year's issues and expand the vision. Recently, seventy-five legal professionals throughout the country volunteered to serve as reviewers for *Green Bag*'s latest project: a book celebrating the best legal writing.

As one law-firm partner has said, "*Green Bag* is different, in part because its aim is to start up an interesting legal discussion rather than trying to have the final word on any subject. It's the journal for people who care about novel legal ideas, not just to help them with a current case but also because the ideas are interesting in their own right. You could say it's a journal for people who don't only work in the law, but enjoy the law as one of their hobbies, too."[18]

Davies, Kosma, and Gossett could have plodded along a manicured path toward success in their profession, working hard, fitting in, perhaps content only to remember the glimmer of excitement of the potential defining moment they had sensed but then disregarded. They didn't. You shouldn't, either.

Key ③ CAPACITY, Not Conformity

**It's not how good you are at copying others
or making incremental improvements,
it's how bold you are at unlocking hidden potential—
in yourself and others—and applying it in new ways.**

*The most amazing powers to change our lives and the world are
waiting just beneath the surface of our daily habits, if only we
could see these hidden powers, awaken them, and put them into
action.*

—ORISON MARDEN

Many summer evenings, my grandfather would return home from
his hospital rounds to pick me up and take me somewhere in his
car. To a park he loved, for example, where he would share with me
his delight and wisdom about things we observed together—trees,
birds, flowers, and people.

On one evening outing, however, I noticed that he seemed to

be driving along a new route. He had brought his medical bag with him, too, which he didn't usually do. I asked him where we were headed and he answered, "Today there's something else I want you to appreciate."

We reached a run-down part of town and parked alongside a bridge. I could make out a group of people milling around under the bridge. As much as I loved and trusted my grandfather, I was anxious. My brain's fear centers must have jumped into high gear, because I suddenly found my heart racing and my hands trembling, unable to stop wondering what bad things would happen if those strangers in the shadows were up to no good.

Under the bridge, we encountered a group of men and women. It was easy to tell that their lives were very hard, and this was now where they lived. They all greeted my grandfather as he approached, and he introduced me to each of them. He knew all their names. They had hung some bedspreads in a corner of their site, apparently knowing he was coming, and one after another he met with them behind the bedspreads, giving them each a medical examination for whatever they told him was ailing them.

I talked with the others as my grandfather conducted his examinations, and they were thoughtfully interested in my school and my other activities. They teased me, as adults will do, about whether I had a girlfriend. In short, we held normal conversations of the sort adults have with youngsters. In the background, I often heard my grandfather laughing and joking with his patients as he examined them.

Normal it was, but normal was not what I had expected. When I asked my grandfather about the experience on our way home, he said, "Robert, not long after I started my medical practice, the Great Depression hit, and times got very rough for practically everyone. People came to me, dressed a lot like the people you see here, who not long before had been farmers or business owners or bankers or schoolteachers. I learned right away to be thankful for what I have, and to recognize that contrary to what today's popular expression says, what you see is not what you get. You have to look deeper to see the best in people, and when you do look that way, what you see can be amazing. I do what I can to help them—and I hope this will help you, too."

Then he tapped me lightly on my shoulder and said, "The same thing applies when you look at yourself. You're a genius in hiding."

FINDING THE GENIUS IN HIDING

From what you've read so far in this book, you can understand why we often fail to find that genius within ourselves and others. During moments of introspection and soul-searching, or when calmly lined up with one of your open-space goals, the amygdala can be a source of implicit knowledge, even wisdom,[1] but more often it lives in the-sky-is-falling mode, primed along with the RAS and other brain areas to root out weaknesses that might threaten your immediate performance rather than recognize strengths of yours that might have some longer-term payoff.

The RAS blares out your "weaknesses" to the rest of your brain like a bullhorn so each part will pay attention to this "problem" and be deafened to anything else. The feeling is a lot like being a second-grader with the meanest teacher ever: "Your penmanship is *terrible!* I've told you a *thousand times, i* comes before e except after c! Sit up straight! Stop daydreaming!"

Your amygdala and RAS are conformity-driven fear mongers, always quick to hit the panic button and let other parts of the brain ask questions later. They see you as one big problem to be fixed, and fixed now, with all kinds of other hidden faults waiting to be discovered and fixed next, before you do something really stupid that makes both of you extinct.

That's fine if conformity—or survival alone—is your goal. If you conform to everything, you're visible to no one—which is just the way the amygdala and RAS want it.

And it's no surprise that we also turn our superb fault-spotting magnifying glasses on others. That guy or gal over there, doing something wrong—or at least differently from how we would do it—our brain's ancient wiring makes sure to emphasize that he or she could turn out to be a threat to our existence, too. Of course, others are often happy to return the favor and let us know all our shortcomings and weaknesses, with a little exaggeration thrown in for good measure.

Our other typical reaction to all that internal and external criticism is to seek conformity: to do things pretty much like everyone else is doing them, to aspire to pretty much the same things as everyone around us. Your brain figures if you're doing what everybody else is doing, you must be doing it right—or at least right enough to get by—and at least if you don't stand up too tall, you won't get knocked down as often.

Yet parts of your brain know that while you might not be able to do everything, there are some things you can do better than practically anyone else. To make your dreams reality, you want to tap into every source of genius available, in yourself and others. You want to collaborate so you get the best from everyone, instead of finding them hiding their best from you. In fact, as we'll see, competing results in you hiding your best not just from everyone else but from yourself, too.

You want your extraordinary capacity for—and thirst for—creativity and innovation to set you soaring, right past the obstacles that are holding everyone else back. You want the disappointments and frustrations that you experience to turn into irresistible itches for progress and fodder for breakthroughs.

You've got it, if you choose wisely. Your heart and gut brains can be particularly valuable in this regard, along with some parts of the brain in your head, and even a brain area in the spine. But instead of enlisting their brilliance, we have learned to stuff them down, shut them up, sedate and ignore them. But when we listen, there's genius there.

Scientists have located the part of the brain that takes pleasure in punishing people who cheat—it's a very powerful impulse.[2] And they think a principal reason that impulse is so powerful is that humans have learned over recent millennia—after many more years before that of do-or-die competition to survive as a species—that cooperation is now more potent than competition, and cheating tears the fabric of cooperation by undermining trust, so it must be dealt with harshly. It may even be that your "conscience" with regard to cheating is wired directly to that brain center.

The first step in bringing out your best capacities for turning "impossible" goals and extraordinary ideas into successful action is to seize the right moments to cooperate with yourself by tuning in to the best your brain offers and tuning out the harsh and punishing static. That also permits you to treat your frustrations and disappointments constructively, as inducements to find a better way instead of indictments of your abilities. From those positive vantage points, you can engage others far more constructively in larger forms of cooperation toward greater things.

In his twelve-volume work, *A Study of History,* Arnold Toynbee analyzed the trajectories of twenty-six civilizations. He concluded that societies advance when what he called "creative minorities" inspire unprecedented effort to solve difficult challenges. Conversely, he determined, "Civilizations in decline are consistently characterized by a tendency toward standardization and uniformity."

In the next chapters, I'll tell you how to be part of that creative minority and how to avoid the stifling effects of standardization and uniformity.

SAVING AMERICA: J. ROBERT OPPENHEIMER

When it came to the flourishing of his own genius and the nurturing of the genius of others, the physicist J. Robert Oppenheimer stood tall. He contributed to the revolutionary theory of quantum mechanics in the 1920s and led the thinking about black holes and neutron stars in the 1930s. During World War II, he was in charge of the secret laboratory at Los Alamos that raced America's enemies to create a nuclear bomb. Under his guidance, the United States won that race, and consequently won the war. It could have been different: In Germany, the brilliant scientist Werner Heisenberg led the Nazi effort to build a nuclear weapon.

As a 2004 biography of Oppenheimer recounts, he was always ready to hear a new idea, never defensive when his own ideas were challenged, always willing to help a younger scientist move ahead, and never recriminatory when ideas failed to pan out.[3] As a result, he attracted and energized physics geniuses like Richard Feynman and Niels Bohr, people with highly unconventional personalities but huge amounts to contribute.

The Nazis' Heisenberg, on the other hand, was egocentric and authoritarian. He lacked Oppenheimer's ability to see and bring out the best in others. He expected others to act and think just like him.

Contrasting Oppenheimer's openness with Heisenberg's self-centered officiousness, the Nobel laureate Steven Weinberg concluded, "I am convinced that one of the reasons the US was successful in developing nuclear weapons during the war and Germany was not is that we had Oppenheimer while the Germans had Heisenberg."[4]

The capacity to surpass the previous best and change the world resides within all of us, within all of our organizations, and within our societies. Conformity is its enemy.

10
Use Your Brains— All Four of Them

Go to your bosom,
Knock there, and ask your heart what it doth know . . .
— WILLIAM SHAKESPEARE, *MEASURE FOR MEASURE*

In the *Devil's Dictionary,* first published in 1911, Ambrose Bierce sarcastically defined "the brain" as "an apparatus with which we think we think." Bierce could be considered a neuroscientist ahead of his time: We do, of course, "think" with our brain—the one in our head—and sometimes, as I've shown, we just think we're thinking. But we also truly think with several other brains throughout our bodies. What we "think" we're thinking within the brain in our head is often actually input coming from our other brains. And, to the extent we disregard that input from our other brains, we're not really thinking to anywhere near the best of our capacities.

Those other brains—real brains, as I said at the beginning of this book, with neuronal structures at least as extensive and complex as those in major areas of the brain in your head—exist in your heart, your gut (the enteric nervous system), and, some evidence suggests, also in your spine. They send vitally important signals that we recognize in everyday speech—"My gut tells me"; "My heart tells me"— but that we too often ignore in favor of the kind of "thinking" that the brain in our head does.

Compelling new research from many different scientific fields shows that for ingenuity, teamwork, and breakthroughs to happen, intellect is a less crucial ingredient than those other forms of intelligence.[1] Unlocking your own distinctive potential and applying it ever more fully in your life and work have remarkably little to do with thinking alone. New research describes how we can make highly intelligent intuitive decisions that depend on our emotions and occur without thought.[2]

As science looks closer, it is coming to see that intuition is not a gift but a skill. And, like any skill, it's something you can learn.

I've already mentioned many ways in which the thinking brain can trap you in the closed space of fears, habits, and misperceptions. Yes, there are ways to overcome that, and parts of that brain like the prefrontal cortex, dorsal striatum, and nucleus accumbens very much want you to do so. But your heart, gut, and spine brains can take you directly to many kinds of awareness that move you into open space. One leading brain scientist has written that in order to significantly move forward we have to learn to rely more on tuning in to the "sensory acuity" of our "other" brains.[3] They form a part of you that's smarter than you are and faster than you are, reading every opportunity and engaging with every goal in your life.

By and large, the vast realm of life's learning happens unconsciously, or implicitly, beneath and beyond your "thinking" brain areas. Long underappreciated for their power to absorb new learning and create street-smart wisdom, the limbic-related areas like the basal ganglia, ACC, hippocampus, and amygdala are actually linked to brains in your gut and heart that along with these limbic-prefrontal circuits give rise to what is called "emotional intelligence."[4]

ALL TOGETHER NOW

Rationality and analysis get machines to run. Intuition invents them. Rationality and analysis produce spreadsheets dissecting past performance. Intuition creates the future. Because all those things are valuable, achieving all you can is not a matter of "losing your head" but of getting the balance right between the thinking brain in your head and the intuitive intelligences in your gut, heart, and spine.

You may remember the account of Michael Ovitz and Michael Eisner from chapter 9: "Something" told both of them that the arrangement they were about to make was a bad idea, which is just the way it turned out. That something was their hearts and guts, but—being smart, accomplished fellows—they let their head brains override the greater wisdom that was coming from elsewhere inside them. They thought they were smarter than the truth. That's a crucial lesson from this chapter: When you find yourself saying or thinking, "Something tells me . . . ," then stop and pay attention. You're not smarter than your collective brains, and trying to be so is a ticket to disappointment or worse.

The brain in your head is not one integrated thinking device, it's a stacked-up series of separate or loosely linked organs that evolved at different times to meet different needs and serve different purposes.[5] Now, more and more, we discover that there are other parts of that same somewhat chaotic circuitry, parts that are not located in our heads. Neuroimaging technologies are now answering questions about how we make snap decisions, where instant instincts rise, why we may feel comfortable or uncomfortable without any obvious reason, what most deeply motivates us, and what makes us feel most satisfied. The sources of many of those vital perceptions are located throughout our bodies.

I have written at some length about these other brains,[6] and in the following pages I'll describe some of the core science about them. In one sense, of course, it doesn't matter so much whether those brains are "real brains" or not: we have known for a long time that there is wisdom outside our heads. In 350 BC, Aristotle wrote, "The brain is not solely in the head. The brain is in the heart and more."[7]

So, attending to your instinctual responses to things is good advice, regardless of neuroscience. The word "emotion" is derived way back from Latin, and it means "the spirit that moves us." Without feeling, we don't tend to move; and without movement, we're not going anywhere—certainly not any closer to our biggest dreams and aspirations. Alternatively, as Norman Vincent Peale said so well, "If you throw your heart over the fence, the rest of you will follow."

We each have exquisite mechanisms outside our heads for sensing and locking on to what's important. As much as 95 percent of thought, emotion, and learning occur somewhere beyond the conscious mind.[8]

BIG BRAINS, NO BUCKS

Yale professor Robert Sternberg has extensively studied the reasons why some people succeed and most don't—what he calls "successful intelligence."[9] He writes, "Between 75 and 96 percent of the variance in real world criteria such as job performance and innovation and wealth creation cannot be accounted for by individual differences in intelligence test scores."[10] Many intellectually bright people care so much about appearing intelligent that they withhold their curiosity, ingenuity and initiative at the very times when those qualities can count the most.[11]

Thomas Stanley, author of *The Millionaire Mind,* calls the fallacy of waiting for superior intellect to make you successful "Big brains, no bucks."[12] The vast majority of millionaires did not have the sharpest intellect or best grades in school, but they learned to use their ingenuity and every other kind of intelligence they could muster. And, it turns out, that is the far greater gift for any kind of success, not just financial, in life and work.

According to Steven Pinker of MIT, "Without the stimulus and guidance of emotion, rational thought slows and disintegrates . . . The emotions are mechanisms that set the brain's highest-level goals."[13] Scientist Gary Klein has studied many top-performing organizations and teams, and he concludes, "Analysis cannot replace the intuition that is at the center of the decision-making process."[14] Richard Farson, psychologist and president of the Western Behavioral Sciences Institute, reports from his research that "the one quality that many of the best leaders agree separates them from their less successful rivals is confidence in their intuition."[15] He says that great leaders have "golden guts."[16]

Emotional intelligence engages not only the gut and heart, but also the cranial brain's limbic system and even the thinking brain.[17] But all of this is not about acting without thinking first; it's about augmenting your cerebral intellect with your other brains and bringing them at least a bit more fully under your conscious control to reap more of their benefits. Let's take a brief look at your other brains and then proceed to some specific advice.

THE BRAIN IN THE GUT

Scientists who study the elaborate systems of nerve cells and neurochemicals found in the intestinal tract now tell us that there are about 100 million neurons in that enteric nervous system (ENS), which is being called the "second brain."[18] All of the more than thirty chemicals that transmit signals to and within the head brain are also found in the ENS. This combination of chemicals and complex circuitry enables the ENS to act independently, learn, remember, and influence our perceptions and behaviors.

Dr. Michael Gershon of Columbia University has said, "The relationship between the cerebral and enteric brains is so close that it is easy to become confused about which is doing the talking."[19] He adds, "The second brain can, whenever it wants, process data picked up by the sensory system and can act on it . . . , thus it is not a slave to the brain [in the head] but a contrarian brain [in its own right], an independent spirit in the nervous system."[20]

The enteric nervous system is far faster than the brain in the head, by some estimates a million times faster.[21] For example, it runs outcome scenarios—if this, then that, then this will likely happen, and so on—thousands to even millions of them, in seconds. Sensory signals go directly to the enteric nervous system, which can respond to those signals before your thinking brain is even aware of them.[22]

The ENS extends its "radar" so intuitively and amazingly that it selects stimuli *before* they appear.[23] The basal ganglia, the deep place in the cranial brain largely outside reach of thinking and words, is one key place you can access life wisdom as you build your actions going forward—*if* you learn to trust your gut, which connects directly to that brain area.[24] The neural circuits involved in confronting complex and puzzling decisions involve neural pathways that link to the basal ganglia and the amygdala, where the brain stores most of its emotional memories.[25]

Encouraged by scientific research on intuition, top managers feel increasingly confident that when faced with complicated choices, they can trust their gut. A recent survey by executive search firm Christian & Timbers reveals that fully 45 percent of corporate executives now rely more on instinct than on facts and figures in running their businesses.[26]

However, I believe it's vital to point out that the brain in the gut benefits from deepening your range of experience in decision-making. You have to use it to grow its power and accuracy, and this seems to increase the neural effectiveness of its connections to many areas of the cranial brain.[27] Think ahead right now to a significant challenge you face—a meeting with your boss, or a job interview, for example. If you think about it for a few moments, the brain in the head will often run outcome probability percentages. It will scan the situation and assign a number for how ready you are: "You're eighty percent prepared for that meeting, and that's just fine," it might say.

Now hold the image of that key meeting in your mind and push the feeling down to your gut. What do you feel, if anything? Your gut will check out vast numbers of possible outcome scenarios in no time at all. And sometimes it will tense right up. Translation? Perhaps something like "*This* meeting's more significant than others. If it goes really well, all kinds of doors will open. Eighty percent readiness is not enough. Get more ingenious!" If you doubt the gut reading, look a bit more closely at the meeting and ask what defining moments might be hidden within it. Chances are, your second brain knows way more than you do.

I'll have more suggestions and recommended actions later, but first let's complete our tour of your brains.

THE BRAIN IN THE HEART

There was something my grandfather Downing wanted his patients, and me, to understand, and so he would say, "Point to yourself." He knew that no one would then point to her head, but always to her heart. He would remind his patients that they usually really knew what was best for them when they looked inside the heart. For centuries, the heart has been known as the source of emotion, courage, and wisdom.[28] New research provides a scientific basis to explain how and why the heart affects mental clarity, emotional balance, creativity, and both personal and interpersonal effectiveness.[29]

When I was young and sitting in my grandfather's office, he would often wait until I responded to his question by pointing to my chest, and then he would put his stethoscope to my ears so I could listen to my own heart, and then to his. He wondered out loud what undetected mysteries were hidden there inside that miraculous organ. Quite a few, it turns out.

In the human fetus, the heart develops before the nervous system and thinking brain; the electrical energy in every heartbeat, and the information contained therein, is pulsed to every cell of the body long before other developmental activities take place.[30] That pattern continues throughout your life: Every one of your heartbeats causes instantaneous whole-body communication as a wave of energy travels through the arteries many times faster than the actual flow of blood.[31] Pressure wave patterns vary with each intricate, rhythmic pattern of the heart, and each of our trillions of cells feels those patterns and is dependent on them in a number of ways.[32]

Recent studies have shown that the coherence of the heart brain's rhythms can change the effectiveness of the thinking brain, often dramatically.[33] That's not so surprising when you realize that the heart is the most powerful generator of rhythmic information patterns in the human body.[34] With every beat, the heart not only pumps blood, but also transmits complex patters of neurological, electromagnetic, hormonal, and pressure information throughout the body.

The heart's electromagnetic field is approximately five thousand times greater than the field produced by the brain.[35] The electrical changes in feelings transmitted by the heart can be felt and measured at least five feet away,[36] sometimes even ten feet or more.[37] The brain in the heart also has powerful, highly sophisticated computational abilities that enable it to intuitively "read" complex situations and their relevance to you and your goals.[38] And like the ENS, the heart brain is very fast: By some estimates, between eighty thousand and 2 million times faster than the brain in the cranium at reading what's going on inside you and around you.[39]

In terms of human ingenuity and initiative, it also turns out that the heart is not only *open* to new possibilities, it actively *scans* for them. It instantaneously searches for new opportunities to grow or learn, establishes a "reading" of what others feel, measures the coherence or congruence of that feeling state, and checks its own inner state of coherent values and passions.[40]

How do you use the brain in your heart? First, you get out of its way. The heart brain's creative "radar" needs to be free to scan the world around you and help you make sense of it. Next time you're ready to make a decision, seek a solution, build a relationship, or search for new opportunities, pause for a moment to sense what your heart tells you. The brain in there is already humming along at high levels, and each time you listen to it more carefully you increase your ability to rapidly monitor more of its messages. Is it always right? No. But it's always a good source for a fresh perspective.

THE BRAIN IN THE SPINE (?)

George Soros, the international financier who has made billions in the risky, intense world of currency arbitrage, feels opportunity in his back. According to his son Robert, "The reason he changes his

position on the market or whatever is because his back starts reacting. It has nothing to do with mental reason."[41]

What exactly is Soros's back reacting to? As Soros himself has observed, the markets where his money is at risk don't yield completely
to rational analysis, even using the most high-powered computers,
because they are continuously and often instantaneously changing in
response to factors that are not just rational but often emotional or
psychological, too. So he needs a reliable source of intelligence outside his head—and he's learned that it's in his back.

A number of scientists have spoken of the possibility of embedded intelligence inside the spine. A major neuropsychology textbook
asserts, "Clearly the spinal cord is not a passive channel for conduct-
ing information but is actively involved in transposing that information through its own internal connections in a way that is consistent
with [life's] continually changing state. . . ."[42]

My own first impression that there might be more to the spine
than an electrical column inside the vertebrae was rooted in the
image my grandmother Cooper conveyed to me after meeting Helen
Keller. My grandmother said Ms. Keller had the best posture she had
ever seen. I wondered why a woman who was blind, deaf, and mute
would care so much about her posture if she couldn't even see herself
in a mirror or observe what others saw when they looked at her.

Later on, I delved more deeply into this to see what was there.
Helen Keller's autobiography, *The Story of My Life*, changed the
world. But *The World I Live In*, Keller's sequel to her autobiography, is
far less known.[43] There she talks about posture and the senses, and
the world they opened to her. "Hold your head high," she writes.
"Look the world straight in the eye." I have a picture of her with
Alexander Graham Bell, and her posture is amazing. What she had
learned was that *all* her senses dimmed the moment she slumped, but
when she was relaxed and upright in the world, all of her senses extended dramatically farther.

In *The World I Live In*, she wrote, "Search out my blindness, it
holds riches past computing." She wrote of the "finer vibrations of life

within us all if only we would awaken and use them," and she was also responding to skeptics who doubted that a girl who was blind, deaf, and mute almost from birth could find words to describe her experience or could experience life as fully as a person with normally functioning senses. William James, nearing the end of his own career, wrote a longhand note to Helen within a week of receiving her book, saying, "You have told so much truth about human nature which nobody had suspected. Sensations as we normally know them form the relatively smaller part of the world we mentally live in."[44]

Are the spinal column and the surrounding network of nerves more than just conduits for neuroeletrical impulses? Is there a relational or positional brain in the spine that connects us to the world and orients us in time and space? No one knows for certain, but right now, slump over and notice what your senses are doing. How far away can you sense the environment or other people? How's your acuity and insight? Now sit upright, relaxed, fluid, head high. What changes in the ways you relate to everything around you?

Ancient martial-arts traditions talk about the spine as a center of energy. They also talk about the knowing energy in the heart and gut (ki or chi). In Understanding the Mysteries, Lao-tzu wrote, "Those who master their posture have intelligence."[45]

George Leonard describes the "special presence of uprightness" in The Silent Pulse: The Search for the Perfect Rhythm in Each of Us.[46] Your "stance" has been used symbolically through the ages to refer to your attitudes and approach to life or work. "Walking tall" refers to posture and also to a perspective on life, as does "walking the walk and not just talking the talk." As with the heart and gut brains, our images and language bespeak the vital importance of the spine to being our best selves. Even if it's not a full-fledged brain, we know that when the spine is open, aligned, and upright, we tend to be, too.

FIVE SECONDS CAN CHANGE EVERYTHING

Routines of living almost solely from the head have taken hold in nearly all of us, and we have come to believe that rationality requires the exclusion of feelings from thoughts and decisions.[47] In fact, exactly the opposite is true: We are built to reason using practically everything inside us. The gray matter in our craniums is amazing—it's just less than all we need to do all that we can, as well as we can.

To say, "Let's leave feelings out of this," while making a decision is not much different from saying, "Let's leave chewing out of this," with regard to your digestive system or "Let's leave the ankles out of this" when you're walking. You can do it, but you're not using the system the way it was intended, you're not doing it to your full capacity, and bad things will probably result.

To both build on and build up your four brains' combined contribution to your capacity, make better use of the pivotal first moment of every interaction. Consciously insert a brief pause and pay special attention. If you leap into action or answer without pausing, you often miss deeper wisdom and better solutions. Tune your senses into what's unique about this interaction, person, or possibility, and put your instincts and intuition first. Then add some analysis if it fits the situation. If you start with analysis or action, you will almost always suppress intuition.

The best decision-makers under pressure rarely think one move at a time.[48] They keep their deeper sources of attention reaching forward toward the solution after next, and you can, too. Before answering or responding to requests in a negative way—or taking on what you don't want to do by automatically saying yes—take a breath and let your instincts and past experience help you see a pattern here and link your answer with your own values and your best possible outcomes or goals.

The process is simple: Whenever an important question or challenge arises, pause for five seconds before you say anything, act, or touch the keyboard. Ask:
- What do my instincts say?
- What does my deeper experience say?
- Are there any gaps here?
- Any hidden breakthroughs?
- What's next? What's deeper? What's more?

Maybe it will take you more than five seconds to ask these questions at first, but after some practice they will begin literally to "ask themselves" without requiring you to deliberately invoke them. The results can be profound—here are some of the findings.[49]

- Increased flexibility in approach by up to 50 percent
- Increased attentiveness by up to 300 percent
- Increased resourcefulness or courage in facing new challenges by up to 100 percent over habitual resistance
- Increased energy by up to 100 percent
- "Ideal performance state" sustained longer and more easily

Because this five-second tool seems so simple, it's worthwhile to touch on some of the neuroscience behind it. On the heels of an important question or challenge, whenever you calmly pause and extend your senses, you quiet the brain's reactive areas like the alarm-bell-ringing RAS and attention-hijacking amygdala, ever ready to assume the worst, play off each other's panicky tendencies, and end up throwing your body chemistry into a stress state.[50] With practice, you mute their reactivity and increase your chances for a productive response to the challenge or question. What helps this happen is the increased activation that a calm five-second pause can bring to the gear-shifters—including the basal ganglia and the anterior cingulate cortex[51]—priming them to redirect your attention, including your gut instincts and heart-brain sensitivity, more fully to the challenge at hand.[52]

When you become more attuned to the intelligence signals from your gut, heart, and spine, and practice having your thinking brain aid you in this collective intelligence, then with each five-second pause your basal ganglia, ACC, hippocampus, and dorsal striatum areas can help you more clearly sense where the best options and choices are. Neurologist Antonio Damasio suggests that the anterior cingulate region is the key to making beneficial changes, especially judging the outcome of behaviors in a split-second.[53]

When the ACC's gear-shifting mechanisms aren't "well-oiled" and aligned with your open-space goals linked to emotional experiential memory, you can easily find yourself locked on habitual thoughts or behaviors and have trouble noticing and responding to signals from outside your thinking brain, particularly seeing options in stressful situations.[54] Every time you practice noticing and acting on new stimuli, you improve the ACC's power to improve your life and work.

DROP YOUR TOOLS

There's an overall principle of this book, magnified in this discussion, that was well expressed by the insightful organizational scholar Karl Weick. Studying the tragic deaths of twenty-seven firefighters in two wildfires, he found that when the blazes unexpectedly turned toward the firefighters and they had to flee, they carried their equipment with them instead of dropping it to be able to run faster, and that was why the blazes caught up with them, even as they were within sight of safety. "Drop your tools," Weick advised his readers, advancing ten reasons why we all tend to cling to our tools even when we should let them go.[55]

Dropping your tools is not the same as throwing them away—you can always come back and pick them up again. But some of the head-brain thinking skills we have acquired and been rewarded for can weigh us down at critical moments, so it's good to test how far you can get without them. Let's look at a few examples.

First, many of us are quite good at looking back and critiquing what's already happened, but not so good at moving forward into the unpredictable, messy future. As often as you can, resist looking backward and deliberately aim all of your brains forward, so they can help you sort out what's next, and what's beyond that, increasing your odds of making wise decisions and of adapting in the best ways to changing conditions.

Second, we can also be quite good at zeroing in on right now, giving it the once-over from every possible perspective of what's wrong, and how that's likely to harm us. Again, at times when you're inclined to do that, use your other brains to extend your awareness and senses farther into what's coming, for as far forward as you can imagine.

Throw in some unexpected twists and turns in your imagination so you build the robustness of your capacity to look forward instead of gazing at your shoetops.

Third, the ancient brains exert great pressure on us to build lives based on safe, secure routine. Your other three brains exist in part to draw distinctions and defy that tendency . . . if you let them.[56] It is the ability to meet new situations with new tools based on fluid openness, and not with the old ones of your fixed attitudes and predetermined reactions, that results in living toward your best and highest goals.

Fourth, many of us can analyze decisions in several linear, rational, analytical ways. Being so thorough is a positive trait, up to a point. But eventually, we must act, and many of us are instinctively inclined to hem and haw, to seek more data, to succumb to what some psychologists have started to call "decidophobia." Putting all your brains to work, from the beginning, makes you more comfortable with choosing and moving forward. Paul Van Riper, a retired Marine Corps lieutenant general who was almost shot in half by enemy fire during his first tour of duty in Vietnam when he took out a North Vietnamese machine-gun emplacement, ran the Marines' leadership and combat-development program in the 1990s. He changed the way decision-making was taught there.[57]

Van Riper noticed that in the swirl and confusion of war simulations—let alone actual combat—rational decisions always seemed to come up short. "We used the classical checklist system," he told an interviewer, "but it never seemed to work. Then we'd criticize ourselves for not using the system well enough. But it still never seemed to work, because it's the wrong system."[58]

Studies by researcher Gary Klein caught Van Riper's attention. Klein found that when the highest performers make decisions they don't logically, sequentially, and systematically compare all available options. Instead, they size up challenging situations almost instantly and then *act,* drawing on gut instincts, intuition, pattern recognition, and some rough simulation of options.[59] To Van Riper, this seemed to correlate to how people had to make decisions on the battlefield.

Leaders there don't ponderously weigh alternatives; they simply notice what's unique, grab the first idea that seems good enough, then the next, and the next after that. To them, it doesn't even feel like "deciding."[60]

When you pause even for a moment to focus on uniqueness, that lets the brain leap into what I have already noted as *fluid intelligence* instead of getting bogged down in *crystallized intelligence,* where all new problems and opportunities are met with old solutions and rigid past attitudes.[61]

Today, the Marine Corps applies what it calls "decision tempo" to beat analysis paralysis. At the heart of decision tempo is the "seventy percent solution": If you have 70 percent of the information and feel 70 percent confident, move forward with a decision. Often a less-than-ideal action, swiftly and expertly executed, stands a good chance of success, whereas no decision and no action stand no chance at all.[62]

SEVERAL OTHER CHANGES TO TEST

Here are a few of the other simple, practical tools I use and teach others to use to profit more fully from the wealth of brains nature has given us.

Recognize your patterns. Ultimately, using all your brains is a process of pattern recognition. The more you practice, the more patterns you intuitively recognize. Take a moment now and then to list decisions you've made that turned out right. Then list some mistakes you've made, and then reconstruct the thinking you went through. Where did intuition come in? Was it right or wrong? Are there patterns for when intuition gives you trustworthy advice and when you have to ask more questions?

Catch warnings earlier. One of the crucial applications of intuition is to alert you to something slipping out of control or going wrong, even if at first you don't know exactly what that is. If something surprises your senses or doesn't "make sense," get more curious rather than trying to dismiss the feeling. Whenever your heart skips a beat sensing trouble, your gut tenses up, or your spine tingles with apprehension or sudden alertness, tune in. Intuition senses a barrier—and perhaps a rapid way to overcome it—long before the conscious mind can sort it out.

Remember how fast your other brains can be. Our "read" on a problem can be acted upon even before we have any conscious awareness that a problem exists.[63]

Value intuition—before you can put it into words. You may see a list of ten factual reasons to make a decision. Your head thinks they look very logical and rational. Then someone says, "Are we all in agreement on this, then?" and you find that somewhere inside you, you are worried. Maybe it's just your thinking brain's fear of trying anything new, but maybe it's deeper. Maybe you should say something like "It all looks logical to me, but for some reason it doesn't feel quite right, and I'd like an extra day to take a closer look at why."

Be wary of intuition about other people's motives or intentions. The thinking brain's powerful drive to mistrust others often creates false "intuitions" about their intentions. Here's a case where you have to consciously double-check what you think you're hearing from inside yourself. Unfortunately, when we try to guess another person's motives or intentions, more than nine times out of ten we may be wrong.[64]

To understand, we first need to ask and observe. Begin observations by saying, "From my point of view . . ." It's vital to own your feelings and views as your own. "Maybe my intuition's off, but I'm sensing that you're under lots of pressure today . . . " Or "I could be wrong, but I'm sensing that you're quite excited about X but not Y . . ." Once you accept your impressions as your own and ask a sincere question, let the other person react: yes, no, or with something specific. This is a respectful way to learn more about someone or engage in a meaningful conversation. It also creates an opportunity for each individual to express distinctive, and perhaps surprising, feelings and opinions.

Adapt! It's great to have a plan, but if you're not careful it will stifle ingenuity and block adaptability. Flashes of creative breakthroughs keep sparking from your intuition. Plans, no matter how carefully laid, go awry. Even if plans include contingencies in advance, there's little chance these can match the range of possible changes and new opportunities that will appear. Using all four of your brains makes you stay more fluid, more tuned in to the changing world around you, seeking and evolving the most effective ways forward as you go, and helps you stop overrelying on plans.[65]

As a leader, dismantle the obstacles that prevent people from using their intuition. Since such feelings are inherently hard to express, don't let people jump on a dissenter who hesitantly says, "I'm not sure . . ." Instead, say, "Tell us more." Some leaders go around the table twice at meetings to give people a chance to put hunches into words. To sharpen your intuitive thinking, you have to get out of your own way; to foster it among those around you, you have to get out of their way, too.

People are very reasonably hesitant to drop their head-brain tools and hear what their gut or heart or spine is trying to tell them. Learn to be all right with a "felt sense" that's telling you or someone else something that can't quite be articulated.

MAKE STEVE JOBS'S "SECRET" YOURS

Steve Jobs founded Apple Computer when he was twenty and changed the world. Then, at thirty, he got fired from Apple by its board of directors. So he started a few more companies, including Pixar Animation Studios, which created the world's first computer-animated feature film, *Toy Story,* and is now the most successful animation studio in the world. Then, twelve years later, he was rehired as Apple's CEO.

His life wasn't just turbulent professionally. He dropped out of college and lived for a while in friends' rooms, returning soft-drink bottles for the deposit so he could buy food. Today, he's one of the world's richest people. His romantic life was often rocky. Today, he's blissfully happy with his marriage and his children.

In 2005, he was the commencement speaker at Stanford University (saying, "Truth be told, this is as close as I've ever gotten to a college graduation"). What he told the graduates is as good a summary of this chapter as you are likely to encounter:

> Your time is limited, so don't waste it living someone else's life. Don't be trapped by dogma—which is living with the results of other people's thinking. Don't let the noise of others' opinions drown out your own inner voice. And most important, have the courage to follow your heart and intuition. They somehow already know what you truly want to become. Everything else is secondary.[66]

11

What You Demonstrate, Becomes Real

Hope doesn't come from calculating whether the good news is winning out over the bad. It's simply a choice to take action.

—ANNA LAPPE

It's deep winter in Wisconsin. Ten degrees outside. Snowbanks line the roads and icy patches on sidewalks make walking hazardous. Frank Daily, fourteen years old, has just boarded city bus number ten along with many of his schoolmates, on his way home from school. The bus driver is John "Kojak" Williams. The bus heads west on Blue Mound Road.

While his schoolmates chatter on in other parts of the bus, Frank sits alone near the front, lost in thought. He's having a hard time fitting in at this new school. He looks down at his new Nike sneakers and remembers the disappointment he felt when he failed to make the school's basketball team. He feels lost, invisible, and it's hard to shake that feeling.

The bus stops and a woman slowly climbs the steps, wearing threadbare clothes, no shoes, and only tattered socks. She settles into a seat behind the bus driver, a few rows in front of Frank. Many of Frank's classmates are laughing; the bus driver yells at them to quiet down.

The driver asks, "Where are your shoes, lady?"

"Can't afford shoes," she answers. "I got on the bus to get my feet warm. If you don't mind, I'll just ride around for a bit."

"Can't afford shoes?" the driver asks.

"I've got kids," she says. "They all have shoes. There's not enough for me, but that's okay. The Lord will take care of me."

Frank looks down at his new Nikes and thinks about this woman, "Another invisible person." Under the seat, he unties his shoes and slips them off. When the bus reaches his stop, he picks up his shoes, walks up to the woman, and hands them to her. As he steps out the door and heads home, he hears what he had feared he would hear— derisive hoots from some of his callous schoolmates.

Frank Daily's story might never have been told except that Kojak, the bus driver, thought it was remarkable enough to contact the local newspaper and tell it to a reporter. "In twenty years driving a bus I've never seen anything like this," he said, adding, "those shoes fit that woman just fine. In my book, that boy's a hero."[1]

I use the word "capacity" in this section of this book because in general it's the right word, but there's a danger in that if anyone sees "capacity" as being just "potential." It's by acting that you manifest capacity, and without action, capacity is useless. Moreover, as I have discussed, acting builds more capacity as new neural connections are wired, new patterns are recognized, parts of your brain that clamor for conformity are hushed for a while, and new learning sharpens both your thinking brain and your intuitive genius.

As Emerson observed, "Character is higher than intellect." Character is not what you think or what you intend; it's what you do. Only through what you demonstrate do you actually grow and deeply live. The eminent neuroscientist Walter Freeman urges us to remember, "We are not merely buffeted by circumstances like stones rolling downhill. We must act and make choices. And every choice we make is deeply personal, arising as a fabric of interlocked influences, desires, and talents that constitute the meaning of everything we do."[2]

It is said of the Japanese fashion designer Rei Kawakubo, "There are few women who have exerted more influence on the history of modern fashion."[3] You may not think of fashion as a world of high importance to you, but it shapes daily experience in ways that not many other fields do, so the fact that Kawakubo works "from the egalitarian premise that a woman should derive from her clothes the ease and confidence that a man does," while her designs are still "intensely feminine" and reject "the hegemony of the thin and the class system that [once] governed fabrication," has an impact on all of us.

When she describes the Paris show that initiated her impact on the fashion world more than twenty years ago, Kawakubo captures the essence of what I'm saying here—she was acting on what she believed, and the rest followed. "I never intended to start a revolution," she says. "I only came to Paris with the intention of showing what I thought was strong and beautiful. It just so happened that my notion was different from everyone else's."

FEEDFORWARD

Once you begin to act on what matters to you, even by making the smallest change in your perspective or behavior, psychological daylight appears. All kinds of change-oriented adjustments take place in your makeup. You shift from potential energy to kinetic energy. Your senses open up. Your neurochemistry becomes more primed to change a bit more, and then more after that.[4]

Our brains have the capacity to sense, reflect, and create ideas continually, but there's a world of difference between imagining a fulfilling life and actually living it. When you know by doing, there is no gap between what you know and what you do. Positive *behaviors* are a primary driver of positive *attitudes,* and not the other way around.[5]

Gandhi had it right when he said, "You must be the change you wish to see in the world."[6] Every aspect of the brightest future you envision, the deepest relationships you crave, and the fullest energy you deserve for life depends on looking ahead and acting along a path that leads toward the end you have in mind—an approach known as *feedforward.*[7]

Whenever you live or work on an emotionally superficial level— when you talk big ideas but hesitate to make even small changes or sacrifices yourself—things can feel relatively easy or comfortable. Your thinking brain equates thinking about something with taking action, so it feels good about itself and you despite the fact that you're actually treading water, behavior-wise, or going backward.[8] Besides, there's no foundation there, nothing to draw upon. And, in one way or another, at one time or another, we end up feeling shallow and lost.

Feedforward changes your brain, causing it to pause here and there in its headlong flight and to wonder about what *you* actually care about, not merely what it wants you to care about. There's early evidence that there's a neuroscience of values, which goes deeper than the brain usually thinks, reaches farther than your neurons are used to firing, and means far more than a paycheck or pat on the back ever could.[9]

MORE CLARITY

Here are several practical strategies for helping your brain keep you moving forward with greater clarity and deeper purpose.

Chase your own dreams, not someone else's. Michael Jordan, probably the best basketball player ever, was cut from his high-school basketball team. A blow that might have ended the hopes of many a young person inspired him. It was *his* goal that had been challenged. He worked harder, learned more, became stronger. He has said, "My advice is find fuel in failure. Sometimes failure gets you closer to where you want to be."[10]

Without that fuel, would Jordan have become as spectacular as he turned out to be? Maybe so, and maybe not. Early success can have a way of producing later mediocrity. Today, in many of our high schools, there are great battles waged over who will be named class valedictorian. It's not just students who clash fiercely over this honor; parents often become intensely involved, too, so much so that schools have tried many ways to defuse all the competition, anxiety, and outright conflict: one high school, for example, named thirty-two valedictorians last year.[11] But what's the value of all that stress? Studies have shown that there's little correlation at all between achieving that honor and any indicator of success in life.[12]

Reflecting back on what I learned from being the last kid picked for all those sports activities when I visited my grandfather, I have often wished I could do a study to find out what became of those who were picked first. A brain that has not faced up to disappointment and found novel ways to deal with it is not as resourceful as one that has.

Override impulses with character. Research in the new field of neuroeconomics, a multidisciplinary research field incorporating neuroscience, economics, and psychology aimed at developing an understanding of how we make choices, shows that when people decide about the distant future, their thinking is basically rational because the prefrontal cortex can prevail over emotion.[13] They can calmly face important decisions that are far off in the distance. But when faced with a choice right now to consume something appealing or delay gratification, we can be as impulsive as chimps. Research on emotional intelligence points out that constraining such impulsiveness is vital to sustained success in life and work.[14]

So make it a point to notice flashes of right-now impulse and pause before you act so you can capture a glimpse of your most emotionally compelling longer-term goals. Putting this moment's impulses into that context triggers the self-regulation drives in emotional experiential memory that make it easier to transcend distractions and the brain's impulsivity and demonstrate character and farsightedness instead.[15]

Make sure your heart's into it. There's a saying that goes "When you follow what you care about, let go and know," and sometimes that's just what you have to do. Many people close down their own ability to access implicit knowledge—from the heart and gut, for example—because they'd rather depend on what is rationally knowable. Then their actions are disconnected from the feedforward potential in using the widest range of intuition and instincts.[16]

One of the most successful programs in the country at turning around the lives of troubled young people is the Anasazi Foundation. There, young people peacefully walk an Arizona wilderness trail with guides who do not bully or threaten them, who are not trying to toughen them up or break them down—who are only trying to help them get back in touch with their own hearts. In the words of one of the organization's founders, Ezekiel Sanchez, "The Anasazi Way is not to change the behavior of the Young Walker, but to provide opportunities for the heart to be touched, so the change can come willingly from the 'one who stands within.' Then the change of heart, like clear water, will flow without compulsion."[17]

Once these young hearts are changed, they start amazing things happening. Interestingly, in a physical reflection of the concept of feedforward, Anasazi refers to unproductive behaviors and attitudes as "walking backward" and productive ones as "walking forward."

Pick something that "can't be done," and do it immediately. While everyone else is trying to judge whether anything different or better can actually be accomplished, go do it. One of my favorite examples is how the movie *Citizen Kane,* which is ranked by the American Film Institute as the greatest American film ever, came about. Orson Welles sat exhausted one evening after seeking funding for the film, having been turned down by everyone he approached. He had a small amount of money for casting but had to beg, bootstrap, and invent ways to get people to help him build sets and film screen tests that eventually comprised nearly a third of the finished movie.

As he did whatever he could to bring about his dream, Welles demonstrated his own unconquerable belief and also created enough bits and pieces of a final film that others could glimpse what was actually possible. Eventually, all kinds of people wanted to fund the movie. Without Welles having shown a way when everyone else said it couldn't be done, *Citizen Kane* would have been just another idea that never became anything.

Whomever you serve—whether it's family, friends, customers, clients, students, citizens, or patients—we are living in an ever-more "show me" and "prove it" culture. The highest-performing individuals and teams base their reputations on behaviors—on coming through, on leading by example, on testing breakthroughs—not on vague promises. So if you want the world to believe more in what you're truly capable of, there's no need to wait for an invitation—you simply must go forward and demonstrate those capabilities.

To win big, skip the trophy. Whenever the stakes are high, the basal ganglia help trigger the brain's dopamine systems—many different neurochemical "highways" in the brain—to flag stimuli in the environment that are reliable predictors of reward: Should you commit to *this,* or that?[18] Those who are motivated by the prospect of winning a prize tend to approach their work in rote—not ingenious—fashion. They aim to defeat others by doing more or less the same thing, only harder, faster, and longer. They do only what is necessary for them to win—or to make sure others lose.[19] Prize-winning becomes the end, not trying something different to find a better way. Following a hunch, playing out a new approach, and diverging to discover the higher path to exceed expectations—or changing the game entirely—are set aside in favor of something to put on the mantel.

Help your nigrostriatal pathway choose the challenges that live inside you and reflect your unique self, not just the ones that might bring you a bit of hardware to polish for the rest of your days.

Turn feedback into feedforward. When you're receiving feedback, replace the need to be right with the need to get better—be a learner, not a knower. When you have that framework, you can face the truth, even when it hurts, and you have a better context for knowing when to listen and care, and when to let the other person's "gotchas" roll off your back. Look through the lens of perspective. What of this will matter a month from now or a year from now?

When you get input that matters, put it to work right away, even in small ways, to show your brain that new pathways need development and you're committed to making that happen. Don't give your brain time to rationalize. Don't wait for that training class two months from now, or for the ideally safe moment (that likely will never come), to start doing small things that lead to appropriate changes.

Track what you've done in simple ways to see how it specifically makes your life or work better. Did it save you time? Free up more energy? Enable you to redirect your focus to higher priorities? Help you come up with more new ideas? What's next, to get more from what you've learned?

OBSTACLES MAKE YOU LIVE WHAT YOU BELIEVE

Earlier, I mentioned the "character arcs" in all great literature, and how you choose a direction and shape for your own arc, ideally one that flows along your strongest line of energy. Much of how your arc actually turns out depends on the actions you take to handle the obstacles between you and what you want to become and accomplish.

Practically every story that engages you, whether that story is fictional or true, has the same essential emotionally rich plot: Someone wants something and then deals with obstacles in trying to attain it. In earlier chapters, we talked about recognizing what you really want, describing it, and identifying milestones on the path to reaching it. We also considered some of the obstacles, particularly those thrown up by your brain, that can keep you from getting there. But there's a deeper part of this story.

Things that get in your way don't just fire up the brain centers where your inherent resistances and fears reside. Following the Brain Displacement Principle that I mentioned earlier, they put the other brain areas under siege as well.[20] But as long as you stay calm and focused forward, you tone down the ultrareactive brain areas and free yourself to enlist more of the unfettered attention and help of the growth-oriented parts of your brain. The former will try and get you to give up, shut down, close in, try what you did before only longer and harder. Which attitude wins is a function of what actions you take.

SEEING WHAT'S REALLY THERE

It's a common fantasy that with enough brainpower and eloquence you can will a desired future into being. In politics, in organizations, in schools, and in families, this fallacy plays itself out until reality sets in, and then the scramble to assign blame begins. Determination and willpower count for a lot, but the more important skills lie in recognizing the real obstacles between you and your dreams and finding the best ways to bypass them. You have to craft your life like an artist or athlete, flowing with new inputs as they emerge, testing new responses.

Your thinking brain can see plenty of obstacles to what your heart wants you to become—it's just that the thinking brain, so skilled at looking backward or outward for the truth, is often wrong. "Is Your Boss A Psychopath?" blares the cover of a popular business magazine.[21] "Is Your Mother-In-Law Wrecking Your Marriage?" asks an Internet site. "Are Your Teachers Holding You Back?" Well, all those things might be true—but so, too, is it true that the only one who's going to fix it is you.

The first thing to realize when judging obstacles and your reactions to them is that your perspective is very narrow. You have a strong desire to see what you're looking for. The more you know—or think you know—about something, the more blinded you can be to what's actually happening. This limitation has been called "educated incapacity."[22]

For example, no one has known more for a longer time about making and selling wine than the French. Yet in the spring of 2005, demand for French wine dipped so low that vast fields of grapes were being plowed under, sold as food for animals, or distilled into industrial alcohol. Wine makers blamed growers in other countries; they blamed the tragic decline in sophistication among wine consumers; they demanded help from the French government. Four hundred thousand free bottles of wine were handed out at tollbooths and on rural roads in an effort to boost demand.[23]

"The rest of the world does not respect anything. Not even the wines that are the pride of our old nation," said one of the "experts."[24] Yet in fact the crisis, which had been predicted for a decade, resulted mainly from greatly increased wine production throughout the world (Australia, in particular) and changes in consumer buying patterns. It was just the French vintners who couldn't, or wouldn't, see it coming.

Some of those vintners, however, found their sales increasing by as much as 12 percent even at the very height of the crisis. Their secret was to abandon the centuries-old French tradition of labeling wine by the area where it is made—Bordeaux, for example—and instead to use labeling that is consistent with the way most of the world's consumers now select wine: by the grape varieties used to make the wine, such as Merlot and Cabernet Sauvignon. The world has changed for French wine makers, but only some of them have seen beyond the limitations of their "educated incapacity"—and those who have changed, have prospered.[25]

WHAT IS ISN'T WHAT'S BEST

The Pulitzer Prize–winning historian Daniel Boorstin has written, "The greatest obstacle to progress is not ignorance but the illusion of knowledge."[26] In his great books, such as *The Discoverers*, Boorstin shows that the best way to know the true shape of things is to step aside from what everyone else believes, leave the comfort of certainty behind for a while, and set sail. There's an important distinction here, which I'll discuss more later, between being an active and open "learner" and being a passive, closed "knower." For now, you might consider what the longshoreman-turned-philosopher Eric Hoffer has said: "In times of change, the learners will inherit the Earth, while the knowers will find themselves beautifully equipped to deal with a world that no longer exists."

Part of your impetus for acting instead of watching might come from curiosity about the true shape of your world. Part of it might come from invention's mother, necessity. Part of it can come from imagining a novel way of overcoming the obstacles standing in the way of your dreams and having the determination to find out whether your new idea works, and if not, to learn how to create an even better idea.

When I think about finding novel ways of overcoming obstacles, I remember a competition held by the schoolchildren's magazine *Weekly Reader* for ideas to get the last dab of peanut butter out of a jar. Many students correctly identified some major obstacles to accomplishing that, such as the shape of the jar or the nature of the readily-available implements, such as spoons or knives. Then they invented new jar shapes and clever new scraping implements. But the winner was an eighth-grader, James R. Wollin, who simply added a second lid at the bottom of the jar!

Addressing a similar problem, the makers of Heinz and Hunt's ketchup finally, in 2002, performed the simple service of turning their ketchup dispensers upside down, so they stand on their closures, and the long wait for ketchup to make its way to the mouth of the bottle and then onto your hamburger came to an end. That simple solution ended the days when hamburger lovers tried to figure out how hard to smack the bottle, whether to tilt it at an angle or hit it from the bottom to loosen the contents.

That is, the true obstacle to rapidly pouring ketchup lay in the distance that the ketchup *started* from the mouth of its container, not in the tactics used to move the ketchup from far away from the container's mouth to someplace nearer to it.

Life can be like that, too. You can spend a lot of time seeing things as more complicated than they should be, and as a consequence you can devote a whole lot of useless energy to getting things moving instead of just letting them flow the way they should in the first place.

GETTING WHERE YOU WANT

For every individual or group, efforts at finding new ways of doing things generally follow a predictable pattern: a bunch of new ideas come forward, and then creative energy peters out as the RAS and the amygdala keep firing away, making noise to the other brain centers, pressing you to believe you'll likely never find a good idea and therefore you shouldn't waste time trying. But then, if you stick with it and put your best capacities back in control—which many individuals and groups don't do—many more new ideas flood out.

There are plenty of creativity-based strategies for identifying obstacles and tackling them effectively, and I have provided you with a list of books and Web sites in an endnote.[27] A few of the most effective methods I have observed, tested, and applied are described below.

Look through metaphors. The brain has a remarkable capacity to use one thing to understand another, as long as it's stimulated to do that. Neuroeconomics also shows that people perceive their life symbolically, not just literally. The great psychologist Milton Erickson found that if he could just find the right metaphor for his patients in therapy, they'd see their problems in a whole new light and come to effective solutions much more quickly.

Nature stories are a great source of provocative metaphors. For example, I often share with my business clients two similar but different ones. The first is the observation that baboons can't hunt in packs. They start out running after some prey—a gazelle, let's say—but they have very short attention spans, and so pretty soon one running baboon hears another baboon running behind him, forgets that they're both running after the gazelle, and instead concludes that the baboon behind him is actually chasing him with a bad intent. So the baboon in front turns around and starts fighting with the baboon behind him, the other baboons join in, and the gazelle escapes.[28]

The second story is about gazelles and why predators smarter than baboons so often pick on gazelles. Gazelles can run faster than most predators, and they can run for quite a long time if they choose to. But gazelles, like baboons, have short attention spans. So a hyena will start pursuing a gazelle and the gazelle will bound effortlessly away. And then the gazelle just forgets why it's running. It sees an attractive clump of grass, and starts nibbling. That's when it becomes lunch for the hyena.

If relating one of those stories metaphorically to a current situation helps you see obstacles in a new light, why not keep playing that fascinating mental game with other stories and images you encounter? How, for example, might James Wollin's clever insight of seeing the bottom of the peanut butter jar as the obstacle, instead of the lack of fancy tools for extracting the peanut butter, be applied to identify ways around obstacles you're facing at work or elsewhere?

Be an alien. To see things differently, grab an entirely different perspective, as, say, an alien with no knowledge of earth's habits, assumptions, or traditions. For example, there is a short story in which an alien sent to scout the earth reports that large parts of the planet are dominated by large metallic beings with four wheels, who force their two-legged subjects to earn money in order to feed them, continually build and repair pathways for them to travel on, and replace them regularly with new generations of bigger, shinier, fancier four-wheeled creatures.[29]

MAKE YOURSELF SOME GOOD LUCK

The thing about overcoming obstacles is that once you've done it, you get to do it all over again. Not everyone likes that, and not everyone does it, but it can be even more satisfying if you have some luck on your side.

The key difference between lucky and unlucky people is that the former embrace new experiences and changes in routine.[30] In fact, they don't just embrace what's novel, they continually seek it out.[31]

Luck is a matter of being in the right place at the right time, with the right attributes. One psychologist has studied the importance and prevalence of chance encounters and luck, noting that, "Some of the most important determinants of life paths often arise through the most trivial circumstances. A chance meeting can alter an entire life."[32] The more places you put yourself in, the more likely you are on some occasions to find yourself in just the right place at just the right time. It also follows that the more capacity you develop for responding appropriately and imaginatively to what you encounter, the more you'll be able to seize opportunities.

1. *Embrace new experiences and change at least one routine every day.* Seeing the world differently, outwitting the brain's natural resistances, and acting differently pays off—in money, ingenuity, and inner happiness.[33] When you change, you shift the firing patterns in neurons and make it easier to keep changing. And it helps set you up for being at the right place at the right time.[34]

2. *Trust your heart and gut more.* According to Richard Wiseman's research in *The Luck Factor,* "Almost 90 percent of lucky people said that they trusted their intuition when it came to their personal relationships, and almost 80 percent said that it played a vital role in their career choices."[35]

3. *Build deeper trust relationships.* Lucky people seem to frequently bump into strangers who open doors for them, or they arrange to meet people who can have a positive influence on their lives or work.[36]

4. *Emphasize open space.* Lucky people tend to break the habit of getting stuck polishing old habits and instead shift their attention toward envisioning and acting on open-space possibilities, and that increases their openness to opportunities. Luckier people tend to have an active imagination tied to possibilities that truly stretch them but are within the realm of coming true, whereas unlucky people either don't look forward or tend to talk a great line about their dreams while their visions remain in the realm of fantasy, never coming to fruition.[37]

THE STORY OF THIS BOOK

Years ago, I had been awarded a contract from a publishing house to write my third book, and I spent the better part of a year doing the research and writing the early drafts. I took a number of risks, both in writing style and format.

It was exciting. I had improvised a new approach to the subject. I was adapting my writing as new research findings appeared, trying to develop a new way to help readers get the most value out of the book, as easily as possible.

In all, I invested nearly a year of my life, going through six complete revised drafts in close collaboration with my senior editor, who had helped many unknown—but she believed worthy—authors. She was pleased with the new direction the book was creating. We both believed it worked. At last I submitted the finished draft to her, and she sent a copy to her boss, the editor in chief.

He read it over the weekend, and on Monday he rejected it.

More than that, he rejected me as an author. He said my experimental style, conversational tone, and writing format were all failures, a disgrace to what he called "the fine traditions of nonfiction writing." He added, "I'm from an Ivy League school. I know what good writing is, and Robert Cooper can't write."

He informed my editor that he was killing the book. He ordered her to terminate my contract, even though it contained a clause that gave me the right to rewrite the book based on input from the editor and editor in chief. He instructed the accounting department not to pay the money that was owed to me for my work that year.

Finally, he ordered my editor not to call me but instead to inform me of all this in a fax. I remember sitting alone in my office as the fax was printing out, then walking over to pick it up, holding it in my hands as I read each line.

This setback not only affected me, it affected my whole family. I might have been able to walk away from it when I was young and single, but by then I had piles of bills, a mortgage, very little savings, and a family with young children who were counting on me. It was right before the December holidays. I was stunned and suddenly broke.

As her own final means of quiet individual protest, my editor quit her job and, in so doing, lost her retirement benefits. In leaving she wrote, "[This publishing house] should never be known for treating an author this way." It was an act of great courage and conscience, which I didn't know about until months later. She has helped me as an editor in countless ways in all the years since then.

I felt the weight of the world on my shoulders. It seemed that I had completely let my family down. If only I had played by the rules and written the book in a standard format, I thought. Then I shook my head—no, exploring a better way was the right thing to try. What would I do next? After mulling things over for a while, I left the office and went home to face my wife, Leslie, and the children, to tell them we would have to find another way to keep going financially. I knew they would be watching how I handled this. Adversity is both a test and a tool.

I remember sitting with them and trying to explain what had happened. I will never forget Leslie's response. It wasn't about our need for money or the bitterness of this setback after all the long hours of work; it wasn't even about the callousness of that editor and his treatment of someone who had given every ounce of his best to fulfill a promise and complete a job.

It was about what matters beneath everything else at times like that. Leslie held my hands and looked into my eyes. All she said was "Are you going to listen to him? Are you going to stop writing?"

I remember looking at her in the kind of amazement we feel for those who love us so deeply that they know our souls, sometimes better than we know them ourselves. She sensed that the fundamental issue was about overcoming a punishing setback to continue to keep alive a means of expression that really mattered to me, that let me advance original ideas and engaged my heart, mind, and spirit.

She knew that together we would find other ways to make a living and a difference and provide for our family. We would not take to heart the words of an Ivy League literary authority. And we would not give up.

Are you going to listen to him? Are you going to stop writing?

You hold in your hands my tenth book.

In moments like that, something deep inside us comes to life ... if we let it. None of us are only what we were born, or what we used to be. We are also what we have it in ourselves to become.

12
Awaken More Genius, "Fix" Fewer Problems

I not only use all the brains that I have, but all that I can borrow.
—Woodrow Wilson

Coming back to work a week before the start of the new school year, an experienced teacher grabbed her preparatory packet, thumbed quickly through the familiar contents, and then pulled out the class roster.[1] Next to each name was a number in a column. Every year she looked at these numbers: standardized IQ test scores. They gave her a feel for which students were smartest and which would likely need extra help.

She was shocked to see all the IQ numbers were above 120, several in the 160s. This was a gifted class, a class of geniuses and near-geniuses! She thought, "Finally, I have been rewarded. No more years spent being a policeman, counselor, disciplinarian. At last I have the chance to work with extraordinary learners."

She spent extra hours gathering together advanced assignments, special projects, and stimulating coursework. No getting by on minimum requirements for this class.

On the opening day of class, she said, "It is an honor to work with students as gifted as each of you. This will be an amazing year."

She went out of her way to prepare a variety of stimulating assignments to fit the diverse nature of these highest-potential students. She provided challenging assignments in every class, she allowed for individual passions and interests to take the fore, she supported different learning styles, she welcomed even the oddest-sounding questions. She sent home encouraging notes to the parents, asking them to stay involved to help develop the full gifts of their children. She added extra creative assignments. There were few complaints. She added content and questions from far above grade level.

The test scores were no surprise to her. They were all high. When the first grading period ended, every single student had an A except a few who had B+s. The parents began calling the principal. The principal called in the teacher.

"This is amazing," he said.

"Not really," she replied. "They are a very special group of students."

"I'm glad you think of them that way."

"Well, why shouldn't I? They are all gifted."

Silence. "What do you mean?"

"I saw their IQ scores. They are all geniuses of one kind or another."

"What IQ scores?"

"The ones on the class roster, next to the student names, just like they always are listed."

The principal reached into his desk and took out a packet of papers. He pulled out a light-blue page. "Didn't you read this?"

She studied it and a puzzled look crossed her face.

"I don't understand."

"Your students are not gifted or geniuses. They are ordinary. Those numbers . . . those are their locker numbers."

FROM WORST TO BEST

About two decades ago, General Motors was faced with the decision of whether to shut down one of its plants, which one GM manager called "the worst in the world."[2] As described in the *Harvard Business Review,* "Productivity was among the lowest of any GM plant, quality was abysmal, and drug and alcohol abuse were rampant both on and off the job. Absenteeism was so high that the plant employed 20%

more workers than it needed just to ensure an adequate labor force on any given day. The backlog of unresolved grievances often exceeded 5,000."[3]

Instead of closing the plant, GM decided to try a wholly new approach based on trust, involvement, and faith in the deeper abilities of each individual. As *HBR* put it, "the logic of coercion" was replaced with "the logic of learning." Among many other things, small teams were used, command-and-control hierarchies were dismantled, and suggestions from everyone were encouraged and heeded.

Within three years, astonishing change occurred at the plant, which was called NUMMI, for New United Motor Manufacturing, Inc. "NUMMI's productivity was higher than that of any other GM facility and more than twice what it had been just a few years previously. . . Quality, as rated by internal GM audits, customer surveys, and *Consumer Reports,* was much higher than at any other GM plant . . . Absenteeism dropped from between 20% and 25% to a steady 3% to 4%; substance abuse is a minimal problem; and participation in the suggestion program has risen steadily from 26% to 92%. The overall proportion of employees describing themselves as 'satisfied' or 'very satisfied' has risen progressively to more than 90%."[4]

You'll have to ask the collective brains at General Motors why the ability to see genius in hiding at its most abysmal plant, and thereby transform it to the best, seems to have had so little lasting impact on GM's operations as a whole. But the proof is there, as it is all around us every day, that when you see people as geniuses in hiding instead of problems to be fixed, everything starts to change.

SEEING EVERYONE'S GENIUS

Since every person's brain is wired differently and we all have unique life experiences, it's important to be open to all kinds of genius in all kinds of talent areas from all kinds of places. Harvard professor Howard Gardner has shown that there are many kinds of intelligence that don't show up in IQ tests but still can change everything in dazzling ways.

So how many dimensions to intelligence are there, anyway? A lot more than we think, says Gardner in his latest research.[5] In addition to "linguistic intelligence" and "logical-mathematical intelligence," Gardner showed that people possess different degrees of spatial intelligence, interpersonal intelligence, musical intelligence, and naturalist intelligence, among other forms. As anyone who has ever worked on a great team knows, it takes all kinds of perspectives and talents to create real and satisfying breakthroughs.

"Imagine you have hundreds of pairs of different eyeglasses," my grandfather used to tell me. "Every time you meet or interact with another person you must find and wear exactly the right lenses to see this one-of-a-kind individual." We live in an increasingly depersonalized world, and yet neuroscience shows that people must be genuinely seen and heard as unique individuals to feel respected and give their fullest genius and capacity. The failure to provide such visibility and valuing, one person at a time, is a primary reason most relationships fail and most people feel underappreciated and resentful.

THE GENIUS OF TEAMS

I would like to add two additional points to what I say in other parts of this book about engaging the leverage power of teams. First, remember what a miracle collaboration can be. Evolutionary biologists can find themselves at a loss to explain how a species that developed in a fierce kill-or-be-killed environment has come to be capable of the high levels of cooperative endeavor required to build great societies.[6]

Second, though, we should also notice how often we still elevate individuals and downplay teams. In the hunter-gatherer environments where our brains developed, it was almost always wisest to side with the most powerful person. There were not teams in the sense I have talked about them here; there were just groups lined up behind leaders. Independent thinking and asking questions could get you into trouble with the leader, who expected loyalty as your principal contribution. Today, even though it's widely recognized that such command-and-control leadership is less effective than involving others, it nonetheless seems that we often prefer to see an individual take charge, even if he or she fails, than to see a team take responsibility and succeed. The craze over the past few decades for exalting "heroic" leadership in business and elsewhere taps into an ancient viewpoint that does not always serve us well today.

Here's a related example that is intriguing as another slant on our views about individuals and teams. Some scholars are now saying that the plays we attribute to Shakespeare, among the greatest works of genius in all civilization, were probably created by a team. Shakespeare was a member of one of the two companies granted permission to stage plays in London. That company, the Lord Chamberlain's Men, remained intact for many years, and each member made a distinct contribution to the way the plays evolved. Richard Burbage, for example, was the company's chief actor, and some scholars believe that he had a large hand in shaping not just how a role was performed, but in the development of the characters themselves over time.

The acclaimed Shakespeare scholar Andrew Gurr, author of many books about Shakespeare and editor of some editions of the plays, writes, "A company of Elizabethan players had to work as a team, and it is misleading to pick out individual members as the key creative forces." William Shakespeare, Gurr says, was an important member of the team, but perhaps not an overarching solo genius whose brilliance left everyone else standing on the sidelines inertly waiting for what he'd come up with next.[7]

It's interesting to consider how generations of Western students might have come to view the world if the possibility of artistic genius as a product of felicitous group collaboration had been presented to them, instead of, or in addition to, our more typical romantic and individualistic perception of the often lonely, even "tortured" sole creator. The same for Edison, whose laboratory in Menlo Park, New Jersey, was filled with highly talented innovators. Nevertheless, he alone took most of the credit for his breakthroughs.[8] Even Vincent van Gogh, perhaps the stereotype of that latter image, was happier and more productive during the days he spent working and living with his friend Paul Gauguin than when he worked alone.[9]

One place to observe this bias toward a focus on the individual—and away from the team—is in the way the very popular "three-hundred-and-sixty-degree reviews" are handled in most organizations. The 360-degree review respects context, a subject we discussed in chapter 7: It flows from the understanding that managers work in a number of different contexts—with their own bosses, with customers, and with peers, for instance, and not just with those who report to them. But the way a 360-degree review is presented contains a contextual message. It might say to an employee something like "Your boss's success is her problem, not yours. You rate her, and then it's up to her to fix things."

How different would the contextual message be if employees were also asked something like, "What specifically have you contributed to better interactions with your boss in the past month?" and at the same time the boss was asked, "What specifically have you contributed to better interactions with your employees in the past month?"

The larger message might become that we're all in this together and, depending on the challenge and our strengths and talents, each of us is responsible—in varying roles as individual champion, mentor, collaborator, or encourager, for example—for each other's success as long as we choose to remain here. Such a message would change the way that everyone understands the context of making things better: It's everyone's challenge to do that, not just someone else's.

That same principle applies anywhere a group of people gathers for a common purpose—in a family, at school, at a 4-H Club or Girl Scouts, in the PTA or at the Rotary Club, on a sports team. Shared responsibility makes the whole more effective than the sum of its parts. We know that in theory, but the brain's wiring toward a focus on individuals can keep us from fully practicing it.

GROW WHAT YOU WANT TO GROW

It's a cardinal rule of your nervous system that what you emphasize, grows.[10] Emphasis is what wires neurons together. Emphasize the negative and you get more excuses, denials, blaming, and resistance, with little if any progress. Keep uncovering and emphasizing the genius in others and you get more genius. Here are some ways to do that.

Check your predilections at the door. How often do you value the single heroic individual, whether that's you or someone else, over the possibilities of what a team could accomplish? How often do you disparage someone else's unique potential for genius, perhaps in order to puff up your own a little more? We have plenty of negative terms for each of the distinct kinds of intelligence that Howard Gardner has identified—egghead, tree hugger, geek, New Ager, artsy-craftsy—and each time you speak or think one of those terms you intensify the brain circuitry that makes you less able to see genius when it's staring you in the face. You isolate yourself more from people who could help you make your dreams come true.

Every time your brain puts someone in a box, get them out of it. Because the amygdala and RAS can be blindingly fast to judge first and empathize later, this can spill over into making snap judgments about people, usually based on little true insight.[11] Recall from chapter 10 that one of the times to question your intuition is when you make a snap assumption about someone's motives or intentions. The same principle applies here: Retrain your brain to pause before categorizing someone. Whenever you start doing it, calmly but firmly guide your attention back to staying curious a bit longer to see the hidden genius and unseen potential inside him. This momentary pause automatically activates value-centered brain areas that prompt you to respect others;[12] it also expands your power of empathy, which has been ranked the number one practical competency of exceptional leaders.[13]

Relentlessly feedforward, not back. Remember from the preceding chapter that feedforward is a powerful driver of growth inside the brain.[14] Our interactions with others can be based on feedforward, but they usually aren't. Most of the feedback we give others is actually payback for some perceived offense or irritation, and that just activates fear centers and stimulates the often-discussed fight-or-flight response.[15] Neither fighting nor fleeing is a helpful reaction for the change you're hoping will take place. Remember that what you want to affect, and all you can change, is how the future plays out; focusing on the past stunts learning and growth. You may derive a quick, nasty pleasure from dropping a "gotcha" on someone else, but you're firing and wiring all the wrong neurons in yourself and that other person.

Know the maximum frequency of recognition. Mark Twain once said, "I can live a month on a good compliment," but most of us can't do that—a maximum of fourteen days between genuine, specific, clear appreciation and recognition may be the limit for many of our work and personal relationships.[16]

If you consider the four people whose genius is most vital to your new and greater success in the next year, chances are that they will each need something different—a different kind of heartfelt acknowledgment of their value in your life, a particular kind of recognition that feels best to them. By focusing on each of these people, one to one, you can begin to tailor what they need in order to feel genuinely valued by you, and how often they need it. See the discussion of the Power of One Passport earlier in this book for specific ideas about doing all this.

Keep coming up with small surprises, and twists that make interactions with you even better than before. Provide at least a small "wow" every time you can.

Get out of brain ruts. Frequently used brain patterns get fired and wired so deeply they can end up like the Grand Canyon: You might feel like cutting a different path higher up through the rock walls, but unless you have a few hundred years to keep at it, it won't work. Recently, while I was rock climbing in Joshua Tree National Park in California with my youngest daughter, we stumbled upon a large rusted iron door on hinges hidden at the side of a massive boulder. When we opened the door, there was a small space inside the rock about five feet on each side. Rumor had it that an old prospector used to lock himself in there. I guess he had the right to do that; it was his life.

But inside our brains there's that insistent clamor for a similarly small box to fit everyone inside. We place people, based on very little real information, into all sorts of categories. The pervasiveness of this tendency is shown by studies that ask adults to watch videotapes of toddlers and describe what they see. In one, a toddler is startled when a jack-in-the-box pops open. Some people say the toddler is "scared"; others say the toddler is "angry." The difference: In the first case, the toddler in the video had been assigned a girl's name (Jessica); whereas in the second case, using the exact same video, the toddler was given a boy's name (David). The "girl" was "scared"; the "boy" was "angry." In similar studies, when children were assigned a male name, they were more likely to be rated as strong, intelligent, and active, while those same children, when they were assigned female names, were more likely to be rated as little, soft, and easygoing.[17]

Some of our favorite sets of brain boxes for people have the labels "good" and "bad." Not much pleases us more than to be able to say who's good and who's bad. So we construct rating systems and fit people into them. For most of us, this is pretty unconscious, but if we're asked we can quickly classify people we know—people at work, acquaintances, teammates, book club members, party-givers—from A to F. More and more businesses are using this kind of grading system. What happens in business when this system is put in place happens everywhere: to be given an A rating is actually a serious problem.

In my work with a number of large companies, the 20 percent, say, of people rated A see that rightly as a zero-sum game: Someone else has to lose for them to win. They now have a vested interest in not letting any B- or C-rated people into their group. If they can keep the B/C/D-rated people from moving up, they, by default, "win." So, by deeply wired human instinct, instead of collaborating and driving highest-performing teamwork, they do the opposite: playing politics, going passive-aggressive, undermining everyone else, trying to protect their own position. They know that if someone else looks good, they, in comparison, will look worse. Even worse, no A has any incentive to rise above the current "best" level, so they try to stop anyone else from doing the "impossible."

Even the best intentioned, most elaborately constructed boxes are still just that, and their effects are malign.

Which pill do you want? In his book *Republic.com*, University of Chicago legal scholar Cass Sunstein observes that we increasingly live in a world where practically no one has to think beyond his or her current beliefs and predilections. With zillions of television and radio outlets, Internet sites, blogs, and interest-group publications, we can spend all our free time, all the time, hearing nothing but what we already agree with.[18] This is very comforting and satisfying for our brains, but it's very unhelpful for our ability to appreciate others who differ from you.

How curious can you become about what's hidden, what's deeper, what's better, what's next? How can you bring that excitement and wonder to others? Most adults have a hard time unless they practice this, even though at one time it was natural to all of us, as you know if you have ever dealt with the endless questions children can concoct.

In the film *The Matrix,* the central character played by Keanu Reeves is given two pills to choose between: The blue one permits him to continue living within the comfortable and controlled matrix, the red one lets him see more of what's real and make his own choices about how he will live, with all the exhilaration and frustration that accompanies those choices. Which pill do you want?

Forget about that bus. Whether you're in business or in school or running a bake sale or raising a family, your images matter. Pick one that captures the élan and initiative with which you aim to succeed and inspires others with those same feelings. For example, there's a lot of talk in business these days "having the right people on the bus."[19] Why a bus, of all things? Why not a speedboat or highly maneuverable jet or helicopter or some turbo SUV? You can have amazing talent on that big bus, but the moment you fail to make that first hairpin turn in the dark while everyone sings in harmony, it's all over.

And who, exactly, are "the right people"? You can spend years trying to figure out where to find the talent and get it all in the right seats on the bus. By then a hundred others—solo, in small groups, or large-scale organizations—will have run rings around you on their motor scooters, bullet-trains, or rocket ships in terms of defying the odds and innovating. There's far more leverage in creating a team made up of individuals with the greatest drive and ingenuity to accomplish what everyone else thinks they can't.

Get yourself out of the way. One of my favorite questions, which I ask regularly of everyone important in my life, is "Is there anything, no matter how small, that I do that gets in the way of your best work (or life, or happiness)?" I have been surprised at how many times small things I do inadvertently sabotage someone else's progress (and often my own progress along with it, since these are people I'm connected with in important ways). Having acknowledged that I do such things, I can then reverse the question, asking others to ask me the same thing so I can respond. If your experience with these questions is anything like mine, I think you'll be amazed at what you find.

Give yourself the scents test. Brain scans show that when people sense or feel they're being treated unfairly, a small area of the brain called the anterior insula lights up, producing the same kind of disgust that we feel when smelling a skunk.[20] That disgust overwhelms the prefrontal cortex and its deliberations, causing people to automatically say no to whatever we say or ask and turn away, feeling ripped off.

The antidote is to live your beliefs in every action you take, to stay curious and open to new views and different perspectives. Demonstrate clearly and transparently what you believe. Come through on every promise, immediately take responsibility for any oversights or mistakes, and in every other respect hold yourself accountable.

AGAINST THE ODDS

At the A. B. Combs Leadership Magnet Elementary School in Raleigh, North Carolina, seeing all children as geniuses has transformed a once-dismal institution into a national model for excellence.

Here's what Combs School was like in 1997, in the words of the school's principal, Muriel Summers: "Only a little over half of our students were passing end-of-grade tests, magnet enrollment was stagnant, and apathy had spread like a cancer through our community of students, parents, and teachers. The school district had issued a mandate to reinvent ourselves or cease and desist as a magnet school."[21]

Then the school, in Summers's words, developed "a dream to create a school where every child would see within themselves hidden genius and the array of life's possibilities." As she says, "Most schools look at what students can't do. We look at what they can do! Honoring the greatest in each of our students is a lesson that continues to change the lives of those we are so honored to teach."

Honoring the greatness in others is not an inherent skill for most people: I've already discussed in this book many reasons why the brain doesn't naturally work that way. Combs had dedicated administrators and teachers, but many of them had found their zeal considerably diminished by years of disappointment in the classroom and criticism from all quarters. Parents, too—as you and I might also do in such circumstances—tended to look for what was wrong in the school and then issue demands for correcting it. There were, as Summers writes, "skeptics and naysayers at every turn."

Always on the lookout for new ideas for fulfilling her dreams for the children, teachers, and parents of her school, Muriel Summers attended a workshop that I presented. After the workshop, she applied many of the tools and ideas you are reading about in this book. Inspired by the quality of her commitment, her verve, and her ingenuity, I continued to suggest ideas, many of which she also applied, along with many others she gleaned from many other sources.

And now—again as Muriel Summers tells it—"Today we *are* the school that seven years ago was but a dream! Our scores have risen from the 60th percentile to the 90th! 96.8 percent of our students perform above grade level in reading and mathematics. We are honored to hold recognition as a National Blue Ribbon School, a National School of Character, and a National Magnet School of Excellence."

Can you learn anything from the transformation Muriel Summers achieved by, as she puts it, "seeing a light within each child and striving to make sure it shines ever brighter"? Is her challenge somehow easier than what you might face every day at work or in your other endeavors? Consider one final bit of information: The 660 students at Combs come from fifty-seven different countries and speak twenty-eight different languages.

13

Constructive Discontent
Drives Growth

*The best games are not those in which all goes smoothly to
conclusion, but those in which the outcome is always in doubt. The
geometry of life is designed to keep us on the crux between certainty
and uncertainty, order and chaos.*

—GEORGE LEONARD

I walked into my grandfather's medical office one day when I was
about thirteen—unannounced, as usual, since he had given me permission to come by any time I wanted—to find him sketching on a
notepad, as he often did. Before he noticed me, I saw an intense scowl
on his face, as though he was really angry. I hesitated to approach
him. He looked up at me and sensed my discomfort.

"I didn't want to disturb you," I said. "You looked . . ."

"I looked what?"

"Angry."

He smiled. "Is that what you thought?"

I said, "It's the look I sometimes see on your face when I can't
sleep and I come downstairs to the kitchen and see you in the den
with the light on, reading or making notes or sketching on your pad."

"That's not anger," he said softly, nodding to acknowledge that
he understood why I might perceive it that way. "It's different. I'm
sorry I didn't notice you come in. Sometimes I get really intense

about trying to solve something—like solving a mystery. When that happens I'm not happy with the way things are. But to me, that's a good feeling."

"How can not being happy feel good?"

"Because it dares me to find a better way. I think that kind of un-happiness is one of the most powerful human drives: being unsatis-fied because the best answer you have, or the only answer, is not good enough.

"Now today, for example," he continued, "I had just come back from the hospital when I got a call from a friend who's one of the head surgeons at the Mayo Clinic. He's going to operate on a little girl tomorrow morning. She has a malformed intestine and he's going to try to fix it. But no one's ever done that specific operation successfully before. And he and I don't want this little girl to die."

He rubbed his forehead, thinking about it. "We take it personally— we *really* don't want her to die. So instead of just worrying or hoping or accepting that there's no other way but the ways that have failed before, he and I spent some time on the phone being really curious about discovering another way to keep her alive. That was an hour ago, and I'm still here sketching, asking myself questions, looking deeper for what everyone else might have missed."

He had me come sit next to him and he turned his pad to a new page where he diagrammed a normal small intestine and its connec-tions to the adjoining organs. Then he drew her intestine. He showed me the traditional way to operate, and why it wouldn't work for her. Then he showed me two or three different approaches he was think-ing about.

He loved to diagram possible new ways of performing surgeries, or to look at the connections between ideas in visual ways, seeking to discover something unexpected that had escaped him in other formats.

I've never forgotten the feeling of sitting beside him that day, sharing his thoughts as we both stared at what existed and tried to find what might be possible to save a little girl's life.

THE POWER OF CONSTRUCTIVE DISCONTENT

I call this inner drive "constructive discontent," and it can take many forms. It bespeaks commitment to daring growth instead of slow stagnation, to responsibility instead of resignation, and to building your own new capacity instead of waiting for the world to want whatever you already have.

In its strongest forms, constructive discontent is not an easy feeling to live with. The Nobel Prize–winning physicist James Franck once remarked that he always recognized a great idea by the feeling of "terror" it caused in him.[1] For most of us, the feeling might not be so severe, but still, we have generally learned to choose comfort over anxiety. When you learn to abide discontent and even prize it instead of shutting it down, big things start to happen.

The signal that arouses your constructive discontent can come from anywhere—a feeling inside yourself, challenge or criticism from others, a reaction to things you see in the world at large. What turns the initial feeling into action is the strength of those brain areas that want to move you constructively forward into the choppy seas of new discoveries instead of remaining stuck in your easy chair.

With practice, you can strengthen and embolden the more forward-looking inventive parts of your brain, the places that see the world as it could be and ask, Why not? And, then, linked to your emotional experiential memory, they will drive you toward it. Then it becomes more natural to take a contrarian view or test a different approach without outcry from your own old reactionary brain areas. What you're now more clearly conveying neurologically to your brain is "This is important to me. This deeply matters."[2] Such a message can awaken those farther-reaching, meaning-producing areas like the nucleus accumbens and the deeper part of the amygdala, and mobilize them to help you find what's better and deeper, not just what's easiest or most popular.[3]

THE DANGERS OF LOYALTY

Loyalty is a big deal these days. But if you're not careful, loyalty can make the brain and senses blind to what is right, worthy, different, and possible.[4] Many executives put loyalty right up there on their list of expectations along with integrity and trust and daring initiative, but it shouldn't be.[5] I once was asked to advise a leadership council for a well-known company. The first day, the CEO, in talking about his senior leaders, said to me, "This work on excelling under pressure and teamwork and breakthroughs is all fine, but what I *really* want is loyalty. Find out for me—are they *on* the team or not?"

This had nothing to do with his leaders lacking integrity or drive or creative courage or effective collaboration toward worthy goals. It was all about loyalty to whatever the CEO wanted, and nothing else. All his brain wanted were sycophants, marching in step to his orders, echoing agreement with his own limited vision, and emulating his habits. In this case, loyalty was a code word for a culture of obedience and fear of reprisal for being different, not a culture of innovation and respect. That's when the push for loyalty becomes a huge mistake.

Independent people with creative courage to lead change and drive new growth tend to leave obedience-based cultures so they can work with other daring, committed people. To the brain of an executive or politician or volunteer head of your neighborhood watch group, who wouldn't want to have their own Republican Guard? But the truth is we'd all be better served by behavior that many people would regard as discontented and disloyal: unvarnished honesty about exactly what's going right *and* wrong, delivered straight and early, not in some watered-down version at the eleventh hour.

Alfred Sloan, onetime head of General Motors and an icon of American leadership, understood that principle. Once, in a board meeting when an important decision was about to be made, he said, "I take it that everyone is in agreement with this decision." All heads in the room nodded in assent. Sloan looked around and said, "Then I propose we postpone further discussion of this matter until our next meeting to give ourselves time to develop disagreement and perhaps gain some understanding of what the decision is all about."[6]

There's a psychological paralysis that seeks to overtake the brain without conscious awareness. In his extraordinary novel *The Feast of Love*, Charles Baxter calls it an attitude of "lethal neutrality and immobility."[7] In the brain's self-protectionist and often self-righteous tendency to try to avoid conflict by having no opinion and taking no stance, it in fact defers to those more dominant—even when they are wrong—and leaves you both invisible and immobilized. The Nobel laureate Elie Wiesel, who survived the Holocaust, has said that the opposite of courage is not cowardice, it's indifference.[8]

As William Blake put it, "Without contraries there is no progression." More friction and contrariness in America's boardrooms over the past decades might well have saved some big companies from collapse and spared their employees and shareholders a great deal of pain. More friction in your life can fire up your brains to become more ingeniously constructive. Someone criticizes you? Be inspired by it. Someone doubts you? You'll never succeed? You're not talented enough to run your own company? You're not smart enough to write a book? You're not graduate-school material? Never . . . Can't . . . Impossible . . . The nucleus accumbens and heart brain, for example, live for such challenges . . . if you let them.

MOBILIZING DEFIANCE

A spirit of defiance often underlies constructive discontent, a steely insistence that the best, which has not yet been found, can and will be found. By you. Gary Hall Jr. won his tenth Olympic medal, and fifth gold medal, in 2004, swimming fifty meters faster than anyone in the world, again earning the title as the fastest person on water. Twenty-nine years old, Hall's chances against younger opponents had been discounted. A diabetic who had to inject himself with insulin eight times between getting up in the morning and the start of his gold-medal race, his body was considered suspect. The Olympic coach inexplicably left him off the Olympic relay team he should have anchored, his replacement swam poorly, and the team finished third in a race it probably would have won if Hall had swum.

Was Hall left out by his coach because he's different? Perhaps so. As one writer put it, Hall "doesn't train like other athletes, think like other athletes, or feel like other athletes."[9]

But whatever he does, it works. Asked what fires him competitively, Hall answered, "Defiance." Explaining, he said of his three Olympics, "The first time, they said I was too immature, too much of a loose cannon. The second time, they said you have diabetes, you can't do it. This time, you're too old, you have diabetes, you can't do it. They keep on tacking on more excuses and, well, you know—defiance."[10]

As Hall says, he had plenty of excuses for settling for less than his best, excuses within himself and excuses provided by others. We all do: Conjuring up or buying into excuses is one of our brains' core competencies. But Hall's kind of defiance is within us all, too, providing the energy to shove aside not just excuses but habits, routines, and others' "impossibilities."[11] So the next time you start feeling that your age or health or past or nonconformist attitude limit your future, you might take a moment to think of Gary Hall Jr.

A framework that can help us think about ourselves in this regard is the one I mentioned earlier: the difference between *knowers* and *learners*. Knowers place paramount importance on being right; learners primarily want to find new, different tools that take them to a higher level of rightness. Business writer Fred Kofman describes being a knower as a "virus," and that's a good way to think about it— as a germ that weakens your resilience and can do you great harm if it isn't treated. We always have to ask ourselves whether our intent is to grow or to defend, to be right or to move forward, to sidestep the puddles of discontent in our lives or to splash in them.

IT'S RIGHT TO BE WRONG

Much of your thinking brain sees life almost wholly as a conflict you must win—and for you to win, whatever you think must be right, and anyone at odds with that view must lose. That ancient survival instinct, from the days when winning may have meant living and losing may have meant dying, now keeps us stuck repeating the past instead of creating the future.[12] The desirable alternative to being right isn't being wrong; it's being right in a way that advances new understanding instead of just proving that you already have all the answers. It's learning, not just knowing.

In the early 1800s, a French artillery officer named Charles Barbier came up with a novel solution to a deadly problem.[13] Reading a message at night in wartime required lighting a lantern, and doing that created a great target for enemy fire. Barbier poked a series of raised dots onto paper—in a simple code of twelve dots—and created "night writing." When he left military service, he decided to promote his raised-dot writing as an aid for blind people.

A thirteen-year-old at the Royal Institute for the Blind was among the first to be taught the new system. He was excited by it but found it complicated. He went ahead on his own and created some ways to simplify it. He offered his ideas to Barbier, but Barbier was convinced his method could not be improved, and he was insulted at the very notion that a boy could improve it. The blind boy, nervous at being ridiculed, spoke haltingly to explain his ideas. Barbier stormed from the room and slammed the door, his mind closed.

Instead of losing heart at being told he was wrong, the boy determined to develop his ideas further. By the time he was twenty, Louis Braille had created the system named for him that has benefited millions of people. Charles Barbier had to be right, and as a result his contribution was practically nothing; Louis Braille wouldn't give in to being told he was wrong, and he changed the world.

Douglas Adams, author of *The Hitchhiker's Guide to the Galaxy* and other great whimsical challenges to status quo thinking, frequently used the metaphor of a puddle to express the dangers of thinking you're right when you're not:

> Imagine a puddle waking up one morning and thinking, "This is an interesting world I find myself in—an interesting hole I find myself in—fits me rather neatly, doesn't it? In fact it fits me staggeringly well, must have been made to have me in it!" This is such a powerful idea that as the sun rises in the sky and the air heats up and as, gradually, the puddle gets smaller and smaller, it's still frantically hanging on to the notion that everything's going to be all right, because this world was meant to have him in it, was built to have him in it. So the moment he disappears catches him rather by surprise.[14]

Ask yourself every once in a while whether that hole you're in is really as pleasant and desirable as it seems. Permitting yourself to be wrong can be wonderfully liberating. When you're wrong, everything is possible. You're outside old habits and perspectives, into the unknown. People afraid to be wrong are protecting the past. When you commit to unlocking and applying hidden capacity instead of insisting on conformity, being wrong—and therefore curious and creative—is the right place to be. If you are willing to test new approaches, to find what works better and what doesn't, being wrong puts you on the active path to creating a better future.

It took a whole lot of constructive discontent to fuel America's Revolutionary War, in the days when most residents of the colonies thought of themselves as British citizens and wanted only a better relationship with the mother country across the ocean, not a deadly, costly war of independence. Benjamin Franklin wrote an article in 1767, titled "Right, Wrong, and Reasonable," in which he satirized British ideas of right and wrong, showing how what was "right" to the British served only the interests of the British and was harmfully "wrong" for the colonists, and what the British considered "wrong" was precisely what was in the best interest of the colonists. The pamphlet contained passages like this:

It is *wrong,* O ye Americans! for you to expect hereafter, any protection or countenance from us, in return for the loyalty and zeal you manifested, and the blood and treasure you have expended in our cause . . . or that we will make any acts of parliament relating to you, . . . but such as are calculated for impoverishing you and enriching us.[15]

That article was one of the factors that enabled the fledgling Americans to recognize how others' ideas of right and wrong did not fit with their best interests in their special circumstances.

WELCOME THOSE WHO DISPUTE THE PASSAGE WITH YOU

We often admire the courage and wit in Franklin's saying at the time of the signing of the Declaration of Independence that "we must all hang together, or assuredly we shall all hang separately." And yet today, 70 percent of all Americans say they are afraid to speak up at work for fear of making "career limiting utterances."[16]

Adams's story of the puddle also captures our brains' craving to fit in: The cerebral cortex is filled with areas that monitor doubts about whether you're "in" or "out."[17] We unconsciously and overpoweringly seek the approval of others. You hear people whispering as you walk by them in the hallway and you instantly assume they're talking about you. That's why peer pressure to conform—the desire to be whatever "they" want—so often prevails. Go along, get by, make do, play it safe, don't make waves. And the story of the puddle also captures just what's wrong with that—you start drying up, and you don't even know it.

To keep that from happening, you may need help from others. Walt Whitman wrote a poem that I strive to keep in mind, called "Stronger Lessons":

Have you learn'd lessons only of those who admired you, and were tender with you, and stood aside for you?

Have you not learn'd great lessons from those who reject you, and brace themselves against you? or who treat you with contempt, or dispute the passage with you?

Your best allies for growth can be those people who constructively bug you and make unreasonable demands on you: difficult colleagues; eccentric neighbors; disgruntled customers; questioning children; demanding investors; challenging coaches; nagging mentors. They are true allies.

Recognizing that the comfy place you've found yourself in until now just isn't really working out is the first step toward correcting the situation. The sooner you get that news, the better off you are, but there are many reasons why bad news doesn't always get through to us, or why it often doesn't have much impact when it does.

One reason is that the more powerful you are in a situation, the less bad news you have to listen to. That's true whether you're a business executive, a parent, a coach, a teacher, or a crossing guard. You might hear it—employees will grumble, kids will gripe, players will complain, cars will honk—but it's a lot easier to dismiss all that when so many rationalizations based on your own importance are available to you: "They don't really understand what I'm going through"; "Sure, it's hard for them, but it's in their best interest"; "I don't have time to deal with every petty complaint of everyone who's dissatisfied."

To move anything forward, from the basics of your life to the strategic direction of a giant corporation, you have to acknowledge the gap between the way it could be and the way it is, and then light the spark, in yourself and others, for doing something about it. Most people start with the outer world and ask how they can adapt to it, but the most exceptional people start with their internal drive to achieve what everyone else thinks they can't.

Recent research on innovation confirms the power of constructive discontent, showing that in working relationships "productive friction" accelerates breakthroughs.[18]

CRANK UP YOUR CONTRARIAN MOXIE

Here are some ways to keep the spirit of constructive discontent surging through your system.

Put the Z Effect on your side. While sitting in a restaurant in Vienna, psychologist Bluma Zeigarnik noticed that a waiter could remember a seemingly endless number of items that had been ordered by his customers. However, once he had delivered the orders to the waiting diners, he no longer remembered what he had just served.

What Zeigarnik witnessed was the fact that people remember the particulars of an incomplete task, but once they complete that task they forget about it and about its associated odds and ends. In the case of Zeigarnik's waiter, after delivering the orders to his patrons, he forgot about the orders—and often the patrons who had placed them.

Though Zeigarnik didn't get a second serving of dessert or even get her coffee refilled following her meal, she did get into the annals of psychology for recognizing that an incomplete task or unfinished business creates "psychic creative tension" within us.[19] That tension acts as a motivator in the brain to drive us toward completing the task or finishing the business. Then, once completed or finished, the tension dissipates and we move on to other open issues.

In essence, once something is checked off your to-do list, your brain tends to forget it—no more curiosity or stretch to create anything better. In contrast, constructive discontent works part of its magic by embracing the "Not Quite Finished," or Z (for Zeigarnik), Effect. You set high goals and move toward them at the same time you keep raising those same goals whenever you approach them. On this path, you are willing to have more of the big things unfinished but growing day after day—as if leaving a string of lights on inside the nervous system and senses—instead of succumbing to the brain's automatic tendency to solve the problem in the fastest way and just be done with it. Studies of self-made millionaires and highly successful entrepreneurs show they resist the brain's need for certainty so they can keep options open as long as possible, and thereby arrive at more breakthroughs.[20]

Say "I don't know." A corollary of the Z Effect is admitting, readily and easily, that you don't know the answer to everything. Even though the brain is wired to try to "look good" and wants to appear smart, this takes a lot of the stress off. Studies of the most successful people show that they are often first and fastest to simply say, "I don't know"— and, if the problem or opportunity is important, at once they turn attention toward discovering an answer.[21]

Build the story of your life around growth. Everyone has some story, or narrative, about what their life has been, what it means, and what it will become. That story guides our choices. Many of us grew up with the idea that we should seek calm and comfort, and there's nothing particularly wrong with that, except that with too much of it your narrative—your life's arc—becomes less than it could be. My colleague Terry O'Connor describes his life as a swim in a choppy ocean dotted with lovely islands: periods of hard work cutting through the waves, followed by some lovely relaxing moments savoring the islands' pleasures—and then back into the ocean.

"For many in my parents' generation, the goal was to get to the island and never leave, except for maybe dipping your toes once in a while in warm, calm waters," Terry says, "but for me, I feel more like the islands are out there as temporary rewards for the next challenge I learn to overcome, not as ends in themselves." What image might clarify your attitude toward life and help give you more resolve to seek out and tackle its tough but rewarding challenges?

Choose honesty over harmony. Something within us responds deeply to people who level with us. As a family member or member of a team working on something important, ask yourself, What holds the highest value: Dealing with each other honestly, or harmony—getting along with each other?

I come from a family with a mother wholly committed to harmony and a father to honesty. Fireworks. Many people who believe they place the highest value on honesty actually discover, when observing their own attitudes and behaviors, that they spend lots more energy and attention trying to smooth everything over. They have learned to feel at ease the way the brain does, when everything is figured out and on autopilot, and everyone is happy. But almost always that harmony isn't, it's a surface tranquillity only. So look deeper.

This is not to say that harmony is not sometimes a worthy aim. There are times when just settling things down makes sense. But acknowledge that: "I am choosing harmony over honesty right now."

Be direct in the first person. One of the most diluted ways to deliver recognition or mentoring is to convert the person you are talking about—who may be sitting five feet away from you—into a third-person pronoun: "I would like to express a word of appreciation for Julie. She went out of her way to . . ." Research by Robert Kegan and Lisa Laskow Lahey indicates that although it may be a bit more uncomfortable to speak directly to Julie, especially in front of others, such communication is far more powerful and its impact lasts far longer.[22] "Julie, you have made all the difference. You went out of your way to . . ."

Be specific and build forward. A related point for giving recognition or growth-oriented support to others is to be specific.[23] I talked about this in several ways in earlier chapters, but it's worth mentioning again. Make certain to frame your positive comments with why this matters—how exactly, for example, something the person has done (or can do) will help you move toward a worthy goal that you and/or this other person have.

LIBERATE YOURSELF FROM WHAT'S BEST

"What if I do it a different way?" the little girl high up on the rock face asked her more experienced climbing partner.

"Don't. This is the best way. That's what I'm here to teach you." He had been climbing for close to thirty years; she was eleven years old.

"Why can't I change it?"

"Because it's a great technique used by great guides. It's safer and easier."

"What if I find a better way?" asked the small voice.

"Better than the best?"

"Yes," came the immediate reply.

The girl's teacher laughed. He peered up the slope, considered the situation, and then subtly signaled to the guide above and belayer below to double-check the safety of the ropes. A small, completely safe slip might help her learn that she did not yet know enough to challenge the best current knowledge in this sport.

"Go ahead," he told her. "Try it your own way."

Which is exactly what the young girl did. She crossed the crux in a totally new way, one her companion had never seen before. He smiled and tried the new way himself.

That little girl was my youngest daughter, Shanna. Her companion and "teacher" was me. I found myself, once more, learning how constructive discontent shapes the progression from good to great to what's possible.

Key ④ ENERGY, Not Effort

It's not how hard you try or how long you work, it's how effortlessly you get more of the right things done.

When doing the most work, those of lofty genius are the least active.
—LEONARDO DA VINCI

Some years back, my passions for visiting distant lands and for rock climbing brought me to the Himalayas. I had trained hard for this once-in-a-lifetime experience, and I had made sure to get the very best gear, especially footwear. Beyond training and mental toughness, every climber knows how much footwear matters. It's crucial for gripping the mountain, so I had sifted through all the available varieties of high-tech boot designs to choose the ones that would assure me an extra margin of safety.

When I met my guides, one of them, named Pasang, stood out right away. In contrast to the lean and wiry builds of most of the guides, Pasang was big and beefy. He looked more like an NFL line-backer than a masterful mountaineer.

His footwear stood out, too. He wore—as he would wear every day of our climb—an old and beat-up pair of black patent leather Florsheim dress shoes over thin black dress socks. I learned later that he had received the shoes several years earlier as a gift.

I had my doubts about Pasang, and my doubts increased as the first day of climbing wore on. As I braced myself against the high winds and paid attention to practically nothing besides keeping my balance on the narrow trails covered with slick layers of broken rock, Pasang, just in front of me, slipped and slid from side to side, laughing all the while, in his dancing shoes.

To me, despite his obviously superb balance, he always seemed on the brink of a needless crash or fatal fall. To him, my exhausting efforts seemed counterproductive. At the end of the day, as I sat at our campsite barely able to keep my weary eyes open, he and his compatriots were laughing, singing, and playing Tibetan games, which they would do far into the night.

"Florsheim!" he exclaimed the next morning as he put on his shoes, his smile brighter than the sun that glistened on the mountain walls. Sometime later in the climb when I asked him about those shoes, he told me, "I love how they feel. Lighter on my feet. I am more flexible when I have them on." During that trip I never saw him stumble or slip without recovering well, and never for a moment did he lose his sense of humor or his sheer joy at being alive.

We all know people who excel and, as the saying goes, "make it look easy," even though what they are doing is in fact darn difficult. Not just great athletes or instinctive leaders, but people who ride out tough times while still brightening instead of depressing those around them, or who can get up at dawn to prepare a Thanksgiving meal and still cherish fellowship with their guests, or who find the moments during a hectic and stressful day to bring a smile to the faces of others.

It's all about applying energy instead of effort whenever that is possible. And it's possible much more often than our brains would have us believe.

THAT BUSYNESS TRAP

By now, I think you've come to see how much your brain likes busy-ness and effort, how delighted it feels about itself and its powers as it calls for putting your nose even closer to the grindstone, and how happy it is to keep cracking the whip over you to do more, more, and more, lest you fall behind.

Unless you recognize this and choose a better way, your brain gets free rein for its maddening tendency to favor willpower over skillpower. You may numbly try to climb the mountains in your life when you could have ascended far more easily to the top. Our an-cient brains' wiring actually makes us feel proud of being exhausted and stressed. If something seems too easy, our neural wiring hums with warning signals, worrying that we've somehow been tricked—after all, life's a struggle and *nothing* can be easy, can it?

Yes, it can.

Thomas Edison did the world a disservice when he famously said that genius is 1 percent inspiration and 99 percent perspira-tion.[1] Not that perspiration doesn't matter, but too many of us have come to accept that perspiring is practically all there is. Edison just underestimated his own genius, as so many of us do, failing to rec-ognize how much of his perspiration started from the energy of inspired ideas, not brute-force effort.

You go a lot faster with a lot less friction, generating more en-ergy to hit higher targets and do it in less time and with less stress and strain, when you streamline your efforts, finding the precise mechanisms and catalysts that zoom progress forward, and jetti-soning all the rest that's just perspiration. Nothing wears you down like trying harder instead of smarter. There's great wisdom in the adage that insanity consists in trying the same thing over and over, or faster and faster, and expecting different results.

In later chapters, I will show you how to more effortlessly activate some of your brain and body's key "energy switches," at any time of day, wherever you are, for increased innovation and insight at the right moments, so you don't deplete precious energy in repeated frontal assaults on that wall that's not going to give way.[2] Or maybe it will finally give way—but will you have any energy left to celebrate, let alone move farther forward, after you've finally knocked it down?

TURN UP YOUR META-STAT

The truth is, no matter how much energy you want, you can't hoard it or store it, you have to get really good at producing it, not once in a while but every half hour or so, all day every day. Energy starts in your nervous system and connects to all the other systems of the body. Your brains have a powerful, integrated set of areas that help govern your alertness, balance, resilience, and energy production. The basal ganglia, for example, help control your body's idling speed and enhance motivation[3] at the same time as they integrate your feelings, thoughts, and movement.[4]

These brain areas connect to what I call the *meta-stat*.[5] The term derives from *meta,* as in *metabolic*—energy-producing, fat-burning, life-giving—and *stat,* as in *thermostat*—ever-adjusting (and also medical shorthand for quick). Meta-stat is a shorthand summation of the overall functions that set your rate of energy production, continually raising or lowering it like a thermostat in response to the signals you give it.[6]

Twenty-four hours a day, your meta-stat signals the mitochondria, little cellular furnaces—energy factories—contained in every one of your body's trillions of cells. Every one of the mitochondria are in effect listening for and responding to metabolic signals that you give them—or, more likely, fail to give them. Depending on the signal they get from your actions, they'll either fire up—which results in growth and renewal—or they'll dampen down. Good things happen when they're fired up. But when they dampen down, the cells fatigue, underproducing energy and even becoming extinguished altogether. Then even if you want more energy, you can't have it, and instead you must rely on greater effort, tension, fear, rushing, caffeine, and deadlines to keep you going.

Over 99.9 percent of your genetic makeup was formed prior to the beginning of the agricultural age, which was hundreds of generations, or thousands of years, ago.[7] Your genes and biochemistry are deeply, even stubbornly, designed to function just as they did long ago, based on ancient cycles of feast and famine, energy and survival.[8]

You and I inherited this master system. As part of our genes, we have a blueprint for staying active and lean, fit, and full of energy. Yet, in a matter of a few recent generations, most of us have all but lost our awareness of it or the ability to use it.

Mind you, we're not to blame for a bit of instinctive regression. When you can ride in a car or bus, you don't need the energy once required to flee predators or stay one step ahead of other natural risks. Turning lights on and off at will has made us far less conscious of how our bodies respond to light and darkness, and has also thrown off the natural wake-and-sleep patterns (controlled by darkness and daylight) that controlled our energy reserves for so many millennia. Food comes from the grocery shelf or fast-food window, not from hunting and foraging, so the ratio of energy expended to energy consumed is way out of whack. And the advent of powerful medicines has even altered our immune systems—definitely extending our life expectancy, but also making us rely more on pills than body-generated disease-fighters.

But despite all these changes in lifestyle, your metabolic physiology has been designed to respond with exquisite precision to your signals. *Your* actions still govern the choices those cellular furnaces make. Your meta-stat has been intricately programmed over endless generations to carefully monitor and respond to whatever signals it receives or fails to receive throughout the day. All you need to do is practice using those signals, and the upcoming chapters introduce ways to do that.

TURN DOWN YOUR UPTIGHTNESS

Decreasing physical tension also increases energy. Sounds simple, but when you let your life be run mostly on autopilot, your basal ganglia ramp up your body's idling speed and, with it, muscle tension levels. So there's a good chance you may have unwittingly conditioned yourself to let your tension-creating brain areas dominate you, causing you to overreact to everyday hassles and feel tense and tired much of the time—and accept this as "normal."

But when you learn to stay cool and collected more often instead of becoming caught up in the drama of everyday "emergencies," you calm down your ancient reactionary brain areas and strengthen the parts of your brain that want to take the long view and cut needless stress and strain so you have more energy for the truly important things.

THE PERILS OF PERSISTENCE

You can put more energy into the right places and take out the needless effort. I'll show you how. But many people then just apply the energy into doing more of the same old things they did before. That's the wrong kind of persistence for achieving your breakthrough goals. Persistence is wonderful in theory, but there are times when it can be dangerous in application. Too much persistence can turn into what psychologists call *perseveration*—the repetition of unproductive behaviors even after the stimulus for them has passed. As one author has put it, "Perseveration is a medical term for a brain dysfunction which causes people to persist in a task even though they know rationally that the chosen strategy is doomed and may even be mortally dangerous."[9]

Much of the stress that people experience results from a form of perseveration, as we keep trying to achieve new and better results with behaviors that aren't up to getting us where we want to go. We do that even though we all know by now that stress is, in fact, "mortally dangerous," a leading cause of so many deadly and debilitating ailments.[10]

In serene moments, you dream of shaping amazing break-throughs, and then a single stressful turn arrives and you start see-ing imaginary evils, trying harder to prevent everything that could go wrong, feeling like a victim of circumstances. Every time your mind belabors a problem or challenge in the same old ways under pressure, the brain cells handling it undergo intense activity. They rapidly exchange ions between their inner chemistry and the brain's fluids. It takes lots of energy to recharge all those ions. As neuroscientist Michael Chafetz describes it, "If brain cells conduct too many messages in too short a period of time, they will exchange so many ions that they can no longer recover easily. These nerves are now fatigued and the symptoms include increased effort, irri-tability, inability to concentrate, mental slowness, and increased mistakes."[11]

Fatigue targets weak points in the brain and nervous system.[12] The harder you try, the more fatigued you become. The mind tries to take over and your memory gets clogged, disrupting your fluid intelligence and blocking your ability to retrieve your best perfor-mance skills from your primary memory.[13] In athletes, the result of these combined factors is called "tanking" or "choking"; for the rest of us, whatever our situations, the consequences of this fatigue are similar: We not only lose access to new ideas and skills, but the old ones we used to be able to call on don't work either.

Our stress levels keep going up. When a 1983 *Time* magazine cover story called stress "the epidemic of the '80s," 55 percent of re-spondents to a related survey said they experienced great stress at least once a week. By 1996, 75 percent of survey respondents re-ported being stressed in that way.[14] What do you imagine the level is today? If you're a businessperson dealing with international part-ners or customers, prepare to hear more and more about stress from them: The consulting firm Grant Thornton International, which has offices in 109 countries, found in a worldwide survey conducted in 2005 that stress levels among people in business had increased, often dramatically, in every major industrial country over the levels from just a year before.[15]

You can use the techniques in the following chapters to greatly increase your energy levels and step down your stress. But if you give in to your brain's drives and just use your new energy to add more layers of stress, you'll quickly wind up back where you started—or worse.

A KINGDOM FOR A WHEEL

In his recent book, *Collapse*, the Pulitzer Prize–winning author Jared Diamond provides a cautionary tale about how dangerous the wrong kind of persistence can be.

Diamond explores the reasons why once-flourishing societies died out. One of those civilizations existed on Easter Island. Today Easter Island is a treeless wasteland with no living animals; but when the first Polynesians landed there, it was quite the opposite: heavily forested and teeming with life, fertile enough to support a population as large as thirty thousand.

But in order to erect the nine hundred huge stone statues that now form the island's only remaining "population," much wood was required: the Easter Islanders possessed neither wheels nor large animals, so each statue, after it was carved in a quarry, was dragged by hundreds of people on sledges made from tree trunks, using ropes made from other trees. As the trees disappeared, so did the rest of the island's vegetation and animal life, until there was nothing left to support the inhabitants.

"I have often asked myself," Diamond writes, " 'What did the Easter Islander who cut down the last palm tree say while he was doing it?' "[16]

Think of those Easter Islanders hauling on ropes to drag hundred-ton statues out of quarries and then all across the island on sledges made from logs. Plenty of perspiration there, lots of exhausting, back-breaking, persistent toil to be proud of at the end of each day. And proud their ancient-wired brains, much like ours today, must have been—never realizing that the harder they tried, the longer they worked, the more numbly they sacrificed, the faster the future for themselves and their children was vanishing.

And, apparently, no one, not even the quarriers, carvers, and sculptors who spent all day shaping rocks, thought to invent a wheel (reinvent it, really, since wheels had been invented in Mesopotamia four thousand years earlier). It's hard to imagine how much that single inspiration might have changed life on Easter Island—maybe, by preventing the island's deforestation, it might even have preserved the Easter Islanders from the descent into chaos and cannibalism that marked their civilization's last days.

As Malcolm Gladwell observes, "The lesson of *Collapse* is that societies, as often as not, aren't murdered. They commit suicide: they slit their wrists and then, in the course of many decades, stand by passively and watch themselves bleed to death."[17]

Effort without consideration of how energy can wisely be increased and leveraged will drain your life force in that same way, no matter how much stamina and resilience you have. Hard work is good. Smart work is a whole lot better, and a whole lot better for you.

14

Excel
Under Pressure

*The exceptional life depends not on working harder, but on
different, even opposite, actions from habit and the crowd.*
—RALPH WALDO EMERSON[1]

Maybe from time to time you've watched a television show like *Jeopardy!* from the comfort of your easy chair and figured that in the right circumstances you could play pretty well, maybe even win. So let's say you pass all the rigorous qualifying tests and wind up right there on stage about to compete, with two other highly qualified folks standing beside you. They look a lot more confident than you feel. There's a big audience out there, and all your friends and relatives are going to see how you stand up to this test.

Then you learn a couple of things you hadn't really considered before: You can only buzz in with your answer when a light goes on above the *Jeopardy!* board, something that can't be seen when you're watching it on TV; and, more disconcertingly, you aren't buzzed in until you *release* the buzzer you're holding—not just when you press it down.

So now you not only have the pressures of being smarter faster than two worthy adversaries, and doing so in the glare of the studio lights in front of millions; you also have to quickly master a whole new, counterintuitive, way of communicating. Some people can step right up and handle all that with ease; many others fall far short of their best.

Or imagine you have arrived at a make-or-break moment in your love relationship, and right now it's your chance to try to get a fresh viewpoint or solution across. Or you're facing a momentous and un-expected crisis in clarifying values in raising your child. Or you're standing in front of your boss about to ask for a raise based on what you perceive as exceptional performance but you have just heard that others have rated you a C performer. You're at a community hearing on an environmental issue that deeply matters to you and the vote is about to be taken and you feel your final comment may make or break the decision. . . Suddenly there is silence, and it's your turn to express—in a matter of moments or minutes—what you believe and why you believe it, and to persuade others to let go of their resistance at least briefly and see things from your view. Would you shine?

Maybe you're standing on a smaller-than-normal basketball court wedged into a corner of the intersection at West Fourth Street and Sixth Avenue in New York's Greenwich Village, surrounded by a twenty-foot-high fence, known as the Cage. This is one of the world's best-known basketball showplaces, attracting movie stars, sports agents, and international scouts to scope out the talent who play there each summer in the extremely intense, emotional West Fourth Street Tournament. The Cage attracts a very competitive group of city kids, many of whom do, did, or will play at major universities.

The court's unique dimensions foster a demanding, adaptive style of play, and dominance in the standard game is far from a guarantee you can prevail here. A thirty-year history of furious competition and a host of stalwart old-timers—like Moneybags, the homeless scorekeeper, and the instant-nickname-bestowing announcer, Dee Foreman—lend electricity to the Cage and run the always spirited and often rambunctious games.[2] And now it's your turn, to stand out, or not.

How will you respond? Will you be at your best? Better than your best? Or will you "choke," like almost everyone does, afterward muttering something like "If only you could have seen me when I'm at my best . . ."?[3]

As John Kao, former Harvard Business School professor and successful entrepreneur in many fields, has said, "The focus of human history has evolved. Now it's about the chemistry of the brain and the people whose neurons fire fastest and best in changing conditions."[4]

ALL ON THE LINE?

Pressure points may be brief in duration, but they can make or break your dreams. Your trajectory through life is largely influenced by the battle between your brain's homeostasis mechanisms, which fight to make you stay the same and repeat what has worked for you in the past, and the growth drive that rises through pressure, a drive that is deep within certain brain areas and called *syntropy*—"the drive in living matter to perfect itself."[5] But syntropy rarely surfaces on its own; you must consciously unlock it and keep aiming it at your best future.

Your homeostasis mechanisms are fiercely dedicated to accumulating things, not releasing them, to carrying more baggage—including emotional baggage and mental habits, and physical overtrying—and these keep-everything-the-way-it-was tendencies consume way too much energy into defending what's already habit. You call on willpower. You may tell yourself, "No problem," but when you slip or start to fall, all that extra baggage makes everything way more difficult than it has to be.

The hypothalamus, for example, is located beneath the basal ganglia, and is the dominant force in maintaining everything about the status quo.[6] Sudden changes, even minor shifts, in your habits or attitudes or routines can throw it into alarm mode, which is why how you handle pressure situations is so vital. At the moment that any part of your homeostasis gets messed with, the hypothalamus is primed to trigger the release of chemical signals from your brain into your bloodstream, instantly influencing both feelings and behaviors.[7] Your adrenal glands pump out stress hormones including adrenaline and cortisol—and the level of pressure you're facing suddenly rises even higher.[8]

Usually, you can't even see how hard you are making things on yourself unless you stand outside yourself and observe. Once you do see it, you can learn to transcend it. If you panic or fly into anger or get all tensed up over a challenge, you throw the hypothalamus into overdrive, triggering a flood of stress chemicals instead of a trickle, shocking your systems and consuming lots of energy. This can leave you overwhelmed not just by the situation but by your own internal chemistry. But when you're calm under pressure and make smooth, well-chosen moves, it's easier to keep the hypothalamus alert but not overreacting, and that makes handling the pressure far easier.[9]

In every moment of a pressure-packed situation, your strongest habit steals the show unless you practice in advance to change your response patterns. Your mind, emotions, body, and spirit will follow, in a single instant, the brain and nervous system pathways that are most developed by your past choices and practices. In the absence of new learned-response pathways, under conflict the brain will revert to ancient, fear-driven reactions that incapacitate you or plunge you into counterproductive, even life-threatening, outcomes. Why not start now to build new, more effective pathways? Here's one of the most reliable places to begin.

CALM *IS* WHAT CALM *DOES*

The crucial factor in applying energy and not effort is something I've discussed in various ways throughout the book: *self-directed learning*—intentionally testing, choosing, and strengthening the skills that move you forward into more of what you want to be and become, rather than letting your ingrained brain patterns run you on autopilot reactionary patterns the old way.

To make rapid progress under pressure, you have to not only desire calm and think calm, you also have to condition your brain and nervous system to *be* calm and thereby *keep* you calm.[10]

Here are six ways to begin accomplishing this:

1. *Observe your interaction with the pressure point.* Catch yourself the moment you start trying harder, and, instead, shift gears and come at everything differently. This significantly increases the chances you'll come through successfully, with minimal struggle and strain.[11]

2. *Increase your skill at doing the opposite of what everyone else does under pressure.* Loosen up, flow more, extend your senses (instead of letting the amygdala, the RAS, and the hypothalamus narrow them and blind you to opportunities popping up in the midst of turmoil and stress), travel lighter, and stay curious. This lets your prefrontal cortex stay free to serve you so you can more effortlessly change course and improvise in the face of the unexpected twists, turns, and stumbles going forward.[12] It also helps the hippocampus succeed in its real-time shaping of better responses going forward through the pressure.[13] It's easier to manage life's pressure points when you're standing outside your old ruts and routines looking in.

3. *Toughen up—practice putting yourself under increased pressure.* Yes, actually invite brief installments of increased pressure into your life and work.[14] Doing so toughens the resiliency pathways in your brain and body, making you better able to handle pressure smoothly and recover from it rapidly.[15] The central attribute of such toughness is "calm energy," where you keep your energy high and your muscle tension low.[16]

Two systems that begin at the hypothalamus are crucial for toughness and calm energy. In one, the hypothalamus responds to stress by signaling for the release of adrenaline from the adrenal glands. In the other, stimulus from the hypothalamus triggers the release of cortisol from the adrenal glands. Adrenaline and cortisol are both stress hormones. In individuals who have developed toughness, the normal level of activity in both systems is steady and low: tough people are at relative ease under most everyday circumstances, and their physiological responses reflect their calm energy. When tough people face a sudden threat or spike in pressure, the hypothalamus-adrenaline system goes into action smoothly and effectively and the hypothalamus-cortisol system remains relatively stable. As soon as the emergency is over, the hypothalamus-adrenaline system readily returns to normal, and the hypothalamus-cortisol system stays low.

Such a calm and appropriate reaction prevents depletion of the brain neurotransmitters, called catecholamines, that affect mood and motivation. That means that people with toughness return to a balanced and productive state of mind quickly, even after intensely stressful or threatening situations.

Not so for people lacking toughness. Their unproductive reactions tend to be stronger and longer-lasting, even in the face of the ordinary hassles of everyday life. The amygdala and RAS get involved, too, blaring warnings that ramp the stress even higher. Those catecholamines that I just mentioned can become so depleted that feelings of helplessness and depression are created. With each challenge, small or large, people lacking toughness overrespond, feeling the neurochemical aftershocks throughout their mental, physical, and emotional systems, and they end up with not only poor effectiveness in the moment but with less confidence in their future ability to cope with pressure.

The first key for toughness is to practice staying calm no matter what, and progressively challenge yourself to get better at it. Watch a scary movie—whatever level of fright that's just above your current comfort zone, for example—and consciously practice staying calm and curious throughout. If you get too uptight, turn off the movie and calm down. Repeat, increasing your toughness for suspense and uncertainty.

Depending on your fitness level, you might consider gradually speeding up during exercise and then slowing down, then speeding up again.[17] See chapter 16 for more tools and ideas.

Your goal is to increasingly turn moments of rising pressure into a catalyst for ingenuity and solution-finding. Instead of being immobilized by body-gripping tension, raging anger, a pounding heartbeat, or gut-wrenching panic, when you toughen up and learn to stay calmer, your prefrontal cortex can help you use pressure as a prompt to flow with things for a bit or get really curious about inventing a better way through it. As you build confidence in your ability to stay calm and

effective in an expanded range of situations, your two toughness response systems waste less effort in the face of each new threat or challenge. More effective responses lead to better coping, which in turn
makes for an even smoother mind-body response pattern. Result: You
get really tough and life's craziness is much easier to manage.

4. *Envision calm effectiveness.* One of the ways you change the
brain into more of an ally is to periodically mentally rehearse for
pressure situations. Even for half a minute or a minute, imagine pressure hitting and see yourself staying calmer, on top of things, seeking
solutions instead of resisting. Recall that whenever you envision a
better way of responding, you activate your prefrontal cortex, and the
greater the activation of the PFC through advance imagery, the more
successful you will be at making the action possible and succeeding at
it.[18] This rehearsal also fires up your brain's Broca's Area to activate
and improve the pathways of both mirror neurons and motor neurons required to actually perform that action.[19]

5. *Develop instant calming skills.* It is absolutely vital for you to be
able to nip excessive physical tension in the bud the moment it rears
its head. The truth is, only 5 of your body's 684 muscles are designed
to hold you effortlessly upright.[20] The other 679 should mostly be on
holiday. Yet most people have unconsciously learned to tense dozens,
even hundreds, of extra muscles all day long. They're so used to this
level of tense-energy that it has become "normal."[21] But this not only
wastes energy, it overprimes your nervous system for constant readiness to emergencies, overstimulates the hypothalamus and other reactive brain areas, and leaves you both exhausted and all but
powerless when stress hits. So get very aware of your tension levels.
Unhinge your jaw. It's no mistake that elite athletes have a signature
slack jaw. When the jaw is relaxed, that relaxation generalizes to the
neck and shoulders, keeping you looser.[22]

6. *Get past the past—in a single second.* If a problem hits and you
mishandle it at first, insert a pause in the action and reboot your nervous system for a few key seconds. Relax your eyes, jaw, tongue, and
hands, releasing all tension. These specific areas prompt deepened relaxation throughout the body. If you can safely close your eyes for a

moment, do it. Think of absolutely nothing, as if your mind is a blank screen. Now open your eyes and switch back into gear. Aim your full attention forward.

There's a reason you rarely see consistent top performers throwing temper tantrums.[23] Like them, you want to take a few very calm moments after a missed shot or wrong answer or other muffed action to consciously release the feeling of that negative experience before the RAS can magnify it out of proportion. Then redirect your full focus ahead to what's next, or briefly visualize—see step four above—the action-replay happening perfectly as if it had actually succeeded, which primes your nervous system to come at everything better from this moment on.

FURTHER TOOLS

Like most people, you've doubtless had the experience of being truly "on"—handling stressful situations with grace and sudden changes with ingenuity instead of resistance. And yet there are times when you are not on.

From three decades of research and application I have identified three additional mental switches that enable you—once you've toughened up—to take charge in ways that eliminate much of the effort and add more energy and success. When you learn to flow and respond in these new ways, they provide a quick charge of oxygen and nutrients and the right stimulation to your brain cells, keeping energy higher and reducing effort.

All in all, your brain likes everything neat and tidy, with no surprises: it wants you to identify ad infinitum what could possibly go wrong, and then create a fixed solution to each and every imaginable problem, so that every time a new one arises you can just slap the right solution on it. But in high-pressure situations, the forward-moving feeling of flow gets easily derailed by this resistance to new approaches. The moment pressures rise, preconscious signals from your senses and the lightning-quick gut, spine, and heart brains trigger a cascade of hormones designed thousands of years ago to move

you, ducking or leaping, out of danger's path. Unless you can understand and override some of these stress reactions in today's world,
they become counterproductive and break down the other hidden capacities of your brain, memory, and body, resulting in a wide range of
conditions from fatigue and tension to disease.[24]

Here are three other core skills for excelling under pressure.

1. Find the Hottest Spark

My first switch for trying differently under pressure is to look for
what the pioneering psychologist Abraham Maslow called "the
hottest spark of life."[25] In this place and circumstance, what's the
hottest spark, what excites you most? Finding and focusing on this
positive emotional energy instead of being ground down by the
negative activates your best brain pathways to come to the fore by
mobilizing emotional experiential memory, enabling you to judge information and opportunities more effectively, to turn down irrelevant distractions, and to persist through obstacles toward your most
deeply desired outcomes.[26]

Remember, too, that when, as many of us do under pressure, you
start just trying to prevent bad outcomes instead of bringing about
good ones, your brain is more likely to make those bad outcomes
happen. Focusing on what you want from the situation, not what you
don't want, keeps that nasty negative boomerang from happening.

I mentioned earlier how your brain responds to stimuli that are
predictors of rewards for staying engaged and being innovative, and
then mobilize inner reserves to go achieve the reward.[27] When you
find what's potentially rewarding for you in the midst of a mess, lock
onto that and keep it stimulating not only your best but also new and
even more creative responses.

A neurotransmitter in the brain, norepinephrine, mediates your
level of alertness and ingenuity.[28] Your senses have a kind of radar that
constantly scans for novel stimuli. Whenever something new and important appears, neurons in your sympathetic nervous system activate the norepinephrine neurons in the midbrain's command center,
known as the locus coeruleus. This interrupts whatever else you're

doing and wholly focuses your unified attention on the important stimulus, and your behavior changes.[29]

Transforming negative or unproductive energy into something improbable and positive is the essence of trying differently instead of just harder. As Viktor Frankl wrote, "You do not simply exist, but always decide what your life will be, and what you will become in the next moment."[30]

When he found the hottest spark in his own life, Bill Strickland went from being an alienated, directionless teenager to eventually shaping lives throughout the United States for the better. As one writer puts it, "Strickland, then a 16-year-old black kid, was bored by school and hemmed in by life in a decaying Pittsburgh neighborhood. He wanted a way out, but he didn't have a clue about how to find it."[31] Walking into a high-school crafts classroom, he spotted a teacher shaping clay on a pottery wheel. Strickland tells what happened at that moment:

> I saw a radiant and hopeful image of how the world ought to be. It opened up a portal for me that suggested that there might be a whole range of possibilities and experiences that I had not explored. It was night and day—literally. I saw a line and I thought: This is dark, and this is light. And I need to go where the light is.[32]

With inspiration and encouragement from that teacher, Frank Ross, Strickland changed his own life, gaining admission to the University of Pittsburgh and graduating cum laude. Later, he returned to his impoverished neighborhood to start an arts center for youth. Then he was asked to take over an employment-training center in that same neighborhood. He used the arts as a way to build self-confidence and self-awareness in the trainees, and the center flourished. With Strickland at the helm, the model has been replicated, with similar success, in cities that include Cincinnati, Baltimore, and San Francisco.

He didn't stop there, either. He opened a jazz concert hall and started a Grammy Award–winning record label. He started the Denali

Initiative, which teaches nonprofit leaders how to think and act entrepreneurially. He won a MacArthur Foundation "genius award."

The light Bill Strickland saw in a moment of deep distress became the spark that ignited a lifetime of service and success. It can come from anywhere for you, too, if you're open to it.

2. Stretch your Strengths

The second switch for trying differently is to apply your strengths in challenging new ways. This doesn't mean repeating what's worked before, it means consciously pushing the edges of your strengths, and doing it regularly.

Whenever you extend yourself in areas that feel rewarding, brain function is significantly enhanced by an extra charge of oxygen and nutrients, and new memories are formed that build even better performance under pressure.[33] So wherever you can, step back and examine what you are doing and why and how you are doing it.[34] Stop doing things that don't truly move you forward. This reduces effort and frees you to reallocate your energy into places that make a bigger difference.

For example, set some higher-than-expected targets. If there are ten competencies required to perform your job, accept that no one can do them all excellently, including you. Chances are, you truly shine at a few of them, and you may really enjoy only one or two. Volunteer to take on greater responsibilities for results in the pursuits that call on your strengths and interests, and delegate the other tasks away. Fred Smith, founder and CEO of FedEx, calls this "loosening your job description and then tailoring it to fit you perfectly as a unique individual."[35]

As you keep raising your own targets, certain brain areas may start resisting. Do it anyway. In fact, whenever you notice yourself lapsing into a routine when pressures hit, you may want to add some extra self-imposed stress. For example, get your heart rate up, literally. This conditions your body to be more uptempo for challenges, instead of taking pressure sitting still or lying down where it can more easily overwhelm your brain.

Besides, mild to moderate stress can provide an optimal kind of developmental stimulation. It can be used to make you feel alert and increasingly ingenious.[36] Periodically increasing stress levels—for example, by reaching toward higher goals or stepping outside normal routines or varying the pace of your exercise—can make you more resilient and healthy in body, emotions, and mind.[37]

As noted in chapter 10, it can really pay to know when to trust your gut and heart brains, and in doing so your basal ganglia—which are neurally wired to the gut—give you access to more and more of your life's implicit, unconscious wisdom as you build your actions going forward.[38] When you toughen up by voluntarily increasing pressure while practicing new responses, the basal ganglia absorb this new learning, ramping up their own ability to help initiate more effective actions, helping you better prepare to stay confident and inventive the next time you face a similar challenge, uncertainty, or pressure-packed decision point.[39] Other brain areas also feed in sensory inputs to shape them into actionable knowledge.[40]

3. Apply White-Water Logic

Here's a final twist: Make the unexpected your ally. You can do everything right, and then sooner or later, wham, your life feels like you're in a kayak hurtling through white water. It's just going to be that way sometimes, and to resist it only makes it more of a problem. Water is whirling and crashing in all directions, the currents are dangerous just beneath the surface, spray is lashing your eyes. It all spins out of control in the brain, and you wind up unsure of what stroke to make next, which direction to go . . .

Remember the mountain guide Pasang, his voice delightfully ringing out with "Florsheim!" What works best and freest for you to shine is what's right for you—how calm can you get with maximal poise and energy? What helps you do it? Then start observing yourself whenever pressures rise and see how you can make your response even more calmly effective.

What doesn't work in this situation is overthinking what you should do, or trying to protect yourself. Your best hope by far is to calmly be two or three moves ahead. Not "think" two or three moves ahead; thinking's so slow that it's out of the question. You can, and should, calmly think two or three moves ahead *before* you get into the kayak, headed for white water—but be prepared to abandon that plan as circumstances change, and to just be there, making the best of all your resources in the moment. This includes every iota of your expertise, and, just as important, every ounce of your instincts, brought freely to bear on the next challenge, and the next unexpected twist in the river. None of this is easy, and it rarely ever occurs without presetting adaptability into your nervous system.

I remember asking an executive several years ago, "What do you do if your old ways aren't working?" In response, he reached into a desk drawer and handed me a much-photocopied page headed "What To Do If You're Riding A Dead Horse: The Top Ten List," which contained the following items:[41]

10. Buy a stronger whip.
9. Change riders.
8. Declare, "This is the way we have always ridden this horse."
7. Appoint a team to revive the dead horse.
6. Ignore the dead horse . . . What dead horse?
5. Create a training session to improve your riding skills.
4. Outsource contractors to ride the dead horse.
3. Appoint a committee to study the dead horse.
2. Arrange to visit other sites to see how they ride dead horses.
1. Harness several dead horses together for increased speed.

The correct answer to the question, according to a Native American saying, is "dismount." But the brain loves to stick to a plan, even when it isn't working. At least you have *something,* but as mentioned earlier, that is a shortcoming called the "fallacy of predetermination."[42] Many of us like to act as though we can predict the future and influence its course through our vision and action. But the truth is, while you can set out an innovative course for the future, you don't know what's going to happen next. You have to adapt.

There are two basic forms of adapting as things change, and it's important to recognize the difference. One way is the brain's automatic reaction: trying harder, tensing up, hunkering down, getting defensive, stonewalling, tuning out, doing the same thing as before except doing it harder and faster. Although at times this reaction may help you to cope or at least survive, if you repeatedly adapt in that way your mind and body become reshaped over time by what is called the "general adaptation syndrome," a process that increases tension (which soon comes to feel "normal") and leads to exhaustion.[43] You end up impervious to learning and blocked from growth, wishing things would just cooperate and go back to what you expected earlier on. This is not good adapting.

The other form of adaptation is the application of fluid intelligence to find new, and even better, ways to achieve your dreams. Quintessential inventor Ray Kurzweil, who founded nine companies in thirty-nine years, says that there can be a dreamlike element in great adaptation: "The most interesting thing about dreams," he notes, "is that you don't consider it unusual when unusual things happen. You accept this lack of logic, and this faculty is vital for creative thinking."[44]

Suppose you were sitting in a lovely street-side café in San Francisco and someone bet you that you couldn't drive to New York in less than three months. You'd be foolish, probably, not to take them up on it. Suppose, however, that the year is 1903, the total extent of paved roadways between San Francisco and New York is about 150 miles, you don't even own a car, and any car you might purchase would not only be highly unreliable, but its twenty-horsepower engine could barely achieve a maximum speed, pedal to the metal, of about thirty miles per hour.[45]

You'd think twice, and maybe think a few more times when you considered that no one had ever made such a trip before, there were no gas stations, no road maps, no tow trucks, no roadside eateries or lodging. No roof and no windshield on your car, either—they didn't make them then.

After thinking however many times he had to, a Maine doctor named Horatio Jackson took up the wager.

At every moment on his journey, Jackson had to improvise. He would master one challenge, speeding up to cross a creek, for example, only to find that at the next creek speeding up might mean ramming into a submerged boulder. Cowboys on horseback pulled him out of mudholes. He and his companion, a bicycle mechanic named Sewall Crocker, acquired a dog and outfitted "Bud" with goggles. Jackson's free-flowing adaptability and humor often saved the day. He wrote to his wife, for example, about Bud: "He was the one member of the trio who used no profanity the entire trip."

Each challenge was new, and many were life-threatening. (No cell phones to call for an ambulance. No ambulances. No road markers to direct an ambulance to if there had been one.) Jackson met each one with calm inventiveness in the moment, handling what was in front of him, learning from it, and then handling what came next. He thought about quitting, but the goal and the challenge were important to him, and he was determined to see them through. He made it to New York in a little over sixty-three days. He never collected on the $50 bet, instead thanking the friend who had encouraged him to make his journey, because it changed his life in a hundred ways for the better.

There are some everyday lessons to be learned from Dr. Jackson's extraordinary journey. Among them are these.

- *Recognize and move beyond your fear.* Everyone experiences fear. The key when pressures rise is to not let the fear grow as you stand there, frozen by the barrier, but instead to consciously see the fear as a gift, a catalyst, and channel the *energy*—and feeling—of fear into something that sparks your ingenuity and moves you forward, to create a solution or breakthrough.
- *Make "forward" your only option.* If you do, the brain will take it when things get tough.
- *Concentrate your energies and focus on your primary target,* not everything at once.
- *No matter what, remain calm and composed,* for even in the worst situations you will find opportunities. Staying calm under pressure produces crucial amounts of a key neurochemical, nitric oxide,

throughout the body.[46] Nitric oxide is the unusually small but powerful molecule that switches on the glowing light in fireflies. Inside humans, it neutralizes the negative effects of stress hormones such as norepinephrine that cause rapid heart rate, high blood pressure, tension, anger, and anxiety. Nitric oxide signals the brain to release calming neurochemicals such as dopamine and endorphins. Often this enables you to reach a heightened level of action, mood, creativity, or performance. To master this kind of attention under pressure instead of just relying on expending energy to move you forward, you must engage with your challenges by keeping physical tension levels low, freeing yourself to try differently instead of harder.

Invention *in the moment* is the source of much of what is new. A flash of inspiration and breakthrough appears as if from out of nowhere. But it's not out of nowhere at all; rather, it comes from the nervous system of anyone who has practiced white-water logic.

People are learning to apply this kind of logic in many organizations today. The U.S. military, facing "fourth-generation warfare" (4GW)—a new type of combat that isn't susceptible to old tactics—is teaching its commanders that "what 'wins' at the tactical and physical levels may lose at the operational, strategic, mental, and moral levels, where 4GW is decided."[47] That means making complex decisions, in the moment, that take into account all six of those factors and not just the first two. Much learning and training has been invested in creating the capacity to respond in those ways. Dr. James Crupi, who holds the title "Strategic Advisor to The Chief of Staff of the Army for Leader Development, Innovation, and Army Transformation," says about reacting properly in those situations, "The issue is not what you've been taught, but what you're able to learn."[48]

But you can teach yourself in advance how to learn under even the most intense forms of pressure. Breakthroughs happen most often when you're calm and curious as pressures rise. This is when the relaxed nervous system makes new (and better) neuronal connections.[49] When you bring this into the way you live every day, your network of neural circuits can change and grow every moment of your life.[50] So make some room in your heart and mind to keep asking two questions about things you observe: "What would I do?" and "What *could* I do?" Keep considering how other actions might have created different outcomes. Mentally rehearsing new ways of behaving changes your brain, preparing you to come up with better solutions when new challenges arise.

SUN THE MUTILATED

When I'm facing tough challenges and looking for calm energy to deal with them, I find it helpful to remember from how far back a human being can come and still make a difference. One of the stories providing that point of reference for me is of the man who was known in his earlier years as Master Sun. His grandfather, General Sun-tzu, wrote the strategy classic *The Art of War.* Master Sun grew up in China in the third century BCE, during the Era of the Warring States, a time of chaos and brutal competition, not so unlike the way parts of our world may seem to us today. As one writer has described it:

> Usurpers set themselves up as lords and kings; states that were run by pretenders and plotters established armies to make themselves into major powers. They imitated each other at this more and more, and those who came after them also followed their example. Eventually they overwhelmed and destroyed one another, conspiring with larger domains to annex smaller domains, spending years at violent military operations, filling the fields with blood. . . . No one could safeguard his or her life. Integrity disappeared. Eventually things reached the chaotic extreme where seven large states and five smaller states contested with each other for power, forming unstable and ever-shifting alliances in the pursuit of greed and personal ambition.[51]

In such circumstances, military and political strategists were in great demand, and when he was young, Master Sun studied warfare and strategy under the mysterious sage Wang Li, author of one of the most intricate and sophisticated of strategic classics.[52] When a fellow student, Pang Juan, was hired as military adviser to the state of Wei, he invited Master Sun to Wei on the pretext of consulting with him. In reality, Pang Juan, aware that his own abilities as a strategist were not equal to Master Sun's, wanted to eliminate him, and when Master Sun arrived, Pang Juan had him arrested as a criminal and condemned to the severest torture. Both of young Master Sun's feet were cut off and his face was horribly disfigured so he would be reduced to the status of a permanent outcast. Left maimed, hemorrhaging profusely and dying, he somehow survived and from that day onward he was known as Sun Bin—Sun the Mutilated.

His story was far from over, however.

Sun Bin believed that he could still make a difference with his life, despite this horrible setback, his new limitations, and the treachery and terror around him. In his darkest hour, he found the drive to let go of what he no longer had, flow with the changes, and transcend his tortured self. While still imprisoned, he managed to obtain a brief, secret meeting with an emissary from the state of Qi.

Although hideously maimed and in excruciating pain, Sun Bin quickly astounded the envoy not only with his courage but also with his keen wisdom about strategy and warfare. The emissary smuggled him out of prison and into Qi, where Sun Bin soon proved himself and won appointment as military strategist to the famed general Tian Ji.[53]

The new tactics Sun Bin devised centered on securing victory with minimal harm and at minimal cost. Eventually, they changed the nature of war in his day. If possible, both sides would end the conflict without humiliation. His teachings, entitled *The Lost Art of War*, were indeed lost for nearly two thousand years until a nearly complete version, recorded on 232 small bamboo tablets, was discovered in 1972 in an ancient tomb in Shandong Province.

Sun the Mutilated found the best within himself under circumstances far worse than most of us will ever encounter. When his life changed, he changed with it, finding the hottest spark that moved him forward and using his strengths in altogether new ways. Time and again, his own version of white-water logic enabled him to shape far more of the world's future than his enemy who left him for dead could ever have imagined.

You build your own inner reserves and innovativeness for times of trial right now. *Are you trying harder or trying differently? What are you becoming?*

15
Streamline

The greatest carver does the least cutting.

—LAO-TZU, UNDERSTANDING THE MYSTERIES

Your brain consumes a lot of your energy: Although it makes up only about one-fiftieth of your total body weight, it accounts for ten times its weight in energy consumption at any given moment.[1] The more stress, anxiety, or frustration you're dealing with, the more energy gets consumed, and the less there is for more constructive pursuits. We're geared to respond to rising pressure by trying harder, so the more pressure we put on ourselves, the less effective we become. Streamlining reverses that, putting all your energy on your side as you move toward your goals faster than ever with less strain.

Producing and sustaining that streamlined goal-directed energy requires only some simple changes. By and large, we human beings fail when we feel we're being controlled by others and win when we're in control.[2] One of the most effective ways to gain that in-control power over yourself and your destiny is to master the small, proven techniques that keep your energy high all day long and raise it whenever it starts to fall.

One smart new move—something as simple as an extra few seconds of muscle toning here and there throughout the day, or sipping some ice water, or eating a small, higher-protein snack instead of going hours until the next meal—can set off a domino effect that ramps up your energy-boosting power in a natural way.[3] With a bit of practice, it becomes automatic—your body and senses will detect a slight dip in energy and prompt you to raise it. In this way you both consciously and unconsciously begin to keep your metabolism—your brain and body's energy-production system—set on "high."

Full alertness is the optimal activated state of the brain and nervous system, where creative solutions appear and we can easily pay full attention to what actions to take and what to exclude. Martin Moore-Ede, a former professor of physiology at Harvard Medical School who has extensively studied alertness and fatigue, says, "A person's alertness is triggered by key internal and external factors that can be considered the switches on the brain's control panel. Understanding these key switches and how to manipulate them is the secret of gaining power over one of the most important attributes of the human brain."[4]

I have written extensively about these switches and the science behind them.[5] Here are several of the many simple, practical ways for you to start turning them on, right now.

Breathe the most air, live the most life. To a remarkable extent, how you breathe is how you live: Oxygen molecules are the central fuel for energy molecules.[6] Most of us barely breathe at all. Instead of only filling your chest with air, allow your lower ribs to expand, opening your diaphragm so you really fill your lungs. Every time you do that, you turn up your energy engine another notch. Deeper, very relaxed respiration enables you to stay on top of stress. With practice, you'll automatically monitor your breathing.

Uplift your posture. There are few more powerful ways to raise and sustain energy than to ease your posture *up*ward, which frees your breathing and raises your energy level.[7] Much of our technology prompts us to assume a head-forward posture, and all our neck-bending pursuits—like reading, watching TV, and peering at a computer monitor—numb the spine and constrict our breathing. It seems like everyone is slumping these days. That posture exacts a toll on our energy and alertness.

Zero tension, maximum flow. If you live and work with tense people during the day, it's easy to end up feeling more tense yourself. But if you want the best kind of energy, calm energy, then take charge of tension by releasing it, fast.[8] Do a quick check of your muscle tension right now. First, tense and relax your shoulders. Then shift attention to other parts of your body in sequence, tensing and relaxing your jaw, then your neck, your back, your arms, and so on, right to the tips of your toes. Even your tongue is probably carrying excess tension, whether or not you're talking! This kind of tension wastes energy and can throw your body chemistry out of whack.[9] Monitor your physical tension level, and whenever you're tensed up, calm down.

Sip ice water. Fluids move hormones into exactly the right places for sustaining energy, and those same fluids eliminate toxic wastes that can accumulate and wear you down. As little as a 4 to 5 percent reduction below optimal water requirements can reduce your concentration and performance by as much as 30 percent.[10] Sipping just over two cups of ice-cold water raises metabolism by 30 percent for the next 90 minutes and burns an average of 25 calories.[11] Forty percent of these calories are burned primarily from abdominal fat (more in men than women) to warm the water in the stomach to body temperature before absorption.[12] Sipping four 16-ounce glasses of ice water during the day will burn approximately 100 extra calories. That may not sound like much but it's the equivalent of running about 10 to 15 minutes a day. In a year, this 100 calories a day amounts to 36,000 calories—burned preferentially from abdominal fat,[13] and that means you could theoretically burn off about 10 extra pounds of abdominal fat just by sipping ice water or some other sugar- and calorie-free beverage.[14] This doesn't mean you can skip the exercise, of course, but sipping a bit of extra cold water every half hour during the day adds an extra source of energy to your life.

Move more. Inactivity is an unnatural state for us, and it limits energy production. To make matters worse, people who sit still for long periods of time are more likely to feel depressed and anxious than those who have regular exercise.[15] Get up regularly and move: Any type of muscular activity stimulates your sympathetic nervous system and helps keep your alertness high.[16] Think of your muscle fibers as energy-producing furnaces. They need to be stoked throughout the day, not just once in a long while. They thrive when they're used. They wither when they're not. After just two weeks of inaction, major muscle groups can begin to lose tone.

It's a mistake to think you have to head to the health club or try to cram all the muscle-toning you need into intense workouts. The alternative is to build in some brief strengthening activities during the day. That way, if you miss a formal workout, you're still fine. In your office, or taking a break from a meeting, you can stand up and loosen up. Do a few toe raises or tense your forearms as you open and close your hands (this builds muscle tone in your forearms and revs up energy). You can do a few modified push-ups (leaning into the wall if you don't like getting down on the floor) or toe curls using your body weight as resistance.

Catch the light. To our ancient metabolism, spending the day indoors is all but equivalent to spending the day in darkness, and it stimulates the inherent physiological processes associated with sleeping.[17] As light increases, brain signals raise your metabolism.[18] More than you might imagine, light switches on your brain and senses. It shifts metabolism upward and gives you a burst of energy. So become a light harvester: Every morning, lunchtime, afternoon, and evening, seek out some bright light. A minute or two outside in sunshine is great. On a cloudy day, you can get a similar benefit by standing or working in an area of increased indoor lighting, even for a few moments here and there.

Snack smart . . . and often. When you eat can matter as much as what you eat for turning up your metabolism and keeping it set on a healthy high level. Whenever you skip between-meal snacks, blood sugar falls and you are likely to experience increased fatigue and tension.[19] Eating smaller, nutritious meals and snacks helps to stabilize blood-sugar levels, which in turn optimizes memory, learning, energy, and performance.[20] When you go four or five hours at a stretch without eating, your blood-sugar levels drop and your energy wanes.

Shift your eyes and mind away. Hour after hour, the tiny muscles in your eyes use more energy than any other muscle fibers in your body. Without a brief rest every half hour or so, they become tired and produce overall fatigue and localized tension in the neck and shoulders.[21]

So change the view. If you've been doing close-up work, take a few moments to blink your eyes and look at more distant objects, such as a picture or poster on the wall, or the scene out a nearby window. If you've been scanning faraway scenery, switch to focusing on something nearby. These easy actions help provide a brief and vital rest for the most active eye muscles, prompting a healthy exchange of fluids in the eyes and providing increased oxygen and other nutrients.

One of the most fascinating, beneficial characteristics of these energy switches in your nervous system is their cumulative effect in keeping you streamlined in moving through your day. With increased alertness, you are better able to catch yourself getting tense or getting sidetracked and fix the problem on the spot. If you take just one of the simple actions I've described, you will notice a subtle but detectable change in your physical and mental responses. If you then use another energy booster after fifteen to thirty minutes—or even the same one—the cumulative effect is even more pronounced.

End the stress-creates-more-stress cycle. When you're moving through everyday hassles with a brain that's hyperreactive to each and every hassle, a negative spiral kicks in. As you automatically and unconsciously make mountains out of molehills, the brain gets more and more anxious about smaller and smaller problems until it actually reacts as if you were under siege from a horde of invaders from a thousand years ago. And all of a sudden that's precisely how it feels. To break this pattern, observe your thinking patterns and actions. Implement a sequence of actions, perhaps tied to the automatic drivers I discussed in chapter 4, that tone muscles, keep you up and moving, and shift your thoughts and attention forward into the future you are building today.

SAY YES TO LESS

Just as there are small, simple ways to change your physical energy level, so, too, are there ways to boost your mental and emotional effectiveness by using the leverage of streamlining. One way is something I mentioned before, but which you might acknowledge more clearly in this context: A stop-doing list can often be just as important as a to-do list. Streamlining results from making small changes that reduce drag and adding other adjustments to increase your speed toward what matters most. So, kindly, clearly, and firmly say no to a lot more and yes to a lot less. Be really picky about where you devote your attention and energy. Move away from people who drain your energy, produce tension, or make it harder for you to advance your life, and move toward those who add to your forward momentum.

As I said earlier, some people respond to new energy by taking on more tasks, and that's often a big mistake. It will only drain your energy again and wholly defeat the purpose of gaining energy, which is to propel you toward new breakthroughs in achieving what matters most for you. Take on fewer relationship responsibilities for people who are off track or you don't deeply care about. Their stress is their stress, not yours. Their negative emotions are their negative emotions, not yours, and you have to distance yourself or else you'll "catch" them and it will bring you down, too.[22] This latter phenomenon is called "open-loop interpersonal limbic regulation," in which one person transmits feelings across time and space that can measurably alter cardiovascular function, hormone levels, sleep patterns, and even immune system functions in another person.[23] So accept fewer commitments that don't fit your strengths and passions or align with your highest goals. It's time to stop equating dedication with overload and exhaustion and get very clear about what you are choosing to place at the heart of your daily life.

A second strategy is to identify a few simple things in the course of each day that rev up your commitment to what really matters amid the din of so much that really doesn't.

My grandfather was a devoted churchgoer, but he didn't always attend one particular house of worship. If he was making house calls on a Sunday, he would drop in someplace nearby to worship. Late at night, after leaving the hospital, he would sometimes stop at a local church or temple to pray. When he had just performed a surgery or visited a sick patient, sometimes he would attend that person's church or synagogue. Expressing his faith every day was one of what he called his "essential core actions," which he shortened to ECAs. Another ECA for him was to stop, every day, to gaze into the eyes of a child. He had a list of about six ECAs, small things he did every day to tap into the deeper energy and meaning in his life. Cumulatively, they took up very little of his time; individually and cumulatively, they affected everything that he did.

I have my own daily ECAs, and I recommend that you should, too. Notice small, brief activities that uplift your energy in ways that reinforce what you truly value, and make a point of doing them each day.

Third, guide the energy of your emotions relentlessly toward the positive. Everything that happens to you, whether it seems good, bad, or somewhere in between, is just energy that your brain is choosing to interpret. You can guide that energy into whatever you want.[24] Even fear can be a gift—it all depends on what you do *next* with the energy of any emotion as it arises.[25]

Managing or eliminating problematic emotions is just not enough for moving forward at challenging times; you must find ways to transform negativity into positive energy. Doing so releases immense inner resources.[26] Whenever dark moods and bleak outlooks clutch your heart or dominate your mind, practice heading in the opposite direction. Deflect or reaim the incoming energy; turn the galvanizing energy of stress into faster streamlining on the path you have chosen. As noted in earlier chapters, the most successful people tend to turn criticisms into progress and to let go of doubts and inner demons after just a few moments. They use these unexpected gifts of energy as catalysts to speed them more smoothly toward a better next step, and a better tomorrow.[27]

YOUR OWN EASTER ISLAND

The longest-range plan anyone really has is the plan he or she is implementing today. Anything else is just a fantasy. Your brain sees through the smoke screens of empty wishes to notice how you act moment by moment, and that's what it magnifies. Little things don't just mean a lot; they can mean the most when you apply them to boosting your energy, raising your focus, and streamlining your path through life.

Doing a lot gets the chores handled and the bills paid. But unless you're deliberately advancing toward what you really want, with as little resistance and wasted energy as possible, how different are you, really, from those Easter Islanders whose devotion to hard work instead of smart work doomed them? We all have to face the fact that sooner or later, we'll be extinct, too.

16
Leap Forward by Doing Nothing

The art of being wise is knowing when to step aside and what to overlook.

—William James[1]

I was in Dublin a few years ago for a meeting with the executives of Guinness, the Irish brewer of one of the world's most popular beers. It was early evening and we were about to board a bus and head out for a tour of the Temple Bar district of Dublin, the newly rebuilt historic section of the city. The marketing director and I were standing in the hallway talking about the results of a global study on why people around the world so quickly develop a deep and enduring allegiance to this dark and intense stout, which, at least from my view, no one instantly loves; it's an acquired taste, which would seem to make popularizing it all the harder.

The marketing director looked surprised when I suggested that I thought marketing the brand might be challenging. "The number one reason people love Guinness," he said, "is they have to wait two minutes after the pint is filled before they can drink it."

Unlike almost every other beer in the world, once a barkeeper pours a Guinness it is left on the bar for two full minutes before being served as "the perfect pint" to the customer.

"They tell us they love Guinness because at the end of the day while everyone else is quaffing other beer straight down, by waiting those two minutes the Guinness customers feel they get their bearings back. They stop feeling so overwhelmed by life's hassles and disappointments and remember that they have family and friends who care about them; I guess it helps them start to relax and set the world right again."

There are many ways to get our bearings back, of course, but one way or another we must do it. One thing I have observed in my research is that many of the most exceptional individuals and leaders know how to do nothing, and they do it *really* well.

They can close the office door, lean back in a chair, and leave the world behind for a long minute just before the most important meetings or most difficult discussions. They can put the world's worries on hold for five minutes and doze off during a taxi ride right before making a decision that will change everything. They can arrive two minutes early to pick up the children, start singing a favorite song off-key, and smile from ear to ear as they tap their toes and provoke an exuberance that's more like being on vacation than doing another chore in a long day. They can sit on a park bench after a bite of lunch and in a dozen long breaths soak in what seems to be all of nature, with absolutely no worry about what's next.

They have learned that doing not just less, but doing nothing at all, restores and builds energy in incomparable ways.[2] Do-nothing choices strengthen the brain, increase circulation, raise energy levels, reduce stress, and sharpen the senses.[3] You can change your whole life by doing nothing at the right times.

Many people buy into the notion that they must keep trying all the time, with every ounce of willpower until exhaustion sets in. The truth, however, is that unless you take breaks from this pressure cooker of intensity, some vital brain components just wither away.[4]

One of the commonest reasons for getting blocked trying to solve problems, for example, is that the brain gets stuck in an old groove that's unhelpful and uncreative. When periods of concentrated focus are interspersed with doing-nothing breaks, our "wrongheaded assumptions have time to dissipate,"[5] and as we return to more intense focus there is a far greater chance of seeing the challenge in a fresh and more productive light.[6]

CREATE BREATHING SPACE

"If only I could get a little breathing space." How often does that wish pass through your mind, and how elusive does it seem? Breathing space is far more important than most people realize. It's where you regain your bearings, raise your vantage point, loosen up, and recharge—but only if you can stay one step ahead of your brain's oldest conditioned habits.

Just as you can catch defining moments by plan and also by paying special attention, you can make breathing space in the same ways.

Plan to come up for air—and then do it. Because we're so used to praising ourselves for our busyness and effort, most of us never build into our schedule even very small gaps for breathing space. It's as if the brain is rushing toward a once-in-a-lifetime around-the-world vacation and thinks it must sacrifice all the small pauses along the way.

One of the simplest strategies is regularly to aim your attention forward into the best possible future and then savor some of the small signs of progress moving from here to there: How have a few of the changes you've tested this past week been moving you toward that better future? Every time you create planned breathing space, you are firing neuron pathways that make it progressively easier to instantly be in that special zone. Science now shows you can learn to be exceptional at pulling back to get ahead.[7]

WHENEVER YOU REST, YOU RISE

There's another reason for doing nothing: your brain's need for deep rest. The hypothalamus and basal ganglia control your body's idling speed, and at least once a day, as well as all night long, you need to send them on holiday.[8] We used to believe that truly renewing rest could only come from long and deep sleep, but even small doses—a few minutes at a time—of doing nothing may ramp up brainpower in the same way that deep rest does.[9]

During deep sleep, your brain sifts through the day's barrage of information and knits it all into memories and new ideas;[10] it appears that brief periods of rest during the day—even just a few minutes at a time—allow some of that work to be performed in advance, making nighttime processing faster and more effective.

We are in fact designed for two sleeps a day, the main one at night and a nap in the afternoon.[11] The parts of the brain that are refreshed by deep sleep actually recover during the earliest stages of sleep, and there's no advantage gained in that regard from additional sleep. According to Dr. James Horne, "Not all of sleep is for recovery. A particular part of sleep occurring in the early part of sleep is most important for brain recovery, and the latter part is not so important in that regard. As we can eat more food than we require and drink more fluids than we require, we may sleep more than we require." His conclusion: "Rather than trying to extend one's sleep, perhaps we should take short naps instead."[12]

All of this is not to say that deep nighttime sleep is not important. That too many people are sleep-deprived is a well-known fact,[13] and state-of-the-art imaging shows that sleep deprivation has dramatic negative effects on brain function.[14] In fact, it seems that your brain may retaliate for inadequate sleep by actually shutting down the very brain functions you're trying to use at any given moment, while leaving the other parts functioning normally![15]

GET YOUR BLOOD FLOWING RIGHT

You can also achieve some significant sustained energy benefits by slowing down your heart rate and dropping your blood pressure.

Let's start with heart rate. Put your index and middle finger gently on the veins on the inside of your wrist and count the beats for ten seconds, and then multiply by six. Your number? Eighty beats per minute? Seventy?

Now breathe out, letting go of excess tension. Trying harder increases your pulse rate. Letting go lowers it. Just relax, releasing stressful thoughts from your mind for a few moments, replacing them with calming thoughts. See if you can bring your heart rate down into the seventies. A sensible goal may be sixty beats per minute. Elite athletes have resting heart rates in the forties and fifties. Stressed-out sedentary people can have resting heart rates in the nineties, and that's a true problem for health and energy recovery.

This feedback loop between letting go and taking your pulse helps your brain sort out ways to back off tension and help the heart work less hard. A number of wristwatches now will accurately check your pulse rate at the push of a button. This allows your mind to let go even faster as you get a quick reading of how fast your heart is beating and perhaps choose to gently guide it lower. Another way to lower your pulse rate at rest is to stay involved with a regular aerobic exercise program, which has been shown to benefit the processes in the hippocampus, potentially doubling the number of new cells within it.[16]

Blood pressure is another indicator of whether your heart is getting the rest it needs. There are some inexpensive yet highly accurate wrist blood pressure and pulse monitors available. Living a long young life depends on staying well and keeping your energy high. Monitoring these heart functions lets you manage your own well-being with far greater ease than has been possible in the past.

DON'T DO IT ANYWAY

Brain strain is as hazardous as a broken-down body, and trying to get your brain to work by brute force is as hazardous as working out too far beyond your body's tolerance. Neuroimages of overused brains show so little activity that they appear to be nearly comatose.[17] These brownouts of the gray matter, even if we've grown accustomed to them and see them as a badge of our hard work and determination, are extremely debilitating.

More often than you're used to doing it, give your brain a break. Pick some key times every day and, to reverse the popular saying, just don't do it. Every day, practice noticing bottlenecks of pressure emerging and step back, disengage, do nothing, in a state of unselfconscious engagement with your surroundings. Smell the coffee or flowers for a full uninterrupted minute. Detach completely from the day's demands as you saunter through the park, gaze at the stars, or watch children play.

Most worries and decisions are of little or no real consequence, after all; your fears about them are mostly misdirected energy. Know when to say when, and then say it.

ALLOW THINGS TO COME TO YOU

When I was very young, my grandmother Cooper read me Winnie the Pooh stories.[18] Her favorite line came when Winnie explained that you must be willing to "allow things to come to you," rather than, like Rabbit, "always going and fetching them." That's a challenging thing to apply, because the brain loves the illusion of progress that effort gives, and it loves how under stress we stick to lines of thought that are clear, conventional, controlled, and secure. This is one way that our own brain's inherent tendencies block us from solving many of life's important problems and challenges.

The brain is built to best explore certain crucial kinds of expansive learning by stepping back from life's rush with a subtle brilliance too easily blunted by thinking too much and trying too hard.[19] Overall, emptiness absorbs the negative and emits the positive. It can serve as a momentary shift into an overdrive gear that reduces strain and glides you forward. In this space of doing nothing healing occurs, our batteries are recharged, our relationships are renewed, and wisdom is found. Aim your mind toward only what's positive, humorous, renewing, affirming. Whenever it wanders back onto the to-do list or worries or doubts, gently redirect it into open, positive space.

More often than before, pull back and come to life. Exertion and effort count far less than the opportunity for neural networks to soak in the world and gain new, energizing information about unforeseen ways to develop.[20]

ABOUT "BALANCE"

One of our challenges today is not that our personal and professional lives are too interconnected, it's that we're mistakenly struggling too hard to disconnect them. What, exactly, does the concept of "balance" mean to you on a personal level? Does it mean that half the waking day is devoted to work and the other half to life off the job?

I think balance has less to do with time or effort than it does with inner commitment of energy: Are you moving steadily toward your highest goals, enthusiastic about life, aware of seizing the moments that matter most, and full of gratitude for your blessings? That's the ideal deployment of your energy. Or are you spinning your wheels, feeling angry, always behind, and unfulfilled? That's the norm, and even if you're spending half your days away from work it won't set life right for you.

Achieving what you're seeking and what almost no one ever finds requires redefining what balance means. The first rule is that personal and professional lives often overlap, and that's not a problem if you're bringing your best self along in both. Some days, if you're managing focus, not time; energy, not effort; impact, not intentions; and so on, you may head home after you have produced in four hours what it took you eight or ten hours to accomplish not long ago. But then once in a while a ten- or twelve-hour workday may be vital to seizing opportunities and making big changes happen.

Find your own best way to make sure that, in any given week, you do amazing things as well as do nothing at the right moments, and that your energy free-flows in the ways that move your values and progress and spirit forward.

17
Stay Hungry,
Stay Foolish

"How did you go bankrupt?"
"Gradually, then suddenly."

—ERNEST HEMINGWAY, *The Sun Also Rises*

In 1968, Stewart Brand, a thirty-year-old Stanford graduate and former Army parachutist, published the first issue of the *Whole Earth Catalog,* an idealistic, practical periodical brimming with provocative thinking and breakthrough tools for doing just about anything. "Access to tools" was the publication's motto, and its mission was to help each reader "find his own inspiration, shape his own environment, and share his adventure with whoever is interested." Even in its large format, with eleven-by-fourteen-inch pages, the catalog sometimes was over an inch thick.

When Brand felt the *Whole Earth Catalog* had run its course, he put out a final issue. On the back cover was a photograph of dawn rising on a country road, the kind you would be drawn to for hiking or bicycling if you were in a traveling mood and had an adventurous spirit. Beneath the photo was Brand's farewell message: "Stay Hungry. Stay Foolish."[1]

I tore off that back cover and taped it first to my car dashboard and then above my desk. For most of my life, I have wished that motto for myself and those I love. Once in a while, I get close to the full expression, but it's just beyond my reach—and ever worth reaching for.

When you stay hungry and foolish, you don't waste much precious energy on someone else's goals that have nothing to do with your own, or on living by someone else's narrow rules that stop you from realizing your own deeper values and purpose. You see dogma for what it is—the control tactics of your old habits or someone else's brain, not your next capacities. You don't let the noise of other's opinions drown out your own inner voice. You listen to your heart and intuition. You dare to do at least a few really big things well, instead of putting them off and settling for just surviving.

100 PERCENT ALIVE

For every thousand people who get trapped in a small corner of their potential life by their hyperactivated ancient brain areas, there's one who stays hungry, stays foolish, and wins big. Take Richard Branson. He's one of those dynamos with the twinkle in their eyes who always know that the next thing—the very next—will be the best ever. He was never supposed to end up like this. He was a British kid with dyslexia who nearly flunked out of one school, was expelled from another, and dropped out at age sixteen to start a youth-culture magazine called *Student* that he hoped might someday become Britain's answer to *Rolling Stone.*[2]

Then, through the years, partly from wandering way off the beaten path and sometimes viewing the world for days on end from a hammock in the Caribbean, he has foisted so many great ideas on the world that his conglomerate of 350 companies generates over $9 billion a year in sales.

I can't think of any other senior executive who has more fun. He aims not to own expensive art collections, a fleet of luxury cars, or a fancy golf-club membership, but rather at shaping a life that fits his passions, stretches his capacities, incorporates his family, and gives him chances to do nothing. It's in his hanging-out time when, he says,

"I come up with more ideas than I ever do in the day-to-day running [of the business from the office]."[3]

He readily admits he has many quirks and spends no effort trying to "fix" them. For example, even though he was invited to speak at a recent Microsoft conference, he doesn't use or own a personal computer. Immediate things he wants to recall he writes on the back of his hand. He couldn't care less about clothes or a Hollywood-style appearance: He carries a gym bag to meetings instead of a briefcase, and was once photographed wearing shoes that didn't match.

He loves disrupting the status quo, pushing the envelope, poking fun at the big shots and rigid incumbents—taking on the industries that hold customers hostage (wireless phone companies) or charge too much (music) or treat them badly and irk them no end (airlines).

He wears a very expensive Breitling watch (a gift from the manufacturer)—not to show off or to check how late he is for his next urgent meeting, as many executives would, but because he's enamored with the small pin on the side that if pulled out signals a rescue helicopter. But his watch rarely tells the correct time because there are two identical pins on the side, and he can't remember which pin sets the time and which signals the helicopter. And he never seems to have any money in his pocket, since he says he hasn't figured out how to use a cash machine, and, even if he could, he thinks he'd probably never remember his PIN.

Branson never set out to be rich or a CEO, and by *not* aiming there—following his passions and aiming to have lots of fun along the way, instead—he became incredibly rich and redefined what being an executive could mean. Almost all of his businesses have seemed foolhardy to the experts, and sometimes those experts have been right, but he's relaxed about that, too, saying, "If something fails, as long as we bow out gracefully and pay off all our debts, and nobody gets hurt, then I don't think people disrespect Virgin for trying."[4]

WHEN MORE IS NOT ENOUGH

There's "hunger," and then there's hunger. Richard Branson's hunger for all the thrills and spills he can pack into his life led him into the business world, where he'll surely remain—at least for as long as he can play the game on his terms. The converse is all too familiar to us—a hunger for more, more, more, however unsatisfying that actually feels, and a willingness to give up life's richness and "foolishness" in order to get it. Tense, stress-driven energy punishing us and then a "reward" that just doesn't feel the way it's supposed to.

Peter Whybrow, director of the Semel Institute of Neuroscience and Human Behavior at the University of California, Los Angeles, has written about what he calls the "American mania," which is that more is not enough.[5] He traces this psychosis back to its roots in our brains, showing how pleasure centers based on minimal satisfactions of basic needs (having enough food to eat or feeling safe) become frenzied when presented with the modern world's glut of potential satisfactions. "I think we've shot through happiness and come out the other end, and we're not quite sure where we are," Whybrow says. "This frenzy we've adopted in search of what we hope is happiness and perfection is in fact a distraction."[6]

EXCITEMENT AND WORTH

Maybe Richard Branson's world of business entrepreneurship isn't for you. Maybe your hunger is something way different—say, traveling the world and making impossible differences on a purely human level wherever you go. Then you could consider the American attorney Inge Fryklund, who over the past five years has found a way to place herself in Kosovo, then in the capital of Tajikistan, Dushanbe, and now in Afghanistan's capital, Kabul.

It's not that her life was so dull before that: She was a prosecutor in Chicago (where she argued a groundbreaking case before the U.S. Supreme Court) and then was tapped to become that city's "parking czar," where she designed an entirely new system for managing parking and doubled the rate of collections of parking tickets. Then she became an independent consultant, where among other things she had the audacity to inform the Chicago political machine that the city's voter registration practices were "antiquated, duplicative, and open to fraud."[7] Imagine that.

Her experience with suspect election practices led her to Kosovo, where in 2001 she helped set up the procedures used to select that region's first democratically elected central government. From there, she joined an ambitious program of the American Bar Association that helps countries that once were part of the Soviet Union set up systems and practices that will help them become healthy independent nations. In Tajikistan, she pushed young lawyers, judges, and others to think about their futures in open-space terms.

She says one of her most moving experiences came late one night in Uzbekistan after a planning session had ended: "An impromptu group of legal professionals, joined by my driver from Kyrgyzstan and a border guard from Uzbekistan, held an impassioned discussion about their visions for the future . . . It was a totally new idea that they could have dreams and choices instead of passively accepting the latest directive from the khan, Soviet, or president."[8]

Now she's in her second year in Afghanistan, helping the citizens of that country imagine their own best futures and bring them about. Some might regard volunteering for the primitive conditions and threat-filled life in Kabul to be "foolish," but for Fryklund, it's part of a pattern. "For most of my career," she says, "I could hardly wait to get to work to find out what interesting things were going to happen that day. Afghanistan is like that, but even more so. I feel that I am really making a difference in Afghanistan. I want to love what I am doing; I don't think I could manage a boring job even if it was important work. Fortunately, there are lots of jobs that combine excitement and worth—it isn't necessary to give up either one."[9]

YOU'RE NEXT

Richard Branson is hungry for all the thrills and spills life can offer him. Inge Fryklund is looking for adventure, engagement, and contribution. What's your hunger? How "foolish" are you willing to be to enjoy it?

As Tom Robbins wrote, "If you insist on leaving your fate to the gods, then the gods will repay your weakness by having a grin or two at your expense. Should you fail to pilot your own ship, don't be surprised at what inappropriate port you will find yourself docked in. . . . To achieve the marvelous, it is precisely the unthinkable that must be thought."[10]

All around the world, there are people, young and old, rising from out of nowhere to prominence in every known and emerging walk of life because they know their hungers, and they're willing to stay foolish enough to enjoy them.

"How did you go bankrupt?" one character in *The Sun Also Rises* asks another. "Gradually, then suddenly" is the answer. That's just the way our lives become bankrupt if we're not paying attention.

Across the street from the art museum in downtown Monterey, California, a redwood seedling is growing toward becoming a giant tree. The seedling was a gift to the city from Alan Shepard, who in 1961 was the first American to fly into space, and ten years later went to the moon. The seedling was aboard that flight to the moon. Shepard planted it to help people recall the grandeur we too often take for granted here on earth, and to put the shortness of our lives and the length of our legacies into perspective. What I remember most about his space journeys, though, is the heroism it took for him to do what he did, and the humanity he showed when he looked back at earth from his space capsule and wept.

As the poet Rainer Maria Rilke observed, "It is breathtaking simply to be here."

MISSING THE PROM, CHANGING HISTORY

Cristen Powell missed an important event in her life—her senior prom. But maybe she didn't mind too much, because as her Beaverton, Oregon, classmates were pinning on their boutonnieres and corsages and stepping into their limos, Cristen was at the other end of the country, in Englishtown, New Jersey, pulling on a fire-resistant drag-racing suit and tugging a yellow helmet down over her long brown hair, on her way to making history.

While her classmates admired the exotic decorations in their gymnasium, eighteen-year-old Cristen climbed into the cockpit of her skinny twenty-five-foot-long dragster, slammed down the throttle, felt the huge tires slip and then grip, and roared forward at a blistering 120 miles per hour. In an eighth of a mile she was going nearly 300 miles per hour.

When her trip down the quarter-mile course ended, Cristen knew she had posted a good time. When the evening ended, she had become the youngest woman ever to win a professional drag-racing event.

Cristen graduated from high school, and she's now a regular on the drag-racing circuit, with her sights on continuing greatness. She recognizes that if others before her had not followed their dreams, the path to hers might have been blocked. She particularly thanks Shirley Muldowney, the first woman to earn a drag-racing license, saying, "She paved the way for people like me."[11]

Maybe Cristen Powell, or Richard Branson, or Inge Fryklund, will be the example that paves the way for you to do what you love, with all the foolish hunger you can muster.

Key **5** **IMPACT,** Not Intentions

It's not how lofty your intentions are or how much you want things to improve, it's how measurable a difference you are making in living your deepest values and achieving your biggest goals.

Obstacles are like wild animals. They are cowards but they will bluff you if they can. If they see you are afraid of them . . . they are liable to spring upon you; but if you look them squarely in the eye, they will slink out of sight.

—ORISON MARDEN

I have mentioned that my grandfather Wendell Downing experienced profound tragedy in his life. As a child of seven, he watched his sister, Helen, a year older than him, die from the effects of diabetes. She passed away in 1901. From all accounts, she was shy but intensely curious about everything around her. One thing she loved was dancing, perhaps because it helped her overcome her shyness.

My grandfather remembered her asking him to dance with her, and he remembered sometimes agreeing and often finding excuses not to.

After he grew up, completed his medical studies, and married, Wendell became father to the girl, Margaret, who would eventually become my mother. His next child, also a daughter, was named Helen. She was bright-eyed, fun-loving, and outgoing, quite different in personality from her namesake. But she, too, loved to dance, twirling around their home in a ballerina costume or stepping out the paces of an intricate waltz.

She would hold up her hands to her father when he returned home from a long physician's day, asking him to join her in this deep source of playfulness, but usually he was too tired or too preoccupied. "Another time," he would say. "I'm sure you can understand."

When his daughter Helen passed her eighth birthday, my grandfather breathed a deep sigh of relief. Her fate, it seemed, would not be the same as his sister's.

Then measles raged through their town. In those days, there was no vaccine against measles, no cure except time. Most children suffered a severe fever and headache and then recovered. But Helen didn't. She contracted spinal meningitis, and she died.

I've written elsewhere about these tragedies and some of the amazing ways in which they came to touch, directly and indirectly, the lives of untold numbers of people—probably even your life or the life of someone you know.[1]

Late in his life, my grandfather felt the full significance of the challenge we are each given to seize the right moments before they are gone forever. What he had missed he didn't want me to miss. He was the first one who encouraged me to decide what mattered most in my life, then move past that into what would be "impossible," and then do it, no matter what excuses my brain automatically dredged up to stop me, as it had him, with the small inner voices that say, "I'm too busy," or "I'm embarrassed," or "I'm sure there will be time later."

Sometimes I accompanied him, late in the evening after his

workday was ended, to visit his daughter's grave. There he would first water two trees he had planted in her memory, an oak and a spruce, and then he would place a fresh flower blossom beside her headstone.

One night he lingered. His silence, and the hushed remoteness of the cemetery, began to make me feel tired. I went back to the car, feeling a bit overwhelmed by all the graves and the quiet. I sat in the front seat to wait for him. Before long I had fallen asleep.

When I awoke, the cemetery was dark. Alarmed, I started to get out of the car to look for my grandfather—then stopped.

In the moonlight, I could see him standing perfectly still, gazing at the sky. I guessed he was searching, in the way he had taught me, to find any trace of shooting stars in the heavens.

As my eyes grew more accustomed to the darkness, I saw him look down at Helen's grave. Then he began moving slowly, almost awkwardly, shifting his weight from one foot to the other. At first, I couldn't understand what he was doing. I didn't realize what it meant.

Then I saw him take a few steps. He reached down, arms extended, his hands enfolding something smaller, invisible—the imaginary hands of a little eight-year-old partner who had joined him under the moon and stars on that gently sloping hill.

He was dancing.

ENDING YOUR BRAIN'S ENDLESS DESIRE TO POSTPONE

The thinking areas of your brain generally love lofty aspirations, well-meaning promises, and good intentions for the future.[2] Where they come up short is in turning those wishes into realities in the here and now.[3] Instead, they wait for things to be immediately relevant to your survival or well-being before paying serious attention to them. Dancing with a little girl can't possibly make a difference to those things, your brain assumes, so why bother? Maybe another day you can squeeze it in.

But the more ingrained your habits become—the more you keep

doing what you've always done instead of something new, the more you delay aiming at breakthroughs until conditions are just right or until you finally catch up on all your day-to-day chores—the more your brain locks on to those habits and defends them against all alternatives. "This is the one way I know to respond," it says, "and since I'm already good at it, I will repeat it."

Breakthroughs, as we've seen, just don't happen that way. Good intentions can float around endlessly in your upper cerebral chambers, making you feel good even though you don't actually do anything or change anything. Until you act with impact and confirm that what you're doing is making a difference right now, your intentions don't amount to anything more than a passing thought. To harness your brainpower to what's actually going to make a difference, you must keep it focused on impact, not intentions. Only when you track progress—one impact point after another—do you mobilize every ounce of your capacity to make the biggest difference.

People who regularly record specific daily and weekly results are nearly 50 percent more likely to make continued progress than those who don't.[4] They also consistently deliver higher levels of performance and ingenuity than those who don't track progress as frequently.[5]

MYTHS OF CHANGE . . . AND BRAIN REALITIES

Because many people are so interested in changing others—at work, at school, at home, in politics and religion, and at the supermarket and the shopping mall—plenty of ideas have been developed for how change can be made to happen. Most of those ideas are myths, unsubstantiated by real experience and inconsistent with how our brains really work. Some change strategies, on the other hand, have demonstrated their worth. In the chapters that follow, I'll dismantle the myths and examine what really works.

A lot of what works depends on measuring impact in ways that are just coming to be understood—ways that go by the label "multi-wave" and involve frequent tracking of signs of progress without waiting for proof of perfection. I'll show you how multiwave progress measurement can help you tap into your brain's demand for immediate, concrete feedback.

And, ultimately, nothing will work for you if it's not grounded in something that really matters. That's why I'll urge you in the concluding chapter to stay close to your soul.

"THIS IS SUCCESS, AND THERE IS NO OTHER"

Orison Marden had it made. A partner at a top New York law firm, he was admired for his legal thinking and sought out for his advice by many of America's wealthiest and most powerful leaders. His father before him had been a big success, too, earning both a law degree and a medical degree from Harvard and going on to found a publishing empire.

One day in the 1930s, as he looked out from his large corner office high above New York City, Marden wondered what his life was really adding up to. Turning his gaze north, toward Harlem, he was reminded of the people who received practically no service from the legal system. That very day, he decided to change all that. He became one of the founders of the Legal Aid Society; he personally volunteered one day each week at the Legal Aid offices in Harlem until his death in 1975; and he so mobilized the legal and political communities to stand up for the poor and the oppressed that he became known as "Mr. Legal Aid."[6]

And he didn't stop there. As the *New York Times* wrote in his obituary, "Mr. Marden's passion for obtaining justice for all spread to national and international levels."[7] Not only was he the first president of the International Legal Aid Organization, his vision also earned him the unprecedented honor of being elected president of the bar associations of New York City, New York State, and the United States. Years after his death, he was still remembered as the "model. . . of the lawyer as a responsible professional and public citizen."[8] The most prestigious award given by the Legal Aid Society is named for him, and an annual Marden Lecture, which has been delivered by Supreme Court justices and other legal notables, still commemorates his passion and calls on lawyers to honor the highest ethical standards.

All lawyers may not follow Orison Marden's example, but he set a standard that before his time was not even considered. He didn't write scholarly articles about change or sit around with his friends discussing how nice change would be—he changed things. Every Tuesday when he showed up at the Legal Aid office in Harlem, he could see the impact he was creating, and that inspired him not just to dream bigger, but to act bigger.

"My father always told me," Marden said, "that the greatest thing a man can do in this world is to make the most possible out of the stuff that has been given him. This is success, and there is no other."

The Neuroscience of Change

It is what we think we know that prevents us from learning something new.

—Claude Bernard

Last summer, a major intersection near my home was closed for nearly a month for repairs and new construction. The usual signs and barricades were set up about a mile away to alert drivers that they'd have to change their usual route: ROAD CLOSED AHEAD. LOCAL TRAFFIC ONLY. Yet every single day, what seemed like hundreds of drivers tried to pass through, going a mile out of their way only to reach the dead end and then be forced to turn around and, with increasing chagrin and concern about time lost, head back to where they'd started so they could catch the long detour.

Change is hard, and the brain always seems to figure it can find a way around it. "Maybe I should change my mind"—when is the last time you heard someone say that? Probably not recently. The brain gets very attached to its own views and habits, reacting to any inkling of change not with fluid adaptation but with increased rigidity.[1] Okay, so then we'll just use willpower to overcome that resistance and . . . and, well, doing that generally just results in the resistance becoming even stronger.[2] It's just a fact: the more we sense that a change might alter our current habits and routines, the more tenaciously we hold on to those habits and routines, and the less likely we are to notice new possibilities for improvement.[3]

The depth of our resistance to change can be seen in patients who have suffered heart problems severe enough to require surgery. Despite painful and debilitating symptoms before their surgeries and the clear understanding after surgery that death can result from failing to change their unhealthy habits, only one person in ten actually makes the lifestyle changes required for heart-healthy living!

That finding was one of those revealed at a recent IBM-sponsored conference devoted to global innovation.[4] The first challenge the luminaries at the conference took on was ending the crisis in health care, and some in the audience were anticipating that a dream team of experts might reveal some stunning scientific or technological advance, maybe an intricate microscopic redesign of the human genome, that would make everything better overnight. Instead, the attendees learned that despite all our society's advances, the root causes of the health crisis haven't changed in half a century. The founder of Global Medical Forum, Dr. Raphael Levey, reported, "When I was in medical school [fifty years ago], many articles demonstrated that 80 percent of the health-care budget was consumed by five behavioral issues, and that's still where we are." (The five issues are, of course, smoking, excessive stress, too much alcohol, overeating and unhealthy foods, and insufficient exercise.)

There is great truth in the saying that the more things change, the more they stay the same. That's your brain's goal: to stay the same, regardless of what you want. And it's remarkably good at achieving that unless you get out of your own way.

The first thing to do is to sidestep eight common myths that often derail change.

EIGHT CHANGE MYTHS

Myth #1: Fear motivates change

The truth is, fear usually backfires. Real, immediate fear—stimulated by a natural disaster, for example—gets us up and moving, but concocted fear does the opposite. When we try to scare ourselves or others into changing, what actually happens inside our nervous system is that we go numb or fatalistic or rebellious against the change, and the brain just hopes it will all go away. We instinctively and persistently deny bad things that might happen to us—something known as stonewalling.[5]

Myth #2: Crisis motivates change

Crisis, a corollary of fear, almost invariably entrenches old habits, which get repeated longer, harder, faster, and louder. We just lose all our energy for change, particularly when faced with one supposed crisis after another, as many businesses are today. We might pretend we're worried, but the brain is actually telling us to just relax, we've heard all this before, and soon it will all blow over.

Myth #3: Giving people facts and analysis about their situation motivates change

Facts and analysis don't move us. The brain is guided by stories and metaphors that we have evolved to make sense of the world and our place in it, not by facts.[6] As a leading scientist explains: "Neuroscience tells us that each of the concepts we have—the long-term concepts that structure how we think—is instantiated in the synapses of the brain. Concepts are not things that can be changed just by someone telling us a fact. We may be presented with facts, but for us to make sense of them, they have to fit what is already in the synapses of the brain. Otherwise, facts go in and then they go right back out. They are not heard, or they are not accepted as facts, or they mystify us: Why would anyone have said that? Then we label the fact as irrational, crazy, or stupid."[7]

In *The Heart of Change,* John Kotter points out, "Behavior change happens mostly by speaking to people's feelings . . . In highly successful change efforts, people find ways to help others see the problems or solutions in ways that influence emotions, not just thought."[8]

Facts are at best secondary factors in making change.[9] If change won't make a difference to your most important narratives, you won't put any real energy into it.

Myth #4: Small, gradual change works best

Sometimes, as you've seen in this book, certain small changes can have significant power to change your behavior and accelerate progress toward your goals. But the vast majority of run-of-the-mill small changes generally don't have enough immediate payoff to persuade your brain that it should pay attention. Major, integrated, farsighted change—such as the open-space breakthroughs we considered earlier in this book—drives self-regulation to advance into a better future despite current stresses and distractions and old habits, influencing the parts of the brain responsible for arousal, engagement, and follow-through and producing faster, more exciting results.[10]

Myth #5: Rewards motivate change

The idea that competition and reward are effective motivators forms the bedrock of our educational, economic, and managerial systems. Problem is, there's virtually no data to support it. Not regarding traditional rewards, anyway, such as money or glory or making others lose so you can win.[11] Changing is based more solidly on going after what is deeply compelling to you personally, because, as mentioned throughout this book, doing that taps into emotional experiential memory and significantly increases your odds for success.[12] Changing is based solidly on values, pride, skills, and intrinsic drive toward achieving "impossible" positive outcomes that connect with an emotional charge to your own best future.

Myth #6: Having a class on change motivates change

I once saw a cartoon in which a man stood at a crossroads, with two directional signs before him. One sign, with an arrow pointing to one of the roads, read "Heaven." The other sign, pointing to the other road, read "Workshops on Getting to Heaven." There are many times when just knowing what you want is far more powerful than having someone tell you about it.

Most of our learning occurs in ways that are called "implicit"— the neurons that construct learning fire and wire without our even being aware of it. "Explicit" learning, of the kind that happens in a classroom, has far less power. Testing new ideas and paying attention to their impacts is much more important and valuable than listening to someone talk about them. Most implicit learning does not occur in the topmost layers of your brain but mainly in the limbic areas toward the center and bottom of your brain, including areas we've talked about earlier that help you rapidly absorb and apply new learning: the second brain in the gut, the heart brain, the basal ganglia, the anterior cingulate cortex, and the hippocampus.[13, 14]

Myth #7: "Just do it" motivates change

While action can change attitude, as we've discussed, you need some kind of meaningful incentive for sustaining change. For example, measurement motivates deeper and more-lasting change, as we'll see in the next chapter.

If you take the phrase "just do it" to mean "do it yourself," you should also recognize that rugged individualism pales in comparison to collaboration when it comes to making change work.[15]

Myth #8: Having a "plan B" motivates change

It's good to know that failing at change won't be the end of the world, but we're way too entrenched in making sure we have what I call a "back door"—an easy way to back out that lets us shirk responsibility for change instead of evolving it as we go forward. Make your escape too easy and your brain will always have one foot out that back door, watering down your commitment to truly testing ideas that could turn out to be better.

HOW REAL CHANGE HAPPENS

From the fact that 90 percent of heart-surgery patients don't change their habits significantly, we learn a lot about how change doesn't work. But from some dramatic interventions with heart-surgery candidates, we acquire an amazing blueprint for change that does work.[16]

In 1993, Dr. Dean Ornish, a professor of medicine at the University of California, San Francisco, set up a clinical trial in which 333 patients with severely clogged arteries were helped to dramatically change the way they lived. The patients attended twice-weekly group support sessions led by a psychologist and received instruction in a variety of healthy practices. They were given help with quitting smoking and adopting a healthy diet.

The trial lasted for only a year. But after three years, more than 75 percent of the patients had stayed with their lifestyle changes, avoiding the bypass or angioplasty surgeries they had been headed for.[17]

Dr. Ornish's program succeeded where other approaches fail in large part because it rejected conventional-wisdom myths about change and instead applied neuroscientifically sound change principles. All these years, physicians had been trying to motivate patients with facts about their desperate straits or with the outright fear of death, and it wasn't working. For a week or so after a heart attack or bypass surgery, patients were scared enough to do whatever their doctors said. But death was too daunting to think about, so their denial or stonewalling would increase, and they'd revert to their old habits and stay there, unchanged.

Informing people who are lonely and stressed—and often depressed—that they're going to live longer if they quit smoking or start exercising or change their diet just isn't inspiring: Who really wants to live longer when they're in emotional distress?

Ornish changed the entire context of change, helping each patient see a new vision of the joy of living, convincing them they could feel better and enjoy an unprecedented richness of living, not just hang on a little longer. Not just convincing them—showing them how they could once again enjoy the things that make daily life joyful, like getting slim and strong again, making love, or even gardening or taking long strolls without the pain caused by their disease. "Joy is a more powerful motivator than fear," he says.[18]

He recognized that bold and comprehensive changes are often simpler and more effective for people to make than small, dabbling, closed-space ones. He saw, for example, that when people try merely to tweak their diets, they lose twice: They feel deprived, alienated, and hungry because they aren't eating everything they want or are used to eating, but they aren't making daring enough changes to immediately see or feel any real benefit either in their energy or their weight, blood pressure, resting heart rate, and cholesterol. The heart patients on Ornish's sweeping program saw immediate and often dramatic results, reporting a 91 percent decrease in occurrence of chest pain in the first thirty days alone.[19] "These rapid improvements are a powerful motivator," Ornish says. "When people who have had so much chest pain that they can't work, or make love, or even walk across the street without intense suffering find that they are able to do all of those things without pain in only a few weeks, then they often say, 'These are choices worth making!' "[20]

Nearly two-thirds of patients who are prescribed cholesterol-lowering "statin" drugs to cut their cholesterol levels following bypass surgery stop taking them within one year.[21] It would seem that taking a pill wouldn't be that difficult a change to make. Yet Ornish contends that patients stop taking the drug because it doesn't actually make them feel any better. So here's further evidence that *emotion*—feeling well, having more energy—matters more to effective change than it's given credit for, and big sweeping changes tend to work way better than small ones.

The support groups made a big difference, too, showing the folks in Ornish's program that they weren't in this alone, not replacing the need for individual willpower but strengthening each person's ability to call on his or her willpower.

AND THEN A MIRACLE HAPPENS

Some time ago, I was in my first day as a consultant to a company that wanted to accomplish some big changes. I like to wander around unannounced and get a feel for the culture of places where I work, and as I did so on that day I came to a cubicle that had a hand-drawn cartoon posted on its outside wall. It showed two people staring at a sign that read:

Step 1: Goal.
Step 2:
Step 3: Change for the Better.

One of the people staring at the sign was saying to the other, "What's step two?" The other was answering, "A miracle happens."

New tools for change, backed by measures of what's working and what isn't, can seem like miracles when they are tailored to your own goals and needs and backed up with effective measurement. Dr. Ornish's work, confirmed by my own team's research on emotional intelligence and change, reveals several crucial factors.

Imagine the best outcome in advance. You will recall that when you vividly envision a change in your behavior, your brain's prefrontal cortex and the auditory cortex region known as Broca's Area fire up new neural pathways that help you be more successful at making the change.[22]

Envisioning a new action or state in vivid, multisensory detail will fire the same brain circuits and cells that are actually involved in doing that activity or making that change.[23] A vivid link between feeling the best outcome and imagining it happening can fire the same brain circuits involved in making the change work. The new brain circuitry appears to actually preshadow the change itself—establishing and strengthening new connections you will need to make the change. This can significantly increase your chances for success with the change.[24] With any potential change, connect the feeling of the positive upside of why it is important to you and your future to these brain centers, because then all kinds of uncommonly accessed inner reserves are mobilized to help move you through the steps of change.

Get as many neurons firing in concert as you can. Big energized change is better than incremental change. So when you decide to change, make sure it's something that emotionally connects with your goals, accept the fact that it will tilt your brain systems out of the ordinary but that it's worth doing, and then wholeheartedly commit to doing it. If you keep the back door open, you'll likely use it. Make sure the change relates to your most powerful lines of talent and energy, so you can move forward right away and create strong, quick, positive results.

Dabbling with change is most tolerable to the brain areas that are deeply primed to block anything that alters homeostasis and the status quo. But this surface action rarely amounts to much. A little bit of this, a little bit of that, and the neurons are firing all over the place, without coordinated alignment in a clear direction for the change. Pay close attention to yourself as you interact with life and its challenges and ask yourself questions like "Is this really the best way to move toward accomplishing my goal?" Then each action you take will link your neuronal connections toward your best outcome.

Team up. Elsewhere in this book, I've encouraged you to announce your change intentions to others and enlist all the others you can find who can help you do what you intend and do it as well as you can. Ornish's work reinforces the importance of those actions.

Stay hot and cool at the same time. Get something happening that shows your brain that *this* change is really worth doing. Otherwise, you won't activate your brain's emotional experiential memory to make lasting change possible.[25] Besides, unless a change captures your heart and fires your enthusiasm—your joy for life—chances are you won't be able to pour your talents and full attention into it, and the change won't work or stick.[26] So give every potential change a temperature reading. If there's no emotional heat, skip it. At the same time, you want to stay cool, personally. Whenever we're stressed, the body secretes the hormone cortisol, which lasts longer than any adrenaline you might get from excitement about your goal and also interferes with new learning.[27]

19
What You Measure, Matters

Wisdom is knowing what to do; virtue is doing it.
—DAVID STARR JORDAN

In the midst of life's expanding complexities and the overloading of nearly everyone's calendar and to-do lists, it's more vital than ever to ask, "What works?" To answer that crucial question, you need measurements. Not just good measurements, but ones that hook your brain on progress and steady improvement.

People who consistently achieve their goals in life and work set up and use those kinds of measures.[1] When properly structured and applied, measurement overcomes the deleterious brain reactions and behavior ruts we've talked about, and it speeds your progress toward your goals.[2] If something is working, you'll know it, and then you have every reason to keep modifying and testing it to make it better.

It's when things aren't working that your brain gets in your way the most. Either it pulls back, says "Never again!" and resists *all* change, or it lands right in a new rut, repeating what isn't working in the hope that determined repetition will improve it sooner or later. That is a waste of time, energy, and impact.[3] The right kinds of measures allow you to see what's not working quickly—before your brain overreacts—and move on to trying something else.

PROGRESS, NOT PERFECTION

Ongoing regular measurement—hourly, daily, and then summarized in weekly progress reports—works best.[4] Anything less frequent is too far off from this moment, this hour, to be compelling enough to engage the parts of your brain that drive you to change your behavior toward a goal.[5] If your brain is permitted to wait for a faraway measurement it has lots of excuses to do little if anything differently.[6]

The traditional model for measuring change has been to check progress against one or two overall indicators. This measurement strategy looks for big chunks of change. But big chunks of change only result from an accumulation of moment-by-moment changes, big and small. What your brain needs to see in order to remain engaged is progress, not perfection, and what you need to make that kind of progress is frequent snapshots that give actionable feedback about the true trajectory and rate of your change.[7]

People who assess, revise, and tailor their actions every day and every week to make them more effective improve themselves forward, instead of just trying to repeat themselves forward.[8] Studies indicate that those who regularly record specific aspirations and track daily results are 32 percent more likely to make progress than those who don't.[9] There are lots of chances in a day to do the small things that create forward momentum. Daily and weekly measures significantly increase self-awareness and demand increased ingenuity, collaboration, and changes now, not someday.

JUST MEASURE IT

Here are the steps for effective, motivating measurement. After a while, you'll start taking these steps automatically.

First, define the types of change that will mean the most to you. Make sure you stay keenly aware of your biggest open-space goals, the ones that are most personally and emotionally meaningful to you. In the next section of this chapter, I'll show you a lot of possible measures that free time and energy to make more progress toward those goals, with many of these measures drawing upon themes from earlier parts of this book.

Second, start every day by glancing at your measures. This keeps them fresher in your mind as ongoing reminders throughout the day.

Third, review your measures every evening. Assess what worked and think about how to improve on that. Dump what didn't work and try something different.

Every Friday, reflect on the week. Share your reflections with a friend, mentor, or colleague who also shares his or her reflections with you. You can do this in whatever way works best for you—in an e-mail or a word-processed document, by phone, or face-to-face.

Each Saturday morning, review your measures, asking whether they might be revised to more accurately reflect your intentions, and also whether there are other measures you might want to add because you have recently realized their particular significance for you.

First thing each Monday, share encouragement and feedforward insights with others to support their distinctive individual progress, and ask for similar input from the other person.

A whole team or family can join together for this, regularly collecting progress markers and sharing them openly. Doing so deepens respect for each other, because you get to see some of the distinctive ways we each come at life and make a difference as we grow. It speeds new learning and sparks collaborative ideas. It also creates a kind of constructive conscience-nudging to keep on instead of languishing or just hoping.

Writing in a personal journal on a daily or regular basis also helps with this process, reinforcing positive experiences and encouraging reflection about them. Regular journaling has been shown to make a surprisingly significant contribution to shedding unproductive habits and acquiring a positive, constructive stance toward change.[10] Journaling works so well because it can bypass the thinking brain with all its rationalizations and excuses and go straight to where your best instincts about betterment reside.

YOUR MEASUREMENT MENU

Here is a list of some measurements you might want to consider. There are others, too: the key is to be specific and discover what's working or not working and how to move forward better and faster toward your open-space goals, today and this week.

Increase energy. How did you increase and sustain your level of energy and engagement all day long?

Save time. Where did you save time? How much time?

Reprioritize focus. How did you redirect the minutes or hours you saved into higher priority areas?

Reprioritize energy. Where, specifically, did you redirect your new-found sources of energy into higher priority areas?

Activate emotional experiential memory. What, specifically, motivated you to take more positive actions to move forward?

Move beyond old habits. How did you notice old habits or rigid mind-sets and change them? How did this help you?

Expand your ingenuity. How did you stretch to test new views and approaches, and what worked?

Apply new automatic drivers. What small, specific actions prompted increased drive toward your open-space goals?

Increase teamwork. How did you collaborate more effectively or support others in hitting their own higher targets?

Make a bigger difference. What was the most exceptional contribution you made or the most exceptional thing you accomplished?

Bring out more of the best in yourself. In what specific ways did you change or grow most?

This weekly measurement approach works because it focuses your attention on what's now and what's next. It provokes you to *test* and *act* your way into new and improved behaviors that turn open-space goals into reality, rather than struggling to *think* your way into these goals, which rarely succeeds on its own.[11] Your actions generate real experiences that help you quickly and accurately learn what works, what doesn't, and why.[12] It takes commitment to monitor and shape your impact, not just intentions, every week. But these measurement minutes are golden. Accept no excuses. As I once wrote on an index card I keep propped up alongside the clock in my office:

> *People say, "I wish I had time for that."*
> *But in the time it takes to*
> > *complain about time*
> > *race against time*
> > *worry about time*
> > *You've already lost it.*
> *Stop wishing for time*
> > *and start measuring progress*
> > *toward your biggest goals*
> > *today, this week.*
> *What you measure, matters.*

20

Stay Close
to the Soul

*Something we were withholding made us weak, until we found it
was ourselves.*

—ROBERT FROST

I remember doing some neuroscience research in the library of the
University of Michigan Medical School many years ago. I gathered a
big pile of books from the stacks and headed for an empty seat at one
of the tables there. As I sat down and steeled myself for some heavy
reading, a nearby book caught my eye. It was open to a page that
showed two photographs. I pulled it over to me so I could look at it
more closely. On the top half of the page there was a photograph of
newborns in a maternity ward—beaming wide-eyed miracles, brimming with the full energy of life's potential.

The bottom half of the page showed a haunting image of passen-
gers on a packed New York subway train, staring numbly ahead, eyes
devoid of miracles or energy or potential, braced for the train to stop,
for work to begin, or just waiting to get the day over with, hurtling
with the sway of the car and clacking of the tracks toward the ends of
their lives.

Two words were printed at the bottom of the page. They asked
simply, "What happened?"

We each began life as one of those newborn miracles of potential.

Between then and now is history. But what happens next is not solely in the hands of habit or fate or the crush of the crowd; it's also in the power of what you dare to imagine and do.

ON INDIVIDUAL HUMAN NATURE, *YOURS*

The poet e. e. cummings wrote, "To be nobody but yourself when the world is trying its best night and day to make you somebody else is to fight the hardest battle any human being will fight."[1] That is, of course, to be your *best* self, evolving.

I have always thought that the slogan that the vibrant, life-loving entrepreneur Dewey Weber selected for his surfboard company said it best: Stay Close to the Soul. It's easy to get so busy doing your job, or just living your life, that you can forget the bigger reason for your job and your life. No matter how many forces try to make you be like everyone else, the scientific truth is that in all of the earth's history there has never been another person exactly like you, and there never will be again.[2]

The dancer Martha Graham expressed this singularity with unmatched eloquence, writing:

> There is a vitality, a life force, an energy, a quickening that is translated through you into action, and because there is only one of you in all of time, this expression is unique. And if you block it, it will never exist through any other medium and be lost. The world will not have it. It is not your business to determine how good it is, nor how valuable, nor how it compares with other expressions. It is your business to keep it yours, clearly and directly, to keep the channel open.... You have to keep open and aware directly to the urge that motivates you. Keep the channel open.[3]

So it all comes down to you, just as it always has, and just as it always will. At your passing some day, the deeper question will never be "How did she die?" but rather "How did she live?"

A BROTHER'S LOVE

Of course, when you stay close to your soul, you're close to others' souls as well. One of the experiences that often reminds me of this happened two summers before my grandfather Downing died. After his evening hospital rounds, we had driven to a nearby park. Two young boys were playing nearby. One was about nine or ten; the other, not more than five, had a deformed leg and arm. As I watched he seemed to be playing wholeheartedly without paying much attention to his limitations.

A brand-new Cadillac drove by the park. It belonged to one of the other surgeons at my grandfather's hospital. The young boys were admiring the sleek lines of the shiny car with the sparkling silver wheels and purring engine as it pulled into a parking space not far from the one occupied by my grandfather's old Buick compact, rusted in the door panels and fenders from the salt on the snowy roads in the winter. "It works just fine," he would say.

The boys ran up to the Cadillac as the surgeon and his wife were getting out to take an evening stroll in the park. In the still air, we could overhear the conversation that followed.

"That's a nice car, mister," the older boy said. His younger brother was up close, admiring the car, peering into the windows, and then tracing the lines of the car's fins with his fingers just an inch away as he walked back toward the taillights.

"Yes, it's mine," answered the surgeon, watching the younger brother warily to be sure he didn't touch anything.

"How much did it cost?" asked the boy.

"I don't think that's any of your business," the surgeon answered gruffly. "I work hard to own such a fine automobile. Now move along, and don't touch my car."

"I'm just dreaming, that's all," the boy said. "Someday I'll work hard, too."

The two boys walked slowly back toward us. "Someday," said the older boy, putting his arm around his younger brother, "I'm going to make enough money to buy you a car just like that."

It's one thing to dream of prosperity; it's another to wish to give it to your brother. The search for larger meaning is innate in us,[4] if we sense deeply enough to notice it, and it drives us to make choices that make a difference, not just a living. About halfway through *Man of La Mancha,* Don Quixote says, "Take a deep breath of your life and consider how it should be lived."

Here are four close-to-the-soul questions about how you live your life that you might ask yourself from time to time. From this moment forward:

1. In what specific new ways can you influence your *family* for the better, compared with what your family would be like if you had never been part of it?

2. In what specific new ways can you influence your *school* for the better—as a student, a teacher, or a parent—compared with what your school would be like if you had never been involved?

3. In what specific new ways can you influence your *organization* for the better, compared with what your organization would be like if you had never worked there?

4. How can you influence your *community* for the better, compared with what your community would be like if you had never lived there?

WHAT'S NEXT: *YOUR* TOOLS

For a long time, scientists asserted that humans were the only species to make and use tools. Even though some recent observations have placed some other species into that category in a very limited way, it is generally true that making and using tools is part of our near-unique humanness.

Using a tool involves anticipating a future different from the present. As Kenneth Norris has written: "Each time we use a tool, we make a set of predictions to ourselves: 'If I turn this screwdriver so far, it will release the window screen, and if I don't step aside now, it will hit me on the head.' We are predictive animals par excellence, and nearly everything we do, from our technology to our language, involves looking at time spans longer than the moment just before us."[5]

Notice that the brain's negativity is hard at work in Norris's example: If I change this, something might hit me on the head. At the same time, the best parts of the brain—the parts that move us forward toward better things—are at work, too, having recognized that replacing the window screen is important, maybe so the bugs don't get in, or maybe taking it down and putting up storm windows because it's time to prepare for winter.

That tension in the brain between changing nothing and building for a different, better future is always with us. How you manage it—what tools you use and how you apply them—determines how close you come to achieving the best of what's possible for you. And achieving your best is the direct route to happiness and satisfaction. As Abraham Maslow wrote, "To be ultimately at peace, a person must keep becoming all that he can potentially become."[6] T. S. Eliot hauntingly described the beauty of that process:

> *We shall not cease from exploration*
> *And the end of all our exploring*
> *Will be to arrive where we started*
> *And know the place for the first time.*[7]

The five keys in this book are a place to begin your own explorations. Take the tools that work for you, use them to shape every moment into something better, and let go of the rest. Let others lead small lives, but not you. Let others argue over small things, but not you. Let others cry over small hurts, but not you. Let others leave their future in someone else's hands, but not you.

1+1=11

When Dick Hoyt's son Rick was born forty-three years ago, something went wrong; he was born brain-damaged and unable to control his arms or legs. When Rick was nine months old, doctors told his parents, "He'll be a vegetable the rest of his life. Put him in an institution." They didn't listen. They cared for him, integrated him into their family (which includes two other sons), and helped him communicate through a computer whose cursor he controls by tapping a lever with the side of his head.

When a classmate of Rick's became paralyzed and the community held a charity run to raise money for his care, Rick sent his father a message: "Dad, I want to do that." Dick, who says that back then he was a "porker" who had never run more than a mile, agreed. He pushed Rick, in his wheelchair, the five-mile length of the race.

It took Dick two weeks to recover, but an amazing journey began when he received a typed message from his son that said, "Dad, when we were running, it felt like I wasn't disabled anymore!" Dick committed himself to bringing as much relief and joy to his son as he possibly could. As of today, he has pushed his son in 85 marathons—26.2 miles each. They have competed in 212 triathlons, which include a lengthy run plus a long swim and bicycle ride, all in the same day. Dick tows Rick in a dinghy for the swims and carries him in a seat on his handlebars for the biking.

Dick has also pulled his son on cross-country skis, climbed mountains with Rick on his back, and crossed the entire United States on a bicycle with Rick on the handlebars. Their best marathon time, recorded in 1992, was thirty-five minutes off the world record.

Rick graduated from high school, and then from Boston College, and he now works at Boston College's computer laboratory, helping to develop a system through which paralyzed people can control devices using their eye movements. This year he and his father completed their twenty-fourth Boston Marathon.

Father and son together call themselves Team Hoyt. Rick has written, "My dad is Father of the Century. Once he sets out to do something, Dad sticks to it whatever it is, until it is done."[8] He might be that, but it's as a team that they inspire each other, and through that, inspire the rest of us. The letters they receive every day are extraordinary[9]:

"Your team has redefined the word LOVE in my dictionary."

"I have never witnessed such heroism. I have served my country as a combat infantryman in Vietnam and still feel that all I witnessed over there pales compared to your devotion and commitment to your son."

"I am only 17 and you have been the only one who has emotionally been able to get through to me. I believe that if you get through to one person you have succeeded, and I just wanted to tell you that you have got through to me."

IMPOSSIBLE IS NOT A FACT

There can only be one Team Hoyt, but we all have it in us to achieve what others think we can't—and to inspire those we come into contact with.

As Winston Churchill said, "We make a living from what we get. We make a life from what we give." Easy to say, of course, but it's a deep and enduring challenge to do. It takes defiance—defiance of norms, of habit, and of much of what your own brain wants. It also takes turning inward, asking what giving your best to the world means to you—and then living it.

More than twenty years ago, I jotted some notes about this challenge in my daybook under the heading "Achieving What Everyone Else Thinks You Can't." Through the years, I have passed these observations along to leaders at a number of organizations, and now I offer them to you:

> *Impossible is not a fact.*
> *It's an attitude.*
> *It's someone else's opinion.*
> *It's something your brain makes up.*
> *It's temporary.*

It's a dare.
It's an open door.

It's up to you to lose
The fear
Groupthink
Yes-people
Pretenders
Old habits
Shoetop gazers
The happy medium
Plan B

It's up to you to defy
Stereotypes
Conformity
Prejudice
Narrow-mindedness
The status quo
Politics
The odds
Doubt

Because what everyone else thinks is impossible, isn't.

Notes

Chapter 1. What Does Your Brain Want, Anyway?

1. See, for example, B. Grind, "Garden of Eden," *Entelechy: Mind and Culture* (2004); G. J. Armelagos, "Human Evolution and the Evolution of Disease," *Ethnic Disease* 1(1991): 21–25; and S. B. Eaton, and M. Konner, *The Paleolithic Prescription* (New York: HarperCollins, 1988).

2. M. D. Gershon, *The Second Brain* (New York: HarperCollins, 1999); S. Blakeslee, "Complex and Hidden Brain in Gut Makes Stomachaches and Butterflies," *New York Times* (Jan. 23, 1996).

3. For more about the heart-brain, see, for example, J. Armour, and J. Ardell, eds., *Neurocardiology* (New York: Oxford University Press, 2004); D. Childre, and H. Martin, *The HeartMath Solution* (New York: HarperCollins, 1999); Institute of HeartMath (www.heartmath.org); and R. McCraty, M. Atkinson, and W. A. Tiller, "New Electrophysiological Correlates Associated with Intentional Heart Focus," *Subtle Energies* 4(3)(1995): 251–268. See also J. J. Lynch, *The Language of the Heart* (New York: Basic Books, 1985). For more on the brain in the intestines, see Gershon, *Second Brain*.

4. Michael Eisner and Tony Schwartz, *Work in Progress: Risking Failure, Surviving Success* (New York: Hyperion, 2002). Digital download available at https://secure.palmdigitalmedia.com/product/book/excerpt/5393.

5. J. LeDoux, *Synaptic Self* (New York: Viking, 2002): 246–247; J. Zull, *The Art of Changing the Brain* (Sterling, VA: Stylus, 2002).

6. G. J. Mogeson, et al (*Progress in Neurobiology* 14(1980): 69–97; R. Nieuwenhuys, *Chemoarchitecture of the Brain* (Berlin: Springer-Verlag, 1985).

7. The "fight-or-flight" response is discussed in many places. Among the more entertaining of those discussions is Robert Sapolsky's *Why Zebras Don't Get Ulcers* (New York: Owl Books, 2004).

8. A Einstein, *Ideas and Opinions* (New York: Wings, 1988).

9. See, for example, K. Haberlandt, "Memory for Skills," in *Human Memory: Exploration and Applications*, chap. 5 (Needham Heights MA: Allyn & Bacon, 1999).

10. John Roach, "Brain Study Shows Why Revenge is Sweet," *National Geographic* (Aug. 27, 2004), available at http://news.nationalgeographic.com/news/2004/08/0827_040827_punishment.html.

11. See, for example, Robert L. Holtz, "Brain's 'God Module' May Affect Religious Intensity," available at http://www.iol.ie/~afifi/BICNews/Health/health19.htm.

12. See http://www.nimh.nih.gov/press/prworkaholicmonkey.cfm.

13. Timothy Ferris, *The Mind's Sky: Human Intelligence in a Cosmic Context* (New York: Bantam Books, 1992): 88. See also Michael Gazzaniga, *Mind Matters* (Boston: Houghton Mifflin, 1988).

14. See, for example, John Kotter, *The Heart of Change: Real-Life Stories of How People Change Their Organizations* (Boston: Harvard Business School Press, 2002).

15. LeDoux, *Synaptic Self:* 253.

16. For more on the cancer link, see http://news-service.stanford.edu/news/2003/october8/psychiatric.html.

17. R. L. Gregory, *Eye and Brain,* 5th Ed. (Princeton, NJ: Princeton University Press, 1997).

Key 1. *Direction*, Not Motion

1. Robert Ornstein, *The Evolution of Consciousness* (Englewood Cliffs, NJ: Prentice-Hall, 1991).

2. Robert Ornstein and Paul Ehrlich, *New World New Mind* (New York: Touchstone, 1989).

3. Paul C. Light, *Sustaining Innovation* (San Francisco: Jossey-Bass, 1998).

4. E. Jaques, *Timespan and Performance* (Falls Church, VA: Cason Hall, 1990); A. R. Luria, *Working Brain: An Introduction to Neuropsychology* (New York: Basic Books, 1973); W. J. Freeman, *How Brains Make Up Their Mind* (New York: Columbia University Press, 2000).

5. M. C. Diamond, *Enriching Heredity: The Impact of Environment on the Anatomy of the Brain* (New York: Free Press, 1988); M. Diamond and J. Hopson, *Magic Trees of the Mind* (New York: Plume, 1999).

6. Jeffrey Kluger, "Robert Goddard," *Time,* available at http://www.time.com/time/time100/scientist/profile/goddard.html.

7. Ibid.

Chapter 2. Good and Great Are the Enemies of Possible

1. For more about the pain in my grandfather's life and how it affected him (and me), see my writings on *Promises to Keep,* available at www.RobertKCooper.com.

2. See http://www.wiu.edu/users/mfbhl/wiu/henry.htm.

3. Masters Forum, Dec. 8, 2004.

4. B. Zander, Masters Forum, Feb. 13, 2003. Also see his book *The Art of Possibility* (New York: Penguin, 2002).

5. M. Le Poncin, *Brain Fitness* (New York: Ballantine, 1992): 65; M. Y. Zhang, et al. "The Prevalence of Dementia and Alzheimer's Disease in Shanghai, China: Impact of Age, Gender, and Education," *Annals of Neurology* 27(4)(Apr. 1990): 428–437.

6. See, for example, M. C. Diamond, *Enriching Heredity: The Impact of Environment on the Anatomy of the Brain* (New York: Free Press, 1988); and K. W. Schaie, "Late Life Potential and Cohort Differences in Mental Abilities," in M. Perlmutter, ed., *Late Life Potential* (Washington, DC: Gerontological Society of America, 1990): 43.

7. J. Zull, *The Art of Changing the Brain* (Sterling, VA: Stylus, 2002); J. LeDoux, *Synaptic Self* (New York: Viking, 2002).

8. See, for example, T. Lewis, F. Amini, and R. Lannon, *A General Theory of Love* (New York: Random House, 2000).

9. M. Storch, "Taking the Reins," *Scientific American Mind* 16(2)(2005): 88–89.

10. G. Kreiman, C. Koch, and I. Fried, "Imagery Neurons in the Human Brain," *Nature* 408(2000): 357–361.

11. M. Diamond, "Response of the Brain to Enrichment," *News from the Neurosciences* (March 2005).

12. Sharon Begley, "Scans of Monks' Brains Show Meditation Alters Structure, Functioning," *Wall Street Journal* (Nov. 5, 2004): B1.

13. Jim Holt, "The Way We Live Now," *The New York Times Magazine* (May 8, 2005): 11, available at http://www.nytimes.com/2005/05/08/magazine/08WWLN.html?pagewanted=all.

14. C. Carter, et al., "How the Brain Gets Ready to Perform," lecture at the 30th Annual Meeting of the Society of Neuroscience, New Orleans (Nov. 2000).

15. "The Human Brain—Imagine Increased Muscle Strength," available at Franklin Institute Online (sln.fi.edu/brain/exercise/neuromuscular.html); *Washington Post* (Dec. 18, 2001): HE03.

16. See http://www.newscientist.com/channel/being-human/mg18625011.900.

17. P. R. Lawrence and N. Nohria, *Driven: How Human Nature Shapes Our Choices* (San Francisco: Jossey-Bass, 2002); D. Amen, *Change Your Brain, Change Your Life* (New York: Times Books, 1998); A. Damasio, *Descartes' Error* (New York: Grosset/Putnam, 1994); A. Bechard, et al., "Deciding Advantageously Before Knowing the Advantageous Strategy," *Science* 275(1997): 1293.

18. Lawrence and Nohria, *Driven;* Amen, *Change Your Brain, Change Your Life.*

19. P. Kennedy, *The Rise and Fall of the Great Powers* (New York: Vintage, 1989).

20. For an in-depth review of this theme, see D. Sull, *Revival of the Fittest* (Boston Harvard Business School Press, 2003): 45–48.

21. See http://seattletimes.nwsource.com/html/opinion/2001798585_suncities23.html.

22. D. Tapscott, *The Digital Economy* (New York: McGraw-Hill, 1995): "Of the companies on that prestigious list [Fortune 500] in 1955, 70% are now out of business. Of the companies on the 1979 list, fully 40% no longer exist."

23. W. C. Kim and R. Mauborgne, *Blue Ocean Strategy* (Boston: Harvard Business School Press, 2005).

24. Ibid.

25. J. LeDoux, *The Emotional Brain* (New York: Putnam, 1997).

26. D. Goleman, et al., *Primal Leadership* (Cambridge, MA: Harvard Business School Press, 2003).

27. B. R. Kada, in J. Field, et al., eds., *Handbook of Physiology* (Washington, DC: American Physiological Society, 1960); R. L. Isaacson, *The Limbic Sysytem* (NY: Plenum Press, 1982); P. D. MacLean, *The Triune Brain in Evolution* (New York: Plenum Press, 1990); LeDoux, *Emotional Brain;* LeDoux, *Synaptic Self.*

28. Storch, "Taking the Reins."

29. Lawrence and Nohria, *Driven.*

30. See, for example, D. N. Sull, "The Dynamics of Standing Still," *Business History Review* 73(3)(1999): 430–464.

31. S. Finkelstein, *Why Smart Executives Fail* (New York: Penguin Portfolio, 2003).

32. R. Passingham, *The Frontal Lobes and Voluntary Action* (Oxford University Press, 1995); R. Restak, *Mozart's Brain and the Fighter Pilot* (New York: Harmony, 2001); LeDoux, *Synaptic Self.*

33. E. De Bono, *New Thinking for the New Millennium* (New York: Viking, 1999): 75.

34. J. Ratey, ed., *The Neuropsychiatry of Personality Disorders* (Cambridge, MA: Blackwell Science, 1995): 153.

35. J. Fuster, *The Prefrontal Cortex,* 3rd ed. (Philadelphia: Lippincott-Raven, 1997); Amen, *Change Your Brain, Change Your Life.*

36. Carter et al., "How the Brain Gets Ready to Perform."

37. C. Sansone and J. M. Harackiewicz, eds., *Intrinsic and Extrinsic Motivation* (New York: Academic Press, 2000): 48.

38. See, for example, W. C. Kim and R. Marborgne, and Kimand Mauborgne, *Blue Ocean Strategy.*

39. R. K. Cooper, *The Other 90%.* (New York: Crown Business, 2001).

40. See, for example, A. Kohn, *No Contest: The Case Against Competition,* rev. ed. (Boston: Houghton Mifflin, 1992); J. F. Moore, *The Death of Competition* (New York: HarperBusiness, 1996); and R. J. Sternberg, *Successful Intelligence* (New York: Simon & Schuster, 1996).

41. See Cooper, *The Other 90%.* See also C. A. O'Reilly and J. Pfeffer, *Hidden Value* (Boston: Harvard Business School Press, 2000); A. Kohn, *No Contest: The Case Against Competition* (Boston: Houghton Mifflin, 1992); and J. Pfeffer, and R. I. Sutton, *The Knowing-Doing Gap* (Boston: Harvard Business School Press, 2000).

42. J. Pfeffer and R. I. Sutton, "When Internal Competition Turns Friends Into Enemies," in *The Knowing-Doing Gap* (Boston: Harvard Business School Press, 2000).

43. K. France, "Competitive vs. Non-Competitive Thinking During Exercise: Effects on Norepinephrine Levels," paper presented at the Annual Meeting of the American Psychological Association (Aug. 1984).

44. Ibid.
45. Kohn, *No Contest:* 55.
46. See C. Jones and J. O'Brien, *Mistakes That Worked* (New York: Doubleday, 1994); C. Jones, *Accidents Happen* (New York: Delacorte, 1998); and C. Thimmesh, and M. Sweet, *Girls Think of Everything* (Boston: Houghton Mifflin, 2000).
47. See http://starbulletin.com/1999/02/13/sports/story2.html.
48. Louis Menand, "Gross Points," *New Yorker* (Feb. 7, 2005): 82.
49. See http://fayette.k12.in.us/~cbeard/cy/patent.html.
50. A. C. Clarke, *Profiles of the Future* (New York: Bantam, 1963).
51. R. Gallistel, *The Organization of Action* (Mahwah, NJ: Lawrence Erlbaum, 1980).
52. S. Ikemoto and J. Panksepp, *Brain Research Review* 31(1999): 6–41.
53. See E. Jaques and K. Cason, *Human Capability* (Falls Church, VA: Cason Hall, 1994); E. Jaques, *Time-Span Handbook* (Falls Church, VA: Cason Hall, 1964); T. J. Stanley, *Millionaire Mind* (Kansas City: Andrews McMeel, 2001); Kim and Marborgne, *Blue Ocean Strategy;* and M. Buckingham, and C. Coffman, *First, Break All the Rules* (New York: Simon & Schuster, 1999).
54. W. J. Freeman, *How Brains Make Up Their Mind* (New York: Columbia University Press, 2000).
55. Storch, "Taking the Reins."
56. B. J. Everitt et al., in J. McGintry, ed., *Advancing from the Ventral Striatum to the Extended Amygdala* (New York: New York Academy of Sciences, 1999): 412–438; B. J. Everitt, and T. W. Robbins, in M. J. Zigmond et al., eds., *Fundamental Neuroscience* (San Diego: Academic Press, 1999); S. Ikemoto, and J. Panksepp, *Brain Research Review* 31(1999): 6–41; P. W. Kalivas and M. Nakamura, *Current Opinions in Neurobiology* 9(1999): 223–227.
57. V. Goetzel and M. D. Goetzel, *Cradles of Eminence* (Boston: Little, Brown, 1962); Kim and Mauborgne, *Blue Ocean Strategy.*
58. Ibid.
59. See, for example, R. E. Thayer, *Calm Energy* (New York: Oxford University Press, 2001); Storch, "Taking the Reins"; and S. E. Thayer, *The Biopsychology of Mood and Arousal* (New York: Oxford University Press, 1989).
60. Kreiman et al., "Imagery Neurons in the Human Brain," 357–361.

Chapter 3. What You Guide, Grows

1. W. J. Holstein, "Best Ideas for CEOs," *Chief Executive* (Aug. 2005): 30–40.
2. E. Jaques, *Timespan and Performance* (Falls Church, VA: Cason Hall, 1989).
3. See, for example, J. LeDoux, *Synaptic Self* (New York: Viking, 2002).
4. E. T. Rolls, *The Brain and Emotion* (Oxford University Press, 1999); D. Gaffan et al. *European Journal of Neuroscience* 5(1993): 968-975.
5. See, for example, P. R. Lawrence, and N. Nohria, *Driven: How Human Nature Shapes Our Choices* (San Francisco: Jossey-Bass, 2002).

6. "Why Logic Often Takes a Backseat," *Business Week* (Mar. 28, 2005): 94–95; J. Fox, "Why Johnny Can't Save for Retirement," *Fortune* (Mar. 21, 2005): 202–210.

7. B. J. Everitt et al., in J. McGintry, ed., *Advancing from the Ventral Striatum to the Extended Amygdala* (New York: New York Academy of Sciences, 1999): 412–438; B. J. Everitt, and T. W. Robbins, in M. J. Zigmond et al., eds., *Fundamental Neuroscience* (San Diego: Academic Press, 1999); S. Ikemoto, and J. Pankseep, *Brain Research Review* 31(1999): 6–41; P. W. Kalivas and M. Nakamura, *Current Opinions in Neurobiology* 9(1999): 223–227; P. La Cerra and R. Bingham, *The Origins of Minds* (New York: Harmony, 2002).

8. W. A. Suzuki and D. G. Amaral, *Journal of Comprehensive Neurology* 350(1994): 497-533; LeDoux, *Synaptic Self*.

9. LeDoux, *Synaptic Self*.

10. Suzuki and Amaral, *Journal of Comprehensive Neurology* 350(1994): 497–533.

11. La Cerra and Bingham, *Origins of Minds*.

12. L. LaRoche, *Life Is Short—Wear Your Party Pants: Ten Simple Truths That Lead to an Amazing Life* (Carlsbad, CA: Hay House, 2003).

13. W. Howat, "Journaling to Self-Evaluation: A Tool for Adult Learners," *International Journal of Reality Therapy* 18(1999): 32–34.

14. E. Jaques and K. Cason, *Human Capability* (Falls Church, VA: Cason Hall, 1994); E. Jaques, *Time-Span Handbook* (Falls Church, VA: Cason Hall, 1964); T. J. Stanley, *Millionaire Mind* (Kansas City: Andrews McMeel, 2001).

15. S. Pinker, *How the Mind Works* (New York: Norton, 1997); D. G. Amaral et al., in J. P. Aggleton, ed., *The Amygdala* (New York: Wiley-Liss, 1992): 1–66; J. Fuster, *The Prefrontal Cortex,* 3rd ed. (Philadelphia: Lippincott-Raven, 1997); M. G. Maioli et al., *Brain Research* 789(1998): 118–125; M. Perides, and D. N. Pandya, *European Journal of Neuroscience* 11(1999): 1011–1036; R. Passingham, *The Frontal Lobes and Voluntary Action* (Oxford University Press, 1995); E.T. Rolls, *The Brain and Emotion* (Oxford University Press, 1999); D. Gaffan et al., *European Journal of Neuroscience* 5(1993): 968–975.

16. A. R. Luria, *Selected Writings of A. R. Luria, Neurosurgeon* (Armonk, NY: M.E. Sharpe, 1987); A.R. Luria, *The Working Brain* (New York: Penguin, 1973).

17. J. Kotter, *Matsushita Leadership* (New York: Free Press, 1997).

18. Ibid.

19. See Jaques and Cason, *Human Capability;* Jaques, *Time-Span Handbook;* M. Buckingham and C. Coffman, *First, Break All the Rules* (New York: Simon & Schuster, 1999); and Stanley, *Millionaire Mind.*

20. D. Sull, *Survival of the Fittest* (Boston: Harvard Business School Press, 2003); S. Finkelstein, *Why Smart Executives Fail* (New York: Penguin Portfolio, 2003): G. Nadler and S. Hibino, *Breakthrough Thinking* (Rocklin, CA: Prima, 1990); G. Nadler and S. Hibino, S. *Creative Solution Finding* (Rocklin, CA: Prima, 1997); R. J. Sternberg, ed., *Why Smart People Can Be So Stupid* (New Haven, CT: Yale University Press, 2002); Jaques and Cason, *Human*

Capability; Jaques, *Time-Span Handbook;* J. Collins, *Good to Great* (New York: HarperBusiness, 2002); Stanley, *Millionaire Mind.*

21. Mintzberg, H. *The Rise and Fall of Strategic Planning* (New York: Free Press, 1994).
22. A. Hargadon, *How Breakthroughs Happen: The Surprising Truth* (Boston: Harvard Business School Press, 2003).
23. M. Storch, "Taking the Reins," *Scientific American Mind* 16(2)(2005): 88–89.
24. Van Dyk, D. "The Coffee Widows," *Time,* spec. sec. (Sep. 2005): A12.
25. Ibid.
26. Ibid.
27. See, for example, J. Dennis, *Money for Nothing* (Davison, MI: Friede Publishing, 1988).
28. See http://money.cnn.com/2005/01/10/news/newsmakers/american_will.reut/ (also in *Barron's,* Jan. 10, 2005: 23).
29. See, for example, D. Bach, *Automatic Millionaire* (New York: Broadway Books, 2004).
30. E. St. James, *Living the Simple Life* (New York: Hyperion, 1998).
31. Special credit to my colleague Dawn Sorenson.
32. Storch, "Taking the Reins."
33. References include L. K. Libby, R. P. Eibach, and T. Gilovich, "Here's looking at me: Memory perspective and assessments of personal change." *Journal of Personality and Social Psychology,* 88, 50–62 (2005).
34. E. Von Hippel et al., *Creating Breakthroughs at 3M* (Boston: Harvard Business School Press, 2001); B. Nelson, *3M's Culture of Innovation* (San Diego: Nelson, 2002); E. Gundling, *The 3M Way to Innovation* (Tokyo: Kodansha, 2000).
35. Personal communications with author; also see N. C. Stokes, *Cool Runnings and Beyond* (Salt Lake City: American Book Business Press, 2002).

Chapter 4. What's Automatic, Accelerates

1. W. James, *Talks to Teachers* (New York: Norton, 1958).
2. See, for example, J. Polivy and C. P. Herman, *International Journal of Eating Disorders* 26(1999): 434–437.
3. E. Sigmund, "Consciously Directing the Creative Process in Business," *Transactional Analysis Journal* 29(1999): 222–227.
4. See, for example, R. J. Sternberg, *Successful Intelligence* (New York: Simon & Schuster, 1997).
5. J. Fuster, *The Prefrontal Cortex,* 3rd Ed. (Philadelphia: Lippincott-Raven, 1997); D.G. Amen, *Change Your Brain, Change Your Life* (New York: Times Books, 1998); D. Goleman et al., *Primal Leadership* (Boston: Harvard Business School Press, 2003); E. Langer, *The Power of Mindful Learning* (Cambridge, MA: De Capo, 1998).

6. J. Pfeffer and R. I. Sutton, *The Knowing-Doing Gap* (Boston : Harvard Business School Press, 2000).
7. An excellent text on this subject is S. McGill, *Low Back Disorders: Evidence-Based Prevention and Rehabilitation* (Champaign, IL: Human Kinetics, 2002).
8. M. A. Adams et al., "Diurnal Variations in the Stresses on the Lumbar Spine," *Spine* 10(1987): 524.
9. T. Reilly et al., "Circadian Variation in Human Nature," *Chronobiology International* 1(1984): 121.
10. C. Carter et al., "How the Brain Gets Ready to Perform," lecture at the 30th Annual Meeting of the Society of Neuroscience, New Orleans (Nov. 2000).
11. Ibid.
12. R. B. Cialdini, *Influence: The Psychology of Persuasion* (New York: Quill, 1993).
13. E. Deci, *Intrinsic Motivation and Self-Determination in Human Behavior* (New York: Kluwer Academic Publishers, 1985).
14. S. Pinker, *How the Mind Works* (New York: Norton, 1997).
15. McGill, *Low Back Disorders.*

Chapter 5. The Shortest Distance Between Two Points Is a Curve

1. See, for example, J. Horn, "Models of Intelligence," in R. Linn, ed., *Intelligence* (Chicago: University of Illinois Press, 1989): 29–73; J. Horn, and R. B. Cattell, "Refinement and Test of Fluid and Crystallized Intelligence," *Journal of Educational Psychology* 57(1966): 253–270.
2. R. Cross and A. Parker, *The Hidden Power of Social Networks: Understanding How Work Really Gets Done in Organizations* (Boston: Harvard Business School Press, 2005).
3. G. Klein, *Intuition at Work* (New York: Doubleday Currency, 2002); J. Katzenbach and D. Smith, *The Wisdom of Teams* (New York: HarperBusiness, 2003).
4. T. Gualtieri, in J. Ratey, ed., *The Neuropsychiatry of Personality Disorders* (Blackwell, 1995): 153.
5. D. G. Amen, *Change Your Brain, Change Your Life* (New York: Times Books, 1998).
6. D. G. Amaral et al., in J. P. Aggleton, ed., *The Amygdala* (New York: Wiley-Liss, 1992): 1–66; J. Fuster, *The Prefrontal Cortex,* 3rd ed. (Philadelphia: Lippincott-Raven, 1997); M. G. Maioli et al., *Brain Research* 789 (1998): 118–125; M. Perides and D. N. Pandya, *European Journal of Neuroscience* 11(1999): 1011–1036; R. Passingham, *The Frontal Lobes and Voluntary Action* (Oxford, England: Oxford University Press, 1995).
7. A. Damasio, *Descartes' Error* (New York: Grosset/Putnam, 1995).
8. Amen, *Change Your Brain, Change Your Life.*
9. Ibid.
10. Ibid.

11. J. Loehr and T. Schwartz, "The Making of a Corporate Athlete," *Harvard Business Review* (Nov. 2000): 120–128.
12. See, for example, T. Lewise, F. Amini, and R. Lannon, *A General Theory of Love* (New York: Random House, 2000).
13. G. Kreiman, C. Koch, and I. Fried, "Imagery Neurons in the Human Brain," *Nature* 408(2000): 357–361.
14. C. Carter et al., "How the Brain Gets Ready to Perform," lecture at the 30th Annual Meeting of the Society of Neuroscience, New Orleans (Nov. 2000).
15. L. White, *Medieval Technology and Social Change*, available at http://www.danderby.com/stirrup.htm.
16. "The Evolution and Future of the Internet," Hamilton Consultants Newsletter, 5th ed. (1998): 4, available at http://www.hamiltonco.com/features/hampub/news5.pdf.
17. See, for example, J. Loehr, *Stress for Success* (New York: TimesBusiness, 1999); J. Loehr and T. Schwartz, *The Power of Full Engagement* (New York: Free Press, 2003); R. A. Dienstbier, in L. Miller, "To Beat Stress, Get Tough," *Psychology Today* (Nov. 1989); R. A. Dienstbier, ed., *Evolutionary Psychology and Motivation* (Lincoln: University of Nebraska Press, 2001).
18. W. C. Dement and V. Vaughan,*The Promise of Sleep* (New York: Dell, 2000); P. Hauri and S. Linde, *No More Sleepless Nights* (New York: Wiley, 1996); J. B. Maas, *PowerSleep* (New York: Collins, 1999); G. Jacobs, *Say Goodnight to Insomnia* (New York: Owl, 1999); J. Horne, *Why We Sleep* (Oxford, 1989).
19. See, for example, M. C. Diamond, *Enriching Heredity: The Impact of Environment on the Anatomy of the Brain* (New York: Free Press, 1988); M. Diamond and J. Hopson, *Magic Trees of the Mind* (New York: Plume, 1999); and A. Montagu, *Growing Young*, 2nd ed. (Los Angeles: Bergin & Garvey, 1989).
20. G. Land, *Grow or Die: The Unifying Principle of Transformation* (New York: Wiley, 1986): 9.
21. D. King-Hele, *Erasmus Darwin* (London: Giles de la Mare, 2000).

Key 2. *Focus*, Not Time

1. Unpublished research by AES, 1987 to present; J. Gleick, *Faster* (New York: Pantheon, 2000).
2. D. Simons and C. Chabris, "Gorillas in Our Midst: Sustained Inattentional Blindness for Dynamic Events," *Perception* 28(1999): 1059–1074.
3. See http://www.telegraph.co.uk/connected/main.jhtml?xml=%2Fconnected %2F2004%2F05%2F05%2Fecfgorilla05.xml.
4. You can see the video at http://viscog.beckman.uiuc.edu/grafs/demos/15.html.
5. "Brain Region Learns to Anticipate Risk, Provide Early Warnings," PhysOrg.com (Feb. 17, 2005).

6. J. LeDoux, *The Emotional Brain* (New York: Putnam, 1997).
7. M. Steriade, "Arousal: Revisiting the Reticular Activating System," *Science* 272(1996): 225–226; G. D. Jacobs, *The Ancestral Brain* (New York: Viking, 2003).
8. J. D. French, "The Reticular Formation," *Scientific American* (May 1957): 2–8.
9. J. Zull, *The Art of Changing the Brain* (Sterling, VA: Stylus, 2002).

Chapter 6. Emphasize the Right Moments, Not the Clock

1. M. Oliver, "A Summer Day," in *House of Light* (Boston: Beacon Press, 1992).
2. See http://www.newscientist.com/channel/being-human/mg18625011.900.
3. See, for example, the chronobiological research cited in E. Rossi, *The Twenty Minute Break* (New York: Tarcher, 1997).
4. Ibid.
5. W. S. Hillis, "The Clock," in J. Brockman, ed., *The Greatest Inventions of the Past 2,000 Years* (New York: Simon & Schuster, 2000).
6. See S. Zuboff, "New Worlds of Computer-Mediated Work," *Harvard Business Review* (Sept.-Oct. 1982): 142–152.
7. Alok Jha, "Society Made Us Smart," *Guardian Weekly* (2005), available at http://www.guardian.co.uk/guardianweekly/story/0,12674,1383787,00.html.
8. "Everything That Can Go Wrong Listed," *Onion* 41(24)(June 15, 2005).
9. J. Zull, *The Art of Changing the Brain* (Sterling, VA: Stylus, 2002).
10. P. R. Lawrence and N. Nohria, *Driven: How Human Nature Shapes Our Choices* (San Francisco: Jossey-Bass, 2002).
11. A. Maslow, seminar at UCLA, personal communication, 1968.
12. J. Gleick, *Faster;* R. Sekular, *Perception* (2002); E. B. Goldstein, *Sensation and Perception* (2001); J. Pfeffer and R. I. Sutton, *The Knowing-Doing Gap* (2000).
13. *Chronicles,* Vol.1: 146–147.
14. M. Storch, "Taking the Reins," *Scientific American Mind* 16(2)(2005): 88–89.
15. J. E. Kihlstron, *Science* 237(1987): 1445–1452.
16. K. H. Pribram, personal communication (1985).
17. A. Damasio, *Descartes' Error* (New York: Grossett/Putnam, 1995).
18. R. E. Thayer, *The Biopsychology of Mood and Arousal* (Oxford University Press, 1989).
19. For an outstanding summation of self-regulation and emotional experiential memory, see Storch, "Taking the Reins."
20. L. K. Libby, R. P. Eibach, and T. Gilovich, "Here's looking at me: Memory perspective and assessments of personal change." *Journal of Personality and Social Psychology,* 88, 50–62 (2005).
21. Kihlstron, *Science* 237(1987): 1445–1452.
22. R. Davidson et al., "Emotion, Plasticity, Context, and Regulation," *Psychological Bulletin* 126(6)(2000): 890–909.
23. P. Drucker, *Creative Living* (Milwaukee, WI: Autumn, 1997).
24. R. B. Zajonc, "Styles of Explanation in Social Psychology," *European Journal*

of Social Psychology (Sep.–Oct. 1989); J. L. Locke, *The De-Voicing of Society* (New York: Simon & Schuster, 1998); N. Nicholson, "How Hardwired Is Human Behavior?" *Harvard Business Review* (July–Aug. 1998): 134–147.

25. Gilovich and Libby, *Journal of Personality and Social Psychology.*
26. G. Klein, *Intuition at Work* (New York: Doubleday Currency, 2003): 60.
27. "Mental Imagery," *Peak Performance Journal* 197(May 2004): 1–4.
28. David Howes, "Body Decoration and Sensory Symbolism in South America," available at http://www.lila.info/document_view.phtml?document_id=47.
29. Zull, *Art of Changing the Brain.*
30. P. La Cerra and R. Bingham, *The Origin of Minds* (New York: Harmony, 2002).
31. Michael Abrams, "Sight Unseen," *Discover* (June 2002), available at http://www.nfb.org/bm/bm02/bm0211/bm0211.htm.
32. Manesha Deveshvar, "Welcome to Blind Cow," Pitara.com (http://pitara.com/magazine/features/152.htm.) In case you were wondering, the waitstaff are all visually impaired, and they find their way around in the darkness without much difficulty. They wear bells, whose jingling prevents collisions in the dark.
33. *Athletic Journal* 57(1976): 74–80.
34. "Mental Imagery."
35. Ibid.

Chapter 7: What You Frame, Engages

1. Quoted in "Lily's Long Bloom," *Washington Post* (Oct. 26, 2003): N01.
2. W. Howat, "Journaling to Self-Evaluation: A Tool for Adult Learners," *International Journal of Reality Therapy* 18(1999): 32–34; M. Storch, "Taking the Reins," *Scientific American Mind* 16(2)(2005): 88–89.
3. J. Gottman, *Why Marriages Succeed or Fail* (New York: Simon & Schuster, 1995); J. Gottman and N. Silver, *The Seven Principles for Making Marriage Work* (New York: Three Rivers Press, 2000).
4. J. Burke and R. Ornstein, *The Axemaker's Gift* (New York: Grosset/Putnam, 1995).
5. M. Moore-Ede, *The Twenty-Four-Hour Society: Understanding Human Limits in a World That Never Stops* (Reading, MA: Addison-Wesley, 1993).
6. K. Arnold, *Lives of Promise: A Fourteen Year Study of Achievement and Life Choices* (San Francisco: Jossey-Bass, 1995).
7. Nathan Rabin, "Lazy Field Goal," *Onion* (May 26–June 1, 2005): 18.
8. G. Samuel, *Civilized Shamans: Buddhism in Tibetan Societies* (Washington, DC: Smithsonian Institution Press, 1993).
9. See, for example, J. L. Oschman, *Energy Medicine: The Scientific Basis* (London: Churchill Livingstone, 2000); and C. B. Pert, *Molecules of Emotion* (New York: Scribner, 1997).

10. See, for example, H. Benson and W. Proctor, *The Break-Out Principle* (New York: Scribner, 2003).
11. C. Sansone and J. M. Harackiewicz, *Intrinsic and Extrinsic Motivation* (San Diego: Academic Press, 2000).
12. A. Damasio, *Descartes' Error* (New York: Grosset/Putnam, 1994); A. Bechard et al., "Deciding Advantageously Before Knowing the Advantageous Strategy," *Science* 275(1997): 12293.
13. "Who's Got the Monkey?" A game by Accoutrements (P.O. Box 30811, Seattle, WA, 98103).
14. K. H. Pribram, personal communication (1989).
15. P. R. Lawrence and N. Nohria, *Driven: How Human Nature Shapes Our Choices* (San Francisco: Jossey-Bass, 2002).
16. *NeuroImage* (Aug. 1, 2001).
17. M. Santosus, "Why More Is Less," *CIO* (Feb. 21, 2005).
18. S. Shellenbarger, "Multitasking Makes You Stupid," *Wall Street Journal* (Feb. 27, 2003): D1.
19. E. Goldberg, *The Wisdom Paradox* (New York: Gotham Books, 2005).
20. D. Norfolk, *Executive Stress* (New York: Warner, 1988).
21. W. E. Deming, personal communication (1983).
22. G. D. Jacobs, *The Ancestral Mind* (New York: Viking, 2004): 178.
23. G. Claxton, *Hare Brain, Tortoise Mind* (New York: Bloomsbury, 1998).
24. E. Langer, *The Power of Mindful Learning* (Cambridge, MA: Perseus, 1998).
25. G. Claxton, *Wise Up* (New York: Bloomsbury, 1999).
26. G. Zull, *The Art of Changing the Brain* (Sterling, VA: Stylus, 2002): 28.
27. Laurel C. Schneider, *Re-Imagining the Divine: Confronting the Backlash against Feminist Theology* (Cleveland: Pilgrim Press: 1998): 87.
28. R. Farson and R. Keyes, *Whoever Makes the Most Mistakes Wins* (New York: Free Press, 2002).
29. A. Miyake and P. Shah, eds., *Models of Working Memory* (Cambridge University Press, 1999).
30. J. LeDoux, *Synaptic Self* (New York: Viking, 2002): 253.
31. Zull, *Art of Changing the Brain;* Langer, *Power of Mindful Learning;* Claxton, *Wise Up;* Claxton, *Hare Brain, Tortoise Mind.*
32. See, for example, C. Pfaffer, *Warrior Soul: The Memoir of a Navy Seal* (New York: Presidio Press, 2004).
33. S. Pinker, *How the Mind Works* (New York: Norton, 1997); S. Pinker, *The Blank Slate* (New York: Penguin, 2002); R. Ornstein, *Evolution of Consciousness* (New York: Prentice Hall, 1991); N. Nicholson, *Executive Instinct* (New York: CrownBusiness, 2003).
34. Zull, *Art of Changing the Brain.*
35. R. A. J. Matthews, "The Science of Murphy's Law," *Scientific American* (April 1997).
36. R. S. Eliot, *Is It Worth Dying For?* (New York: Bantam, 1990).

37. D. Gage, *Mood State-Dependent Memory and the Lateralization of Emotion* (New York: Springer-Verlag, 1992).

38. Nancy Koehn, *Brand New: How Entrepreneurs Earned Customers' Trust from Wedgwood to Dell* (Boston: Harvard Business School Press, 2001): 197. In this book, Koehn tells the stories of Lauder, Josiah Wedgwood, H. J. Heinz, Marshall Field, Starbucks founder Howard Schultz, and Michael Dell.

39. Grace Mirabella, "Builders and Titans: Estée Lauder" *Time* (Dec. 7, 1998), available at http://www.time.com/time/time100/builder/profile/lauder3.html.

Chapter 8. What You Clarify, Unlocks

1. For a memorable exploration of telegrams, see L. Rosenkrantz, *Telegram!* (New York: Holt, 2003).

2. J. Kabat-Zinn, *Wherever You Go, There You Are* (New York: Hyperion, 1995).

3. L. Bossidy and R. Charam, *Confronting Reality* (New York: CrownBusiness, 2004).

4. See, for example, H. Benson and W. Proctor, *The Break-Out Principle* (New York: Scribner, 2003).

5. See, for example, S. W. Lazar et al., *NeuroReport* (May 2000).

6. G. Nadler and S. Hibino, *Breakthrough Thinking* (Rocklin, CA: Prima, 1990); G. Nadler and S. Hibino, *Creative Solution Finding* (Prima, 1997); D. Perkins, *Outsmarting IQ* (New York: Free Press, 1995).

7. Cited in Bennis, W., and Nanus, B. *Leaders* (New York: HarperCollins, 1986).

8. D. Wegner, *White Bears and Other Unwanted Thoughts* (New York: Guilford Press, 1994).

9. R. Restak, *Mozart's Brain and the Fighter Pilot* (New York: Harmony, 2001).

10. S. Pinker, *The Blank Slate* (New York: Penguin, 2002); G. Claxton, *Wise Up* (New York: Bloomsbury, 1999); Wegner, *White Bears*.

11. J. Pfeffer and R. I. Sutton, *The Knowing-Doing Gap* (Boston: Harvard Business School Press, 2000).

12. D. Keefe, *On the Sweet Spot* (New York: Simon & Schuster, 2003).

13. "Hand Gestures Linked to Memory," *Science Daily* (May 11, 2005), available at http://www.sciencedaily.com/releases/2005/05/050511105253.htm.

14. J. Pittam, *Voice in Social Interaction* (Thousand Oaks, CA: Sage, 1994).

15. P. Wallace, *The Psychology of the Internet* (New York: Cambridge University Press, 2001).

Chapter 9. Race Your Own Race, Together

1. Gerald Holton and Yehuda Elkana, eds., *Albert Einstein: Historical and Cultural Aspects* (New York: Dover, 1997).

2. L. Van Praag et al., *Nature Neurosci. Reviews* (Dec. 2000); Diamond, *Enriching Heredity: The Impact of Environment on the Brain* (New York: Free

Press, 1988); M. Diamond and J. Hopson, *Magic Trees of the Mind* (New York: Plume, 1999).

3. See, for example, Dennett, D. "Cognitive Science as Reverse Engineering," available at http://pp.kpnet.fi/seirioa/cdenn/cogscirv.htm.

4. R. D. Hof, "The Power of Us," *Business Week* (June 20, 2005).

5. P. Nutt, *Why Decisions Fail* (San Francisco: Berrett-Koehler, 2002).

6. M. S. Gazzaninga, *The Social Brain* (New York: Basic Books, 1985); E. Aronson et al., *Social Psychology*, 5th ed. (Upper Saddle River, NJ: Prentice Hall, 2004); D. T. Kenrick et al., *Social Psychology: Unraveling the Mystery* 3rd ed. (New York: Allyn & Bacon, 2004).

7. G. Klein, *Sources of Power* (Cambridge, MA: MIT Press, 1999); J. Loehr, and T. Schwartz, *The Power of Full Engagement* (New York: Free Press, 2003); R. Cross, et al. *The Hidden Power of Social Networks: Understanding How Work Really Gets Done in Organizations* (Boston: Harvard Business School Press, 2004).

8. Cross et al., *Hidden Power of Social Networks*.

9. Thomas Haudricourt, "Loose Ways End Losing Days," Milwaukee Journal Sentinel Online (http://www.jsonline.com/sports/brew/oct04/270300.asp?format=print).

10. B. J. Schechter, "My Sportsman Choice: Boston Red Sox" SI.com (http://sportsillustrated.cnn.com/2004/magazine/specials/sportsman/2004/11/19/red.sox/).

11. Tim Sanders. *Love Is the Killer Ap: How to Win Business and Influence Friends*, quoted at http://216.239.57.104/search?q=cache:gabyagIevMgJ:www.gsm.ucdavis.edu/innovator/fall2003/Fall2003Innovator.pdf+lovecat+ap&hl=en#5.

12. James B. Stewart, "Partners" *New Yorker* (Jan. 10, 2005): 57.

13. Ibid.

14. B. Z. Posner and W. H. Schmidt, "Values Congruence and Difference Between the Interplay of Personal and Organizational Value Systems," *Journal of Business Ethics* 12(2)(1992): 171–177; B. Z. Posner and R. I. Westwood, "A Cross-Cultural Investigation of the Shared Values Relationship," *International Journal of Values-Based Management* 11(4)(1995): 1–10.

15. Richard M. Posner, "Against the Law Reviews," *Legal Affairs* (Nov.–Dec. 2004).

16. "Joint Policy Statement on Law Review Articles," available at www.harvardlawreview.org/articles_length_policy.pdf.

17. See http://www.greenbag.org.

18. Brian Brooks, quoted in Gerald de Jaager, "Behind the Green Bag," *University of Chicago Law School Record* (Spring 2005).

Key 3. *Capacity,* Not Conformity

1. D. Goleman et al., *Primal Leadership* (Boston: Harvard Business School Press, 2003).
2. John Roach, "Brain Study Shows Why Revenge Is Sweet," *National Geographic* (Aug. 27, 2004), available at http://news.nationalgeographic.com/news/2004/08/0827_040827_punishment.html.
3. Jeremy Bernstein, *Oppenheimer: Portrait of An Enigma* (Chicago: Ivan R. Dee, 2004).
4. Physics Today Online (Jan. 22, 2005; http://www.physicstoday.org/vol-58/iss-1/p51.html).

Chapter 10. Use Your Brains—All Four of Them

1. See, for example, D. Perkins, *Outsmarting IQ* (New York: Free Press, 1999); and U. Kraft, "Unleashing Creativity," *Scientific American Mind* 16(1)(2005): 17–24.
2. A. Bechard et al., "Deciding Advantageously Before Knowing the Advantageous Strategy," *Science* 275(1997): 12293.
3. S. Pinker, *How the Mind Works* (New York: Norton, 1999); S. Pinker, *The Blank Slate* (New York: Basic Books, 2002).
4. See, for example, M. D. Lieberman, "Intuition: A Social Cognitive Neuroscience Approach," *Psychological Bulletin* 126(2000): 109–137; and J. A. Knowlton et al., "A Neostriatal Habit Learning System in Humans," *Science* 273(1996): 1399–1402; R. K. Cooper, and A. Sawaf, *Executive EQ* (New York: Grossett/Putnam, 1997); and D. Goleman et al., *Primal Leadership* (Boston: Harvard Business School Press, 2001).
5. P. R. Lawrence, and N. Nohria, *Driven: How Human Nature Shapes Our Choices* (San Francisco: Jossey-Bass, 2002).
6. See, for example, R. K. Cooper, *The Other 90%: How to Unlock Your Vast Untapped Potential for Leadership & Life* (New York: CrownBusiness, 2001).
7. *Aristotle's Rhetoric, Book II, Chapter 1,* trans. W. Rhys Roberts; written by Aristotle in 350 BC. Quote taken from first edition galley copy owned by Wendell L. Downing, M.D.
8. D. W. Wegner, *The Illusion of Conscious Will* (Cambridge, MA: MIT Press, 2002).
9. R. J. Sternberg, *Successful Intelligence* (New York: Simon & Schuster, 1997).
10. R. J. Sternberg, "Testing Common Sense," *American Psychologist* (Nov. 1995): 923.
11. R. J. Sternberg, ed., *Why Smart People Can Be So Stupid* (New Haven, CT: Yale University Press, 2002): 32.
12. T. J. Stanley, *The Millionaire Mind* (Kansas City: Andrews McMeel, 2000).
13. Pinker, *How the Mind Works.*
14. G. Klein, *Intuition at Work* (New York: Doubleday Currency, 2003).

15. R. Farson, *Management of the Absurd* (New York: Simon & Schuster, 1996): 148.
16. Ibid: 148.
17. B. R. Kada, in J. Field et al. eds., *Handbook of Physiology* (Washington, DC: American Physiological Society, 1960); R. L. Isaacson, *The Limbic Sysytem* (New York: Plenum Press, 1982); P. D. MacLean, *The Triune Brain in Evolution* (New York: Plenum Press, 1990); J. LeDoux, *Emotional Brain* (New York: Putnam, 1997); J. LeDoux, *Synaptic Self* (New York: Viking, 2002).
18. M. D. Gershon, *The Second Brain* (New York: HarperCollins, 1999); S. Blakeslee, "Complex and Hidden Brain in Gut Makes Stomachaches and Butterflies," *New York Times* (Jan. 23, 1996).
19. Michael Gershon, "The Enteric Nervous System: A Second Brain" *Hospital Practice* (July 1999), available at http://www.hosppract.com/issues/1999/07/gershon.htm.
20. Gershon, *Second Brain:* 17.
21. "Go with Your Gut: Science finds new evidence for gut instincts." *Enlightenment* (May–July 2004); see also Christopher D. Buckingham and Ann Adams, "Classifying Clinical Decision Making: A Unifying Approach," *Journal of Advanced Nursing* 32(4)(1990): 981–989.
22. LeDoux, *Emotional Brain;* LeDoux, *Synaptic Self.*
23. W. J. Freeman, *How the Brain Makes Up Its Mind* (New York: Columbia University Press, 2000).
24. Lieberman, "Intuition."
25. Ibid.
26. See http://www.ctnet.com/pr/releaseDetails.asp?prid=151.
27. G. Klein, *The Power of Intuition: How to Use Your Gut Feelings for Better Decisions at Work* (New York: Doubleday Currency, 2004).
28. R. C. Solomon, *The Passions: Emotions and the Meaning of Life* (Indianapolis: Hackett, 1993).
29. "Science of the Heart," Institute of HeartMath (www.heartmath.org).
30. See, for example, D. Childre and B. Cryer, *From Chaos to Coherence,* Boulder Creek, CA: rev. ed. (HeartMath, 2003); and related studies at www.hearthmath.org.
31. J. Armour, "Neurocardiology: Anatomy and Functional Principles," in R. McCraty, D. Rozman, and D. Childre, *HeartMath: A New Biobehavioral Intervention for Creasing Coherence in the Human System* (Amsterdam: Harwood Academic Publishers, 1999).
32. See, for example, P. Langhorst, G. Schultz, and M. Lambertz, "Oscillating Neuronal Network of the 'Common Brain System,' " in K. Miyakawa et al., *Mechanisms of Blood Pressure Waves* (Tokyo: Japan Scientific Societies Press, 1984): 257–275.
33. See, for example, J. A. Armour and J. L. Ardell, *Basic and Clinical Neurocardiology* (New York: Oxford University Press, 2004); K. H. Pribram and D. Rozman "Early Childhood Development and Learning: What New

Research About the Brain and Heart Tell Us," White House Conference on Human Development and Learning, San Francisco (1997); K. H. Pribram, ed., *Brain and Values* (Mahwah, NJ: Lawrence Erlbaum, 1998).

34. "Science of the Heart."
35. L. Song, G. Schwartz, and L. Russek, "Heart-Focused Attention and Heart-Brain Synchronization: Energetic and Physiological Mechanisms," *Alternative Therapies in Health and Medicine* 4(5)(1998): 44–62.
36. R. McCraty, M. Atkinson, and W. A. Tiller, "The Effects of Emotions on Short-Term Heart Rate Variability Using Power Spectrum Analysis," *American Journal of Cardiology* 76(1995): 1089–1093.
37. Song, Schwartz, and Russek, "Heart-Focused Attention and Heart-Brain Synchronization."
38. See, for example, Armour, and Ardell, *Basic and Clinical Neurocardiology;* D. Childre and B. Cryer, *From Chaos to Coherence;* J. A. Armour, "Anatomy and Function of the Intrathoracic Neurons Regulating the Heart," in I. H. Zucker and J. P. Gilmore, eds., *Reflex Control of the Circulation* (Boca Raton, FL: CRC Press, 1991); and M. Cantin and J. Genest, "The Heart as an Endocrine Gland," *Clinical and Investigative Medicine* 9(4)(1986): 319–327.
39. Cryer and Childre, *From Chaos to Coherence,* rev. ed.
40. See, for example, Song, Schwartz, and Russek, "Heart-Focused Attention and Heart-Brain Synchronization"; Cryer, and Childre, *From Chaos to Coherence,* (rev. ed.); Freeman, *How the Brain Makes Up Its Mind.*
41. Joshua Muravchik, "The Mind of George Soros," *Wall Street Journal* (Mar. 3, 2004), available at http://www.opinionjournal.com/extra/?id=110004764.
42. B. Kolb and I. Whishaw, *Fundamentals of Human Neuropsychology,* 3rd ed. (New York: W. H. Freeman, 1990): 166.
43. H. Keller, *The World I Live In* (New York: New York Review Books, 2003).
44. Ibid.: xxiv.
45. T. Cleary, trans., *Further Teachings of Lao Tzu: Understanding the Mysteries* (Boston: Shambhala, 1991).
46. G. Leonard, *The Silent Pulse: The Search for the Perfect Rhythm in Each of Us* (New York: Dutton, 1978).
47. J. Bargh and T. Chartrand, "The Unbearable Automaticity of Being," *American Psychologist* 54(7)(1999): 462–479.
48. G. Nadler and S. Hibino, *Breakthrough Thinking* (Rocklin, CA: Prima, 1990); G. Nadler and S. Hibino, *Creative Solution Finding* (Rocklin, CA: Prima, 1997).
49. Essi Systems research San Francisco: 1985–2005; Nadler and Hibino, *Creative Solution Finding;* E. Langer, *The Power of Mindful Learning* (Cambridge, MA: DaCapo, 1998); J. Loehr, LGE Performance Science Research, Orlando, FL, *The Power of Full Engagement* (New York: Free Press, 2003); H. Benson, *The Breakout Principle* (New York: Scribner, 2004).
50. See, for example, J. Loehr, *Stress for Success* (New York: TimesBusiness, 1999); Loehr and Schwartz, *Power of Full Engagement;* R. A. Dienstbier quoted in

L. Miller, "To Beat Stress, Get Tough," *Psychology Today* (Nov. 1989); R. A. Dienstbier, ed., *Evolutionary Psychology and Motivation* (Lincoln: University of Nebraska Press, 2001).

51. Damasio, A. *Descartes' Error* (New York: Grosset/Putnam, 1994); D. Amen, *Change Your Brain, Change Your Life* (New York: Times Books, 1998).

52. Damasio, *Descartes' Error;* A. Bechard et al., "Deciding Advantageously Before Knowing the Advantageous Strategy," *Science* 275(1997): 1293; Armour and Ardell, *Basic and Clinical Neurocardiology;* Childre and Cryer, *From Chaos to Coherence;* Lieberman, "Intuition"; Gershon, *Second Brain;* Blakeslee, "Complex and Hidden Brain."

53. Damasio, *Descartes' Error;* Bechard et al., "Deciding Advantageously Before Knowing the Advantageous Strategy."

54. Amen, *Change Your Brain, Change Your Life;* M. Storch, "Taking the Reins," *Scientific American Mind* 16(2)(2005): 88–89; Loehr, *Stress for Success;* Loehr and Schwartz, *Power of Full Engagement;* Dienstbier, in Miller, "To Beat Stress, Get Tough"; Dienstbier, *Evolutionary Psychology and Motivation.*

55. Karl E. Weick, "Drop Your Tools: An Allegory for Organizational Studies," *Administrative Science Quarterly* (June 1996).

56. E. Langer, *The Power of Mindful Learning* (Cambridge, MA: Perseus, 1998): 75–81.

57. See www.pbs.org/wgbh/nova/wartech/nature.html.

58. T. A. Stewart, "How the Geniuses Behind the Osbournes, the Mini, Federal Express, and Starbucks Followed Their Instincts and Reached Success," *Traders Vic* (2005): "Think with Your Gut."

59. G. Klein, *Sources of Power: How People Make Decisions* (Cambridge, MA: MIT Press, 1999).

60. Stewart, "How the Geniuses Behind the Osbournes."

61. See J. Horn and R. B. Cattell, "Refinement and Test of the Theory of Fluid and Crystallized Intelligence," *Journal of Educational Psychology* 57(1966): 253–270.

62. See http://www.govexec.com/dailyfed/0403/040403nj2.htm.

63. Bechard et al., "Deciding Advantageously Before Knowing the Advantageous Strategy."

64. See, for example, R. B. Zajonc, "Styles of Explanation in Social Psychology," *European Journal of Social Psychology* (Sep.–Oct.1989).

65. K. Weick and K. Stucliffe, *Managing the Unexpected* (Ann Arbor: University of Michigan Business School, 2002).

66. S. Jobs, commencement address (June 12, 2005), quoted in *Stanford Report* (June 14, 2005).

Chapter 11. What You Demonstrate, Becomes Real

1. Adapted from B. Lewis, *Kids with Courage: True Stories About Young People Making a Difference* (Minneapolis: Free Spirit Publishing, 1992).

2. W. J. Freeman, *How the Brain Makes Up Its Mind* (New York: Columbia University Press, 2000).
3. All quotes in this section are from Judith Thurman, "The Misfit," *New Yorker* (July 4, 2005): 60–67.
4. J. Loehr, *Stress for Success* (TimesBusiness, 1999); J. Loehr and T. Schwartz, *The Power of Full Engagement* (New York: Free Press, 2003); R. A. Dienstbier, in L. Miller, "To Beat Stress, Get Tough," *Psychology Today* (Nov. 1989).
5. See, for example, E. Aronson, "Self-Justification" in *The Social Animal* (San Francisco: W. H. Freeman, 1972); R. B. Cialdini, "Commitment and Consistency" in *Influence*, 2nd ed. (Glenview, IL: Scott, Foresman, 1988); and J. Pfeffer and R. I. Sutton, *The Knowing-Doing Gap* (Boston: Harvard Business School Press, 2002).
6. M. Gandhi, *The Essential Gandhi: An Anthology* (New York: Vintage, 2002).
7. D. M. MacKay, "Cerebral Organization and the Conscious Control of Action," in J. C. Eccles, ed., *Brain and Conscious Experience* (Berlin: Heidelberg, 1966).
8. S. Pinker, *The Blank Slate* (New York: Penguin, 2002); S. Pinker, *How the Mind Works* (New York: Norton, 1999).
9. K. Pribram, ed., *Brain and Values* (New York: International Neural Network Society, 1996).
10. Michael Jordan, *I Can't Accept Not Trying.* (New York: HarperCollins, 1994).
11. Margaret Talbot, "Best in Class," *New Yorker* (June 6, 2005), available at http://www.newyorker.com/fact/content/articles/050606fa_fact.
12. K. Arnold, *Lives of Promise: What Becomes of High School Valedictorians* (San Francisco: Jossey-Bass, 1995).
13. P. Coy, "Why Logic Often Takes a Backseat," *Business Week* (Mar. 28, 2005): 94–95; J. Fox, "Why Johnny Can't Save for Retirement," *Fortune* (Mar. 21, 2005): 202–210.
14. See D. Goleman, *Emotional Intelligence* (New York: Bantam, 1995); D. Goleman et al., *Primal Leadership* (Boston: Harvard Business School Press, 2003); R. Cooper and A. Swaf, *Executive EQ: Emotional Intelligence in Leadership & Organizations* (New York: Grossett/Putnam, 1997).
15. M. Storch, "Taking the Reins," *Scientific American Mind* 16(2)(2005): 88–89.
16. See, for example, R. J. Sternberg, *Successful Intelligence* (New York: Simon & Schuster, 1997); G. Klein, *Intuition at Work* (New York: Doubleday Currency, 2003); and Goleman et al., *Primal Leadership*.
17. Available at http://www.anasazi.org/index.php?mission_2.
18. P. LaCerra and R. Bingham, *The Origin of Minds* (New York: Harmony, 2002).
19. A. Kohn, *Punished by Rewards* (Boston: Mariner, 1999).
20. E. Barar, *Chaos in Brain Function* (Springer-Verlag, 1990).
21. A. Deutschman, "Is Your Boss a Psychopath?" *Fast Company* (July 2005).
22. At The Masters Forum (Sep. 14, 2004).

23. Deirdre Woolard, "Free Wine in France" (July 15, 2005), available at http://www.luxist.com/entry/1234000967050527/.
24. Oliver Styles, "TV Documentary Highlights French Wine Crisis" (May 12, 2004), available at http://www.decanter.com/news/49149.html.
25. Eleanor Beardsley, "French Wine Industry Faces Uncertain Future," National Public Radio Weekend Edition (April 24, 2005), available at http://www.npr.org/templates/story/story.php?storyId=4617568.
26. Daniel J. Boorstin, interview contained in "In Memoriam: Daniel Boorstin," *NewsHour with Jim Lehrer* (Mar. 21. 2004), transcript available at http://www.pbs.org/newshour/bb/remember/jan-june04/boorstin_03-01.html.
27. Good creativity resources include Jeffrey Mauzy, "Managing Personal Creativity," available at http://www.synecticsworld.com/aboutcreativity.htm. Some good creativity resources include the following: E. DeBono, *Six Thinking Hats* (Back Bay Books, 1999); R. Harriman and J. Mauzy, *Creativity, Inc.: Building an Inventive Organization* (Harvard Business School Press, 2003); G. Prince, *The Practice of Creativity: A Manual for Dynamic Group Problem-Solving* (MacMillan, 1972); M. Ray and R. Myers, *Creativity in Business* (Main Street Books, 1989); R. A. von Oech, *Whack on the Side of the Head: How You Can Be More Creative* (Warner Business Books, 1998); B. Breen, "The Six Myths of Creativity," *Fast Company* (December 2004); R. Florida, and J. Goodnight, "Managing for Creativity," *Harvard Business Review* (July 2005); U. Kraft, "Unleashing Creativity," *Scientific American Mind* 16(1) 17–24, 2005; and J. Mauzy, "Managing Personal Creativity," at http://www.synecticsworld.com/aboutcreativity.htm.
28. "A Bozo of a Baboon: A Talk with Robert Sapolsky," available at http://www.edge.org/3rd_culture/sapolsky03/sapolsky_print.html.
29. At the Masters Forum (Sep. 14, 2004).
30. For the best current review of the scientific insights on luck, see R. Wiseman, *The Luck Factor* (Los Angeles: Miramax, 2003). For a variety of insights on personality traits and luck, see A. Furnham and P. Heaven, *Personality and Social Behaviour* (London: Arnold, 1999).
31. See, for example, M. C. Diamond, *Enriching Heredity: The Impact of the Environment on the Anatomy of the Brain* (New York: Free Press, 1988).
32. A. Bandura, "The Psychology of Chance Encounters and Life Paths," *Amercian Psychologist* 37(7)(1982): 747–755.
33. T. J. Stanley, *The Millionaire Mind* (Kansas City: Andrews McMeel, 2002).
34. See, for example, Diamond, *Enriching Heredity*.
35. Wiseman, *Luck Factor*: 67.
36. R. S. Burt, "The Network Structure of Social Capital," *Research in Organizational Behavior* 22 (May 2000).
37. M. Seligman, *Learned Optimism* (New York: Pocket Books, 1998); M. Seligman, *Authentic Happiness* (New York: Free Press, 2002).

Chapter 12. Awaken More Genius, "Fix" Fewer Problems

1. Commentary on CBS Radio News, December 2002.
2. Paul Adler, "Time and Motion Regained," *Harvard Business Review* (Nov.–Dec. 1993).
3. Ibid.
4. Ibid.
5. H. Gardner, *Intelligence Reframed: Multiple Intelligences for the 21st Century* (New York: Basic Books, 2000).
6. P. W. Mattessich et al., *Collaboration: What Makes It Work*, 2nd ed. (Amherst Wilder Foundation, 2001); R. Cross et al., *The Hidden Power of Social Networks: Understanding How Work Really Gets Done in Organizations* (Boston: Harvard Business School Press, 2004).
7. Andrew Gurr, *The Shakespeare Company: 1594–1642* (New York: Cambridge University Press, 2005).
8. A. Hargadon, *How Breakthroughs Happen: The Surprising Truth* (Boston: Harvard Business School Press, 2003).
9. J. Meier-Graefe, *Vincent van Gogh: A Biography* (New York: Dover, 1967).
10. W. J. Freeman, *How the Brain Makes Up Its Mind* (New York: Columbia University Press, 2002).
11. See, for example, A. Kohn, *The Brighter Side of Human Nature* (New York: Basic Books, 1992); T. Ward, *Empathy: Build Your Business and Your Wealth by Putting Yourself in Other People's Shoes* (Los Angeles: Majestic Books, 2005).
12. J. Fuster, *The Prefrontal Cortex*, 3rd ed. (Philadelphia: Lippincott-Raven, 1997); D. G. Amen, *Change Your Brain, Change Your Life* (New York: Times Books, 1998); D. Goleman et al., *Primal Leadership* (Boston: Harvard Business School Press, 2003); E. Langer, *The Power of Mindful Learning* (Cambridge, MA: DaCapo, 1998).
13. P. Drucker, *Creative Living* (Milwaukee: Autumn, 1997).
14. D. M. MacKay, "Cerebral Organization and the Conscious Control of Action," in J. C. Eccles, ed., *Brain and Conscious Experience* (Berlin: Heidelberg, 1966).
15. The "fight-or-flight" response is discussed in many places. Among the more entertaining of those discussions is Robert Sapolsky's *Why Zebras Don't Get Ulcers* (New York: Owl Books, 2004).
16. R. Blake and R. Sekuler, *Perception* 5th ed. (New York: McGraw-Hill, 2005).
17. Elizabeth Spelke, codirector of the Mind, Brain, and Behavior Initiative at Harvard, from a debate with Steven Pinker about gender brain differences, reported at http://www.edge.org/3rd_culture/debate05/debate05_index.html.
18. Cass Sunnstein, *Republic.com* (Princeton, NJ: Princeton University Press, 2002).
19. J. Collins, *Good to Great* (New York: HarperBusiness, 2003).
20. S. Pinker, *The Blank Slate* (New York: Penguin, 2002); P. Coy, "Why Logic

Often Takes a Backseat: The Study of Neuroeconomics May Topple the Notion of Rational Decision-Making." *Business Week* (Mar. 28, 2005): 94–95.

21. Personal correspondence from Muriel Summers. Ms. Summers kindly credits my earlier book, *The Other 90%*, as a major contribution to the vision and strategies that have helped revitalize the school.

Chapter 13. Constructive Discontent Drives Growth

1. M. Born and J. Franck, *Physiker in Ihrer Zeit : Der Luxus des Gewissens: Ausstellung der Staatsbibliothek* (Berlin: Stiftung Preussischer Kulturbesitz, 1958).

2. J. Zull, *The Art of Changing the Brain* (Sterling, VA: Stylus, 2002); J. LeDoux, *Synaptic Self* (New York: Viking, 2002).

3. Zull, *Art of Changing the Brain*.

4. See, for example, N. Nicholson, *Executive Instinct* (New York: CrownBusiness, 2000); see www.inc.com/magazine/20050401/ahanft.html.

5. M. A. Roberto, *Why Great Leaders Don't Take Yes for an Answer* (Philadelphia: Wharton Business School Press, 2005).

6. See www.sloan.org.

7. C. Baxter, *The Feast of Love* (New York: Vintage, 2001).

8. E. Wiesel, keynote address at "A Tribute to Tibet" at the Warner Theatre, Washington, DC (1996).

9. Ron Judd, "Once Again, Hall Defies All Odds," *Seattle Times* (Aug. 21, 2004).

10. Ibid.

11. See www.theraceclub.net.

12. For further exploration of this, see R. K. Cooper, *The Other 90%* (New York: CrownBusiness, 2001).

13. See R. Freedman, *Out of Darkness* (Clarion Books, 1999); and "Night Writing" in R. Beyer, *The Greatest Stories Never Told* (New York: Collins, 2003).

14. Recounted by Richard Dawkins at http://www.edge.org/documents/adams_index.html.

15. Franklin, Benjamin, "Right, Wrong, and Reasonable," *Gazetteer and New Daily Advertiser* (Apr. 18, 1767), available at http://www.historycarper.com/resources/twobf3/right.htm.

16. Ryan and Oestrich, *Driving Fear Out of the Workplace* (San Francisco: Jossey-Bass, 1999); Locke, *The De-Voicing of Society* (New York: Simon & Schuster, 1999).

17. Nicholson, *Executive Instinct*.

18. J. Hagel II, and J. S. Brown, "Productive Friction," *Harvard Business Review* (Feb., 2005).

19. B. Zeigarnik, "Das behalten erledigter und unerledigter Handlungen," *Psychologische Forschung* 9 (1927):1–85.

20. R. J. Sternberg, *Successful Intelligence* (New York: Simon & Schuster, 1997); T. J. Stanley, *The Millionaire Mind* (Kansas City: Andrews McMeel, 2000);

P. Coy, "Why Logic Often Takes a Backseat," *Business Week* (Mar 28, 2005): 94–95.

21. R. J. Sternberg, ed., *Why Smart People Can Be So Stupid* (New Haven, CT: Yale University Press, 2002): Sternberg, *Successful Intelligence.*

22. R. Kegan and L. L. Lahey, *How the Way We Talk Can Change the Way We Work* (San Francisco: Jossey-Bass, 2001).

23. Ibid.

Key 4. *Energy, Not Effort*

1. N. Baldwin, *Edison, Inventing the Century* (New York: Hyperion, 1995).

2. M. Moore-Ede, *The Twenty-Four-Hour Society* (Reading, MA: Addison-Wesley, 1995).

3. D. G. Amen, *Change Your Brain, Change Your Life* (New York: Times Books, 1998).

4. Ibid.

5. R. Cooper, "Flip the Switch," writings on Metabolism and Energy, available at www.RobertKCooper.com.

6. R. K. Cooper and L. Cooper, *Flip the Switch* (Emmaus, PA: Rodale Books, 2005).

7. S. B. Eaton and M. Konner, "Paleolithic Nutrition: A Consideration of Its Nature and Current Implications," *New England Journal of Medicine* 312(1985): 283–289; S. B. Eaton and M. Konner, *The Paleolithic Prescription* (New York: HarperCollins, 1988).

8. G. J. Armelagos, "Human Evolution and the Evolution of Disease," *Ethnic Disease* 1(1991): 21–25.

9. "BehindTheMedspeak: Perseveration Brought Down the 'Red Baron' " (Oct. 8, 2004) at http://www.bookofjoe.com/2004/10/behindthemedspe_5.html.

10. See, for example, Frederic Luskin and Ken Pelletier, *Stress Free for Good* (San Francisco: HarperSanFrancisco, 2005); and Doc Childre and Deborah Rozman, *Transforming Stress* (San Francisco, CA: New Harbinger, 2005).

11. M. Chafetz, *Smart for Life* (New York: Penguin, 1992): 71.

12. V. P. Zinchenko et al., *The Psychometrics of Fatigue* (London: Taylor & Francis, 1985).

13. Ibid.

14. American Institute of Stress (http://www.stress.org/problem.htm).

15. Grant Thornton International, "Sharp Growth in Stress Levels Among World's Entrepreneurs," available at http://www.citymayors.com/business/stress_survey.html.

16. J. Diamond, *Collapse: How Societies Choose to Fail or Succeed* (New York: Viking, 2005).

17. Malcolm Gladwell, "The Vanishing," *New Yorker* (Dec. 29, 2004).

Chapter 14. Excel Under Pressure

1. Quote from my grandfather Downing's notes. His grandfather attended one of Emerson's final lectures and came home inspired by notes he had taken.
2. W. Martindale, *Inside the Cage: A Season at West 4th Street's Legendary Tournament* (New York: Simon Spotlight, 2005).
3. See, for example, C. Garfield, *Peak Performance* (New York: Warner, 1989); D. Greene, *Fight Your Fear and Win* (New York: Broadway Books, 2002); J. Loehr and P. McLaughlin, *Mentally Tough* (New York: Evans, 1994); J. Loehr, *Stress for Success* (New York: TimesBusiness, 1999).
4. J. Kao, *Jamming* (New York: HarperBusiness, 1996): 4.
5. A. Szent-Gyorgyi, "Syntropy," *Human Nature* (1972).
6. P. La Cerra and R. Bingham, *The Origin of Minds* (New York: Harmony, 2002); J. Zull, *The Art of Changing the Brain* (Sterling, VA: Stylus, 2002); C. Pert, *The Molecules of Emotion* (New York: Scribner, 1999).
7. Zull, *Art of Changing the Brain;* Pert, *Molecules of Emotion.*
8. Zull, *Art of Changing the Brain.*
9. See, for example, Loehr, *Stress for Success;* R. E. Thayer, *The Biopsychology of Mood and Arousal* (New York: Oxford University Press, 1989); R. E. Thayer, *The Origin of Everyday Moods* (New York: Oxford University Press, 1997); and R. E. Thayer, *Calm Energy* (New York: Oxford University Press, 2001).
10. See, for example, J. Pfeffer and R. I. Sutton, *The Knowing-Doing Gap* (Boston: Harvard Business School Press, 1999); E. Aronson, "Self-Justification," in *The Social Animal* (San Francisco: W. H. Freeman, 1972); and R. B. Cialdini, "Commitment and Consistency," in *Influence,* 2nd ed. (Glenview, IL: Scott, Foresman, 1988).
11. References include L. K. Libby, R. P. Eibach, and T. Gilovich, "Here's looking at me: Memory perspective and assessments of personal change." *Journal of Personality and Social Psychology,* 88, 50–62 (2005).
12. T. Gualtieri, in J. Ratey, ed., *The Neuropsychiatry of Personality Disorders* (New York: Blackwell, 1995): 153.
13. W. A. Suzuki and D. G. Amaral, *Journal of Comprehensive Neurology* 350(1994): 497–533.
14. Dienstbier, in Miller, "To Beat Stress, Get Tough;" R. A. Diesntbier, ed., *Evolutionary Psychology and Motivation* (Lincoln, NE: University of Nebraska, 2001).
15. See, for example, Loehr, *Stress for Success;* J. Loehr and T. Schwartz, *The Power of Full Engagement* (New York: Free Press, 2003); Dienstbier, R. A. in L. Miller, "To Beat Stress, Get Tough," *Psychology Today* (Nov. 1989); R. A. Dienstbier, ed., *Evolutionary Psychology and Motivation* (Lincoln: University of Nebraska Press, 2001).
16. Thayer, *The Biopsychology of Mood and Arousal;* Thayer, *The Origin of Everyday Moods;* and Thayer, *Calm Energy.*

17. Stamford, B. *Fitness Without Exercise* (New York: Warner, 1991); J. Loehr, *Stress for Success* (New York: TimesBusiness, 1999); J. Loehr, and T. Schwartz, *The Power of Full Engagement* (New York: Free Press, 2003).

18. C. Carter et al., "How the Brain Gets Ready to Perform," lecture at the 30th Annual Meeting of the Society of Neuroscience, New Orleans (Nov. 2000).

19. G. Kreiman et al., "Imagery Neurons in the Human Brain," *Nature* 408(2000): 357–361.

20. For further explanation and references, see R. K. Cooper, *The Other 90%* (New York: CrownBusiness, 2001).

21. Thayer, *Biopsychology of Mood and Arousal.*

22. Loehr, *Stress for Success;* Loehr and Schwartz, *Power of Full Engagement.*

23. Loehr, *Stress for Success;* Loehr and Schwartz, *Power of Full Engagement;* Thayer, *The Biopsychology of Mood and Arousal;* Thayer, *Origin of Everyday Moods;* Thayer, *Calm Energy.*

24. Ibid.

25. A. Maslow, lecture at UCLA (1970).

26. A. Damasio, *Descartes' Error* (New York: Grosset/Putnam, 1995).

27. La Cerra and Bingham, *Origin of Minds.*

28. Ibid.

29. Ibid.

30. V. Frankl, *Man's Ultimate Search for Meaning* (New York: Perseus, 2000).

31. Sara Terry, "Genius at Work," *Fast Company* (Sept. 1998).

32. Ibid.

33. M. Chafetz, *Smart for Life* (New York: Penguin, 1992).

34. Gilovich and L. Libby, "Here's Looking at Me: Memory Perspective and Assessments of Personal Change," *Journal of Personality and Social Psychology.*

35. F. Smith, in M. Birla, *FedEx Delivers* (Hackensack, NJ: Wiley, 2003).

36. R. Sapolsky, "Stressed-Out Memories," *Scientific American Mind* 14(5)(Jan. 2005): 28–33.

37. See, for example, J. Loehr, *Stress for Success.*

38. M. D. Lieberman, "Intuition: A Social Cognitive Neuroscience Approach," *Psychological Bulletin* 126(2000): 109–137.

39. D. G. Amen, *Change Your Brain, Change Your Life* (New York: Times Books, 1998).

40. W. A. Suzuki and D. G. Amaral, *Journal of Comprehensive Neurology* 350(1994): 497–533.

41. I am not sure who originally created this list. If readers know, and contact me, I will gladly cite the correct source in future editions of this book.

42. H. Mintzberg, *The Rise and Fall of Strategic Planning* (New York: Free Press, 1994).

43. H. Selye, *The Stress of Life* (New York: McGraw-Hill, 1956).

44. R. Kurzweil, in T. Singer, "The Innovation Factor: Your Brain on Innovation," *Inc.* (Sept. 2002).

45. Dayton Duncan and Ken Burns, *Horatio's Drive: America's First Road Trip* (New York: Knopf, 2003). This book is drawn from the PBS documentary film by the same name.
46. G. Stephano, G. Froicchione, B. Slingsby, and H. Benson, *Brain Research Review* 35(2001): 1–19.
47. William Lind, "Understanding Fourth-Generation Warfare." I can't locate the original source for this, but it's on the Web at, for example, http://www.jenex.com/news/news.html.
48. Masters Forum (Nov. 16, 2004).
49. Singer, "Innovation Factor."
50. E. Goldberg, *The Wisdom Paradox* (New York: Gotham, 2005); L. Aiello and P. Wheeler, *Current Anthropology* 36(2)(Apr. 1995): 199–221.
51. Cited in T. Cleary, trans., *Sun Tzu: The Art of War* (Boston: Shambhala, 1988).
52. "The Master of Demon Valley," in T. Cleary, *Thunder in the Sky: On the Acquisition and Exercise of Power* (Boston: Shambhala, 1993).
53. L. Ji, in T. Cleary, *Mastering the Art of War* (Boston: Shambhala, 1989): 96–98.

Chapter 15. Streamline

1. Daniel Drubach, *The Brain Explained* (Englewood Cliffs, NJ: Prentice Hall, 2000).
2. A. Bandura, *Self-Efficacy* (New York: Worth, 1997).
3. R. K. Cooper and L. Cooper, *Flip the Switch* (Emmaus, PA: Rodale Books, 2005).
4. M. Moore-Ede, *The Twenty-Four-Hour Society* (Reading, MA: Addison-Wesley, 1993): 53.
5. See R. Cooper, *The Other 90%: How to Unlock Your Vast Untapped Potential for Leadership and Life* (New York: CrownBusiness, 2001); and Cooper and Cooper, *Flip the Switch*.
6. S. S. Hendler, *The Oxygen Breakthrough* (New York: Pocket Books, 1989).
7. R. Cailliet and L. Gross, *The Rejuvenation Factor* (New York: Doubleday, 1986).
8. Thayer, *The Biopsychology of Mood and Arousal;* Thayer, *The Origin of Everyday Moods*.
9. R. E. Thayer, *Calm Energy* (New York: Oxford University Press, 2001).
10. Scientific paper, Highland Springs Research Institute, Blackford, Perthshire, Scotland (1994–2003).
11. M. Boschmann et al., "Water-Induced Thermogenesis," *Journal of Clinical Endocrinology and Metabolism* 88(12)(2003): 6015–6019.
12. M. A. Siegel and C. Sparks, "The Effect of Ice Water Ingestion," *Heart Lung* 9(2)(1980): 306–310.
13. Studies and review cited in E. Darden, *Two Weeks to a Tighter Tummy* (Dallas: Taylor Publishing, 1992).

14. For more examples, see Cooper and Cooper, *Flip the Switch*.
15. K. Johnsgard, quoted in *Prevention's Lose Weight Guide* (Emmaus, PA: Rodale Books, 1994): 19–20.
16. Moore-Ede, *Twenty-Four-Hour Society:* 55.
17. See, for example, L. Cordain, *The Paleo Diet* (New York: Wiley, 2002); and G. D. Jacobs, *The Ancestral Mind* (New York: Viking, 2003).
18. *European Journal of Pharmacology* 440(2-3)(2002): 85–98; *American Journal of Physiology* 272(Pt 1, 3)(1997): E379–384; *FASEB J* 13(1998): 1391–1396.
19. L. E. Lamb, *The Weighting Game* (New York: Lyle Stuart, 1988): 95–96.
20. E. L. Rossi, with D. Nimmons, *The Twenty-Minute Break* (Los Angeles: Tarcher, 1991): 122–123.
21. J. Stellman and M. S. Henifin, *Office Work* (New York: Fawcett, 1989): 28.
22. E. Hatfield et al., *Emotional Contagion* (New York: Cambridge University Press, 1993).
23. T. Lewis et al., *A General Theory of Love* (New York: Random House, 2000).
24. R. Solomon, *The Passions: Emotions and the Meaning of Life* (Indianapolis: Hackett, 1995).
25. G. De Becker, *The Gift of Fear* (New York: Dell, 1998).
26. H. Bruch and S. Ghoshal, *A Bias for Action* (Boston: Harvard Business School Press, 2004): 76.
27. J. Loehr and T. Schwartz, *The Power of Full Engagement* (New York: Free Press, 2003).

Chapter 16. Leap Forward by Doing Nothing

1. W. James, *Talks to Teachers* (New York: Norton, 1958).
2. R. E. Thayer, *Calm Energy* (New York: Oxford University Press, 2001).
3. R. S. Eliot, *Is It Worth Dying For?* (New York: Bantam, 1999); H. Benson and W. Proctor, *The Breakout Principles* (New York: Scribner, 2003).
4. See, for example, J. LeDoux, *Synaptic Self* (New York: Viking, 2002); W. J. Freeman, *How Brains Make Up Their Minds* (New York: Columbia University Press, 2002); G. Claxton, *Hare Brain, Tortoise Mind* (New York: Bloomsburg, 1999); and G. Zull, *The Art of Changing the Brain* (Sterling, VA: Stylus, 2002).
5. S. Smith, "Getting into and out of Mental Ruts," in R. J. Sternberg and J. Davidson, *The Nature of Insight* (Cambridge, MA: MIT Press, 1996).
6. Jeffrey Mauzy, "Managing Personal Creativity," available at http://www.synecticsworld.com/aboutcreativity.htm.
7. J. Loehr, *Stress for Success* (New York: TimesBusiness, 2000).
8. D. G. Amen, D.G. *Change Your Brain, Change Your Life* (New York: Times Books, 1998).
9. "Scientists Find Brain Areas Affected by Lack of Rest," *Society for Neuroscience* (Nov. 9, 2004).
10. Ibid.

11. See http://www.bbc.co.uk/health/conditions/mental_health/coping_sleep.shtml.

12. Ibid.

13. See, for example, William Dement, *The Promise of Sleep* (New York: Dell, 2000); and James Maas, *Power Sleep* (New York: Perennial, 1999).

14. D. DeNoon, "Lack of Sleep Takes Toll on Brain Power," *WebMD News* (Apr. 2000).

15. "Scientists Find Brain Areas Affected by Lack of Sleep"; T. Steckler, N. H. Kalin, and J.M.H.M. Reul, *Handbook of Stress and the Brain* (New York: Elsevier Science, 2005); DeNoon, "Lack of Sleep Takes Toll on Brain Power."

16. "Exercise and the Brain," *Society for Neuroscience* (Jan. 2000).

17. Steckler, Kalin, and Reul, *Handbook of Stress and the Brain*.

18. A. A. Milne, *The House at Pooh Corner* (New York: Dutton, 1988).

19. G. Claxton, *Wise Up* (New York: Bloomsbury, 1999).

20. Ibid.

Chapter 17. Stay Hungry, Stay Foolish

1. In a recent commencement address (www.news-service-stanford-edu/news/2005/15Jobs; "You've got to find what you love, Jobs says."), Steve Jobs touched on Stewart Brand's "Stay Hungry, Stay Foolish" mantra. One of my friends for many years, Tom Ferguson, M.D., pioneered the medical self-care movement and was a frequent contributor to the *Whole Earth Catalog* and *Last Whole Earth Catalog*. In the '70s and early '80s, he sparked many discussions about the relevance and timelessness of Brand's themes. This one, in particular, struck a lasting chord with me.

2. R. Branson, *How I Lost My Virginity* (New York: Three Rivers Press, 1999); "26 Most Fascinating Entrepreneurs," *Inc.* (Apr. 2005); B. Morris, "Richard Branson: What a Life," *Fortune* (Sep. 23, 2003).

3. Morris, "Richard Branson."

4. R. Branson, quoted in "26 Most Fascinating Entrepreneurs."

5. Peter Whybrow, *American Mania: When More Is Not Enough* (New York: Norton, 2005).

6. Irene Lacher, "In New Book, Professor Sees 'Mania' in U.S," *New York Times* (Mar. 12, 2005), available at http://www.nytimes.com/2005/03/12/books/12happ.html?ex=1122177600&en=96df268ebbb8d27b&ei=5070&oref=login.

7. Burney Simpson, "Study Rips Election Board Practices," *Chicago Reporter* (Mar. 1995), available at http://www.chicagoreporter.com/1995/03-95/0395StudyRipsElectionBoardPracticesComputers.htm.

8. Quoted in Gerald de Jaager, "Building the Rule of Law," *University of Chicago Law School Record* (Spring 2004): 8.

9. Personal communication (July 16, 2005).

10. T. Robbins, *Jitterbug Perfume* (New York: Bantam, 1990).

11. See http://www.womenssportsfoundation.org/cgi-bin/iowa/athletes/article.html?record=12.

Key 5. *Impact, Not Intentions*

1. R. K. Cooper, *Promises to Keep*, available at www.RobertKCooper.com.
2. W. J. Freeman, *How Brains Make Up Their Minds* (New York: Columbia University Press, 2000).
3. J. Pfeffer and R. J. Sutton, *The Knowing-Doing Gap* (Boston: Harvard Business School Press, 2000).
4. W. A. Howatt, "Journaling to Self-Evaluation," *International Journal of Reality Therapy* 18(1999): 32–34.
5. See, for example, R. J. Sternberg, *Successful Intelligence* (New York: Simon & Schuster, 1997).
6. "Orison Marden, a Founder of Legal Aid Society, Dies," *New York Times* (Aug. 26, 1975): 34.
7. Ibid.
8. See http://www.sec.gov/news/speech/spch111703hjg.htm.

Chapter 18. The Neuroscience of Change

1. M. Rokeach, "The Effect of Perception Time upon the Rigidity and Concreteness of Thinking," *Journal of Experimental Psychology* 40(1950): 206–216.
2. R. Ornstein, *The Evolution of Consciousness* (New York: Prentice Hall, 1991); G. Zull, *The Art of Changing the Brain* (Sterling, VA: Stylus, 2002).
3. E. L. Cowen, "The Influence of Varying Degrees of Psychological Stress on Problem-Solving Rigidity," *Journal of Abnormal and Social Psychology* 47(1952): 512–519.
4. See http://www-306.ibm.com/e-business/ondemand/us/innovation/gio.shtml.
5. J. Gottman, *The Relationship Cure* (New York: Three Rivers Press, 2002).
6. See, for example, the neuroscience-based studies of Gerald Zaltman, professor of marketing at Harvard Business School, in G. Zaltman, *How Customers Think* (Boston: Harvard Business School Press, 2003).
7. G. Lakoff and M. Johnson, *Metaphors We Live By*, 2nd ed. (Chicago: University of Chicago Press, 2003).
8. J. Kotter, *The Heart of Change* (Boston: Harvard Business School Press, 2002).
9. Zaltman, *How Customers Think*.
10. M. Storch, "Taking the Reins," *Scientific American Mind* 16(2)(2005): 88–89.
11. See, for example, A. Kohn, *Punished by Rewards* (Boston: Houghton Mifflin, 1999); J. Pfeffer and R. I. Sutton, *The Knowing-Doing Gap* (Boston: Harvard Business School Press, 1999); and R. K. Cooper, *The Other 90%* (New York: CrownBusiness, 2001).

12. Storch, "Taking the Reins."
13. See, for example, M. D. Lieberman, "Intuition: A Social Cognitive Neuroscience Approach," *Psychological Bulletin* 126(2000): 109–137; and J. A. Knowlton et al., "A Neostriatal Habit Learning System in Humans," *Science* 273(1996): 1399–1402; R. K. Cooper and A. Sawaf, *Executive EQ* (New York: Grosset/Putnam, 1997); and D. Goleman et al., *Primal Leadership* (Boston: Harvard Business School Press, 2001).
14. J. LeDoux, *Synaptic Self* (New York: Viking, 2002).
15. A. Hargadon, *How Breakthroughs Happen* (Boston: Harvard Business School Press, 2003).
16. This section is based on Dr. Dean Ornish's pioneering research, IBM's "Global Innovation Outlook" conference in 2004, and "Change or Die," by Alan Deutschman, May 2005, *Fast Company.*
17. D. Ornish, *Dr. Dean Ornish's Program for Reversing Heart Disease* (New York: Random House, 1990); Bill Moyers, "Changing Life Habits: A Conversation with Dean Ornish," in *Healing and the Mind* (New York: Doubleday, 1993); D. Ornish, "Intensive Lifestyle Changes in Management of Coronary Heart Disease," in E. Braunwald, *Harrison's Advances in Cardiology* (New York: McGraw-Hill, 2002); J. Koertge et al., "Improvement in Medical Risk Factors and Quality of Life in Women and Men with Coronary Artery Disease in the Multicenter Lifestyle Demonstration Project," *American Journal of Cardiology* 2003;91:1316–1322.
18. D. Ornish, *Love and Survival: The Scientific Basis* (New York: HarperCollins, 1999); see also http://www.pmri.org/?p=nwr.
19. D. Ornish, personal communication (1995).
20. Ornish, *Reversing Heart Disease;* also see http://www.pmri.org/?p=nwr.
21. C. Cannon et al., "Intensive Versus Moderate Lipid Lowering with Statins after Acute Coronary Syndromes," *New England Journal of Medicine* 350(15)(Apr 8, 2004): 1495–1504.
22. C. Carter et al., "How the Brain Gets Ready to Perform," lecture at the 30th Annual Meeting of the Society of Neuroscience, New Orleans (Nov. 2000).
23. G. Kreiman, C. Kock, and I. Fried, "Imagery Neurons in the Human Brain," *Nature* 408(2000): 357–361.
24. Ibid.
25. Storch, "Taking the Reins."
26. See, for example, Cooper and Sawaf, *Executive EQ.*
27. R. J. Davidson, D. C. Jackson, and N. H. Kalin, "Emotion, Plasticity, Context, and Regulation: Perspectives from Affective Neuroscience," *Psychological Bulletin* 126(6)(2000): 890–909; Zull, J. *The Art of Changing the Brain* (Stylus, 2002): 65.

Chapter 19. What You Measure, Matters

1. P. M. Gollwitzer, "Goal Achievement," in W. Stroebe and M. Hewstone eds., *European Review of Social Psychology* 4(1993): 141–185; P. M. Gollwitzer, and B. Schall, "Metacognition in Action: The Importance of Implementation," *Personality & Social Psychology Review* 2 (1998): 124–136; P. M. Gollwitzer, "Implementation: Strong Effects of Simple Plans," *American Psychologist* 14(1999): 493–503.

2. P. M. Gollwitzer, "Implementation: Strong Effects of Simple Plans," *American Psychologist* 14(1999): 493–503; P. M. Gollwitzer and V. Brandstatter, "Implementation and Effective Goal Pursuit," *Journal of Personality and Social Psychology* 73 (1997): 186–199; P. M. Gollwitzer, "Goal Achievement," in W. Stroebe and M. Hewstone eds., *European Review of Social Psychology* 4 (1993): 141–185; P. M. Gollwitzer and B. Schall, "Metacognition in Action: The Importance of Implementation," *Personality & Social Psychology Review* 2 (1998): 124–136; P. M. Gollwitzer, "Implementation: Strong Effects of Simple Plans," *American Psychologist* 14 (1999): 493–503.

3. J. Zull, *The Art of Changing the Brain* (Stylus, 2002).

4. L. K. Libby and R. Eibach, "Here's Looking at Me: The Effect of Memory Perspective on Assessments of Personal Change," *Journal of Personality and Social Psychology* 88(1) (2005): 50–62; M. Storch, "Taking the Reins," *Scientific American Mind* 16(2) (2005): 88–89.

5. Ibid.

6. T. Lewis et al., *A General Theory of Love* (New York: Random House, 2000).

7. J. B. Willett, "Measuring Change," in E. Amsel and K. A. Renninger eds., *Change and Development Issues of Theory, Method, and Application*, chapt. 11, 213–243.

8. See, for example: R. Sternberg, *Successful Intelligence* (New York: Simon & Schuster, 1997).

9. W. A. Howatt, "Journaling to Self-Evaluation," *International Journal of Reality Therapy* 18(1999): 32–34.

10. See, for example, D. Spiegel, "Healing Words: Emotional Expression and Disease Outcome," *Journal of the American Medical Association,* 281 (1999): 1328–1329. http://jama.ama-assn.org/cgi/content/full/281/14/1328; S. Luttgendorf and P. Ullrich, "Journaling About Stressful Events: Effects of Cognitive Processing and Emotional Expression," *Annals of Behavioral Medicine* 24:2 (2002): 244–248; C. Kalb, "Pen Paper, Power! Confessional Writing Can Be Good for You," *Newsweek* (April 26, 1999); and M. Elias, "You've Got Trauma, but Writing Can Help," *USA Today* (June 30, 2002).

11. See, for example: E. Aronson, "Self-Justification" in *The Social Animal* (San Francisco: W. H. Freeman, 1972); and R. B. Cialdini, "Commitment and Consistency" in *Influence,* 2nd ed. (Glenview, IL: Scott, Foresman, 1988); and Pfeffer and Sutton. *The Knowing-Doing Gap.*

12. J. Pfeffer and R. Sutton, *The Knowing-Doing Gap* (Boston: Harvard Business School Press, 2000).

Chapter 20. Stay Close to the Soul

1. e. e. cummings, *The Enormous Room* (New York: Penguin, 1999).
2. R. Lewontin, *Human Diversity* (New York: Scientific American Library, 1995): 42.
3. Martha Graham, *The Notebooks of Martha Graham* (New York: Harcourt Brace Jovanovich, 1973).
4. R. N. Caine, and G. Caine, "Mind/Brain Learning Principles." *Making Connections: Teaching and the Human Brain* (Reading, MA: Addison-Wesley, 1998).
5. Kenneth S. Norris, "Captain Cook's Porpoises," in *A World Between Waves,* ed. Frank Stewart (Island Press, 1992).
6. A. Maslow, *The Farther Reaches of Human Nature* (New York: Penguin, Reprint, 1993).
7. T. S. Eliot, *Four Quartets* (Harvest Books, 1968).
8. Quoted at http://www.teamhoyt.com/history.shtml.
9. Quoted at http://www.teamhoyt.com/atta_boy.shtml.

Acknowledgments

To God, for the light of hope through all of life's joys and sorrows.
To my family:

My wife, Leslie
My children, Chris, Chelsea, and Shanna
My parents, Hugh and Margaret Cooper
My sister, Mary, and brother, David
My grandmothers, Nora Roby Cooper and Marion Downing
My grandfathers, Hugh Cooper Sr., and Wendell L. Downing, M.D.
Who alone or together
Showed me worlds I never knew.

I am ever grateful for the inspiration and scientific insights I have received from a number of independent-thinking scholars around the world, especially Karl Pribram and Michael Ray at Stanford. I owe special praise to ten pioneers in the practical implications of neuroscience: Karl Pribram, Walter Freeman, Joseph LeDoux, Robert Ornstein, Daniel Amen, Guy Claxton, Jim Loehr, Charles Garfield, Ellen Langer, and James Zull. In addition, the against-the-grain spirit of W. Edwards Deming continues to inspire me, as does the open-space-breakthrough approach championed by one of my early mentors at 3M, Chuck Harstad, the work of Jeffrey Pfeffer and Robert Sutton on closing the knowing-doing gap, and the daring attitude and record-breaking follow-through of five-time Olympic gold medalist Gary Hall Jr.

During the lengthy writing of this book, John Mahaney, executive editor at Crown Business, provided unwavering encouragement and the opportunity to break new ground. Jerry de Jaager read and critiqued every page of every draft, with a keenness of insight, ingenuity, and integration that, as always, has been awesome. Ted Dewan, illustrator extraordinaire, provided his gift in bringing brain images to life for my Web site that expands on this book.

In my business life, I have been privileged to work with colleagues who are among the finest anywhere: Suanne Sandage and LuAnn Freund of Services for Success, Julie Ross of Vivid Edge Productions, and Jerry de

Jaager, along with special mention to Ali Crooks and William Gibbon at
Barclays Bank. I have also had the opportunity to work with some exceptional senior executives, several of whom I wish to mention by name:
Doug Sharp, chairman of BSB Design; Dominic Bruynseels, CEO of Barclays Bank in Africa and the Middle East; Bill Abraham, general manager
at Intel; Larry Taylor, retired president of Pinkerton Security; Julie
Howard, COO and SVP of Navigant Consulting; Mike Remington, re-
gional SVP at Verizon; Susan Duggan, CEO of the Silicon Valley World
Internet Center; Mikel de Irala, vice president of Ford Motor Company;
and Paula Van Ness, former CEO of Make-A-Wish Foundation and current CEO of Starlight Starbright Children's Foundation.

Over the years, many others have provided support, insight, or collaboration in setting off toward one "impossible" goal after another. These
remarkable men and women include Stephen Covey; Ken Blanchard; Ed
Claflin; Stephanie Tade; Dawn Sorenson; Nancy Badore; John Horton,
founder of the Leadership Center; Jim "Murph" Murphy, founder of Afterburner; the board of BSB Design (Doug Sharp, Doug Buster, Larry
Moore, Steve Moore, and Joe Rabin); Paul Winter and Margaret Thomas
of The Leadership Trust; Alan Horton; Deborah Kiley; Peter Samuelson
and Joan Ford at Starlight Starbright Children's Foundation; Howard and
Lynda Schultz; Esther Orioli and the team at Essi Systems and Q-Metrics;
the senior colleagues at the Leigh Bureau; Ilean Galloway, Jim Fleming,
Tim Hendry, Dane Parker, Gaby Ramirez, and Renee Lagos de La Cruz, at
Intel; Will Hildreth; Ayman Sawaf; Allen Goldstein; John Fayad; Mary
Bassett; Martin Lowery; Mary (Bunny) Huller; Mary Louise Hersh-
berger; and Reinhard Woytek.

And to all the others whose courage and spirit continue to brighten
the world we live in alone or together, you inspire me.

Index

About the Author

Driven by a relentless curiosity, ROBERT COOPER is an independent scholar and leadership adviser who has devoted three decades to studying how the most exceptional individuals, teams, and organizations achieve what everyone else thinks they can't. His scientific insights, ultra-practical tools, counterintuitive wisdom, and disciplined metrics have enabled leaders and teams in many industries and fields to produce breakthroughs while everyone else is struggling just to keep from falling behind.

He is the *New York Times* bestselling author of *The Other 90%: How to Unlock Your Vast Untapped Potential for Leadership and Life.* Praised as "a national treasure" by Stanford Business School Professor Michael Ray, and called "the ultimate business guru for the new millennium" by *USA Today,* he has advised executives and rising-star leaders in organizations that include 3M, Barclays Bank, BSB Design, Intel, Starlight Starbright Children's Foundation, Methodist Hospitals of Dallas, Navigant Consulting, Northwestern Mutual, and Verizon.

He has lectured at the Stanford Business School, Stanford Executive Program, Management Centre Europe, Ruling Companies Association (Milan, Italy), and The Leadership Trust (U.K.). For five years he was the highest-rated faculty member in the Lessons in Leadership Distinguished Speaker Series sponsored by universities and business schools from coast to coast.

In a survey of managers and professionals from more than ninety organizations, his work was compared to twenty widely recognized leadership authorities. He rated highest on every scale, including inherent value, usefulness, applicability, and overall results. In an independent rating by professionals and managers in the Senior Management Interchange, the practical value of his work was rated at 4.9 out of 5.0.

He served in the U.S. Marine Corps during the Vietnam War. An All-American swimmer, he received the University of Michigan's Honor Trophy Award for "outstanding achievement in scholarship, athletics, and leadership." He lives in Ann Arbor, Michigan, with his wife and children. His Web site is www.RobertKCooper.com; e-mail: Robert@RobertKCooper.com.